SHAKESPEARE FOCUS

Othello

Text & Notes for Leaving Cert English Higher Level

Martin Kieran & Frances Rocks

Gill & Macmillan

Gill & Macmillan
Hume Avenue
Park West
Dublin 12
with associated companies throughout the world
www.gillmacmillan.ie

© Martin Kieran and Frances Rocks, 2013
978 07171 5684 9

Design by Philip Ryan Graphic Design
Print origination in Ireland by Síofra Murphy

The paper used in this book is made from the wood pulp of managed
forests. For every tree felled, at least one tree is planted, thereby renewing
natural resources.

Any links to external websites should not be construed as an endorsement
by Gill & Macmillan of the content or view of the linked material.

For permission to reproduce photographs, the authors and publisher
gratefully acknowledge the following:

© Alamy: v; © Corbis: 88; © Johan Persson / ArenaPAL: 1, 13, 35, 40,
52, 53, 77, 107, 116, 129, 134, 135, 139, 166, 169, 172, 175, 178, 180;
© Marilyn Kingwill / ArenaPAL: 114; © Nigel Norrington / ArenaPAL:
71, 74, 98, 147.

The authors and publisher have made every effort to trace all copyright
holders, but if any has been inadvertently overlooked we would be pleased
to make the necessary arrangement at the first opportunity.

Contents

Shakespeare's Themes

Style

Sample Essays

End Notes

Shakespeare's text and line numbers

Over the years, Shakespeare's plays have been printed in different formats. Most popular versions nearly always have some modernised spelling and punctuation. Line numbers may also differ slightly, depending on particular editions.

Introduction

- *Othello* is one of Shakespeare's most famous and popular tragedies. Written around 1603, it tells the story of a black general in the Venetian army who murders his wife after being convinced that she is unfaithful. The play has been seen primarily as a domestic or private tragedy that focuses on the downfall of a nobleman and his marriage.

William Shakespeare (1564–1616)

- The play is primarily concerned with the intense relationships between three central characters and explores the universal theme of love. Other enduring themes include jealousy, betrayal, race and gender.

- Drama is usually about tension and conflict of one kind or another. Most Leaving Cert exam questions relate to characters, relationships and themes – all of which are closely interrelated. A good knowledge of the play's key or revealing scenes will provide a solid basis for answering question.

- In studying the play, it is worth remembering that the text was written specifically for theatrical performance. Despite any inconsistencies regarding the plot or timescale, audiences must accept the 'new reality' that Shakespeare has created in order to fully appreciate this intriguing stage drama.

Background

- The likely main source for *Othello, Moor of Venice*, is the *Hecatommithi*, a collection of tales published in Venice in 1566 and written by Giovanni Battista Giraldi (1504–73), an Italian writer also known as Cinthio.
- Shakespeare's *Othello* was probably written between 1602 and 1604.
- First performance: Probably 1 November 1604 before King James I at Whitehall Palace.
- First printing: 1622 in a quarto edition; 1623 as part of the First Folio, the first authorised collection of Shakespeare's plays. The First Folio version omits oaths and curses that appeared in the quarto edition in compliance with a law passed by Parliament that forbade blasphemous language in stage dramas.

Shakespeare's Life

(Dates for plays are approximate)

1564:	Born in Stratford-upon-Avon.
1582:	Marries Anne Hathaway.
1583:	His daughter Susannah is born.
1584:	Birth of twins, Judith and Hamnet.
1585:	Moves to London.
Early 1590s:	Writes first plays, *Richard III* and *Henry VII*.
1593–96:	Continues to write, including *Richard II* and *Romeo and Juliet*.
1596:	Death of his son Hamnet.
1599:	Invests in the Globe Theatre.
1601:	First performance of *Hamlet*.
1603:	Writes *Othello*.
1604:	First performance of *Othello*.
1605–06:	Writes *King Lear* and *Macbeth*.
1609:	Becomes part-owner of the new Blackfriars Theatre.
1612:	Shakespeare retires and returns to Stratford.
1616:	Dies aged 52.

How the Single Text Shakespeare Question is Marked

The Single Text English (Higher Level) question is allocated 60 minutes in the exam and is worth 60 marks in total. These are awarded by reference to the PCLM criteria for assessment (i.e. 3 x 18 marks for each of P, C and L plus 6 marks for M):

P = Clarity of Purpose: 18 marks (30%)

C = Coherence of Delivery: 18 marks (30%)

L = Efficiency of Language Use: 18 marks (30%)

M = Accuracy of Mechanics: 6 marks (10%)

Clarity of Purpose

In assessing Clarity of Purpose, examiners will judge how successfully the candidate has addressed the question and engaged with the set task. This refers to the quality of engagement, relevance, focus, originality and understanding of the appropriate genre.

The marks awarded for Coherence of Delivery and Efficiency of Language Use will not normally be higher than Clarity of Purpose.

Coherence of Delivery

In awarding the marks for Coherence of Delivery, examiners will assess how well the candidate has sustained the response and developed the entire answer. This refers to the quality and management of ideas, supporting points, sequencing and engagement with texts.

Efficiency of Language Use

Marks for Efficiency of Language Use are awarded for the management and control of language. This refers to the quality of language used to achieve clear communication in terms of vocabulary, paragraph structure, syntax, punctuation, fluency, style and expression.

Marks for L are awarded in so far as the candidate's answering is considered appropriate to the delivery of the task.

Accuracy of Mechanics

Marks awarded for Accuracy of Mechanics refer to spelling and grammar, appropriate to the register. Marks for M are essentially independent of P, C and L marks.

Time and Place in Othello

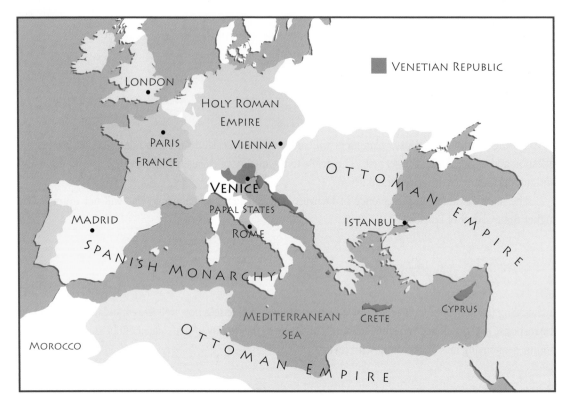

The play takes place during the 16th century in Venice (in northern Italy) and Cyprus (an island in the eastern Mediterranean about 40 miles south of present-day Turkey).

In *Othello*, events happen in a shorter time sequence than is usual with Shakespeare. This results in a greater unity of time, place and action. To some extent, the first act (which takes place over one night) can be seen as a prologue to the main story set in Cyprus. The effect is to make the tragedy seem much more intense. The drama is also heightened due to the lack of a subplot and the almost total absence of comic relief. We know too much about Iago to be entertained by his occasional wit, and any audience laughter is uneasy.

From Act 2 onwards, there is a rush of activity: the wedding celebrations, Cassio's dismissal, Desdemona's pleading on his behalf, Iago's increasing influence, Othello's growing suspicion and its inevitable tragic outcome. Although Othello's whole world seems to disintegrate very quickly, characters make comments that suggest a much longer timescale. Bianca complains to Cassio that he has avoided her for 'seven days and nights'. Othello's belief in Desdemona's adultery 'a thousand times' is also illogical, as there is no opportunity when it could possibly have occurred. Of course, it could be argued that Shakespeare is simply dramatising the power of deranged jealousy by showing Othello's obsessive detachment from reality.

The contrasting settings are also important to the drama. The city of Venice has a sophisticated social class system which welcomes Othello as a military commander but rejects him as a son-in-law. The Moor has little understanding of the finer points of social behaviour and Iago has no trouble convincing him that

women in Venice are all immoral. On the other hand, the Venetian army offers opportunities for a brave soldier such as Othello to gain promotion.

By contrast, Cyprus is symbolically located halfway between the civilised and heathen worlds. The isolated island is close to the danger of invasion. Within this claustrophobic setting, where Othello is in absolute command, he immediately becomes the focus of attention. The loss of the Turkish fleet gives him time for his private life rather than his military duties. It is in this unfamiliar location that passions are let loose and order disappears.

Although there is a tradition in Shakespeare criticism concerning the 'double time' of *Othello*, theatre audiences are largely unaware of any inconsistencies, primarily because they are caught up in the psychological intensity of the play. In effect, two distinct time schemes seem to co-exist. The first of these is the imaginary time sequence that Iago creates to poison Othello's mind. Secondly, there is the tightly compressed time scheme of the main dramatic action. In the end, of course, to fully appreciate *Othello* – and indeed, all of Shakespeare's great dramas – a willing suspension of disbelief is a crucial part of the contract between audience and playwright.

Essential Scenes in Othello

In preparing for the Single Text *Othello* question, it is important to become familiar with the entire play through a close reading of the text. Your written work should show creative thought, supporting the points you make with good reference to key scenes. Some moments in the drama (including the five scenes listed below) are particularly revealing and worth studying in great detail.

Remember that commentaries and study guides are there to be challenged. In responding to exam questions, have confidence in developing your own ideas and always express yourself clearly. Identify the main elements of the question so that your answer is relevant and well structured. Make sure to avoid unfocused narrative. Wherever possible, find your own examples from the text to support your views and use accurate quotations when appropriate.

Act 1, Scene 1

The opening scene takes place on a street in Venice late at night. Iago talks to Roderigo about his hatred for Cassio and Othello. He informs Brabantio that his daughter, Desdemona, has secretly married the Moor, Othello, a successful general in the Venetian army.

Act 1, Scene 3

The Duke of Venice and his senators prepare for war against the Turks. Othello answers Brabantio's accusations of bewitching his daughter and is sent to Cyprus on military duty. Iago initiates his scheme of revenge against the Moor.

Act 2, Scene 1

The scene moves to Cyprus, where Othello, Desdemona and Iago arrive safely. A storm at sea has destroyed the Turkish fleet. Iago involves Roderigo in his plan to discredit Cassio and replace him as Othello's lieutenant. He also swears to ruin the happiness of the newlyweds.

Act 3, Scene 3

In this crucial scene, Desdemona pleads with her husband to reinstate Cassio, who has been dismissed from his post for drinking on duty. Iago persuades Othello that Desdemona and Cassio are secret lovers. Consumed by jealousy, the Moor becomes increasingly controlled by Iago.

Act 5, Scene 2

Othello murders Desdemona in her bed. Emilia reveals the truth about Iago's evil plot. Realising his terrible foolishness, the Moor then kills himself, leaving an unrepentant Iago to be punished by Cassio, who remains in Cyprus as the new governor.

Characters

DUKE OF VENICE

BRABANTIO (a senator), father to Desdemona

GRATIANO, brother to Brabantio

LODOVICO, kinsman to Brabantio

OTHELLO the Moor, a general in the military service of Venice

CASSIO, an honourable lieutenant (to Othello)

IAGO, an ensign to Othello

RODERIGO, a Venetian gentleman

MONTANO, governor of Cyprus (before Othello)

CLOWN (in service to Othello)

DESDEMONA, wife to Othello

EMILIA, wife to Iago

BIANCA, a courtesan (mistress to Cassio)

SENATORS, SAILORS, GENTLEMEN OF CYPRUS (OFFICERS, MESSENGERS, MUSICIANS)

The first act takes place in Venice. The rest of the play takes place in a seaport in Cyprus.

Act 1

SCENE 1 – *Venice: A street at night*

As the play opens, Roderigo and Iago are in the middle of a quarrel over money. Iago complains bitterly about Othello and boasts of taking revenge on him. He informs Brabantio that his daughter, Desdemona, has recently eloped with Othello. An outraged Brabantio organises a search party to find the couple.

'I know my price'

Enter Roderigo and Iago

Roderigo: Tush! Never tell me; I take it much unkindly
That thou, Iago, who hast had my purse
As if the strings were thine, shouldst know of this.

Iago: 'Sblood, but you will not hear me:
If ever I did dream of such a matter,
Abhor me.   5

Roderigo: Thou told'st me thou didst hold him in thy hate.

Iago: Despise me, if I do not. Three great ones of the city,
In personal suit to make me his lieutenant,
Off-capped to him: and, by the faith of man,   10
I know my price, I am worth no worse a place:
But he; as loving his own pride and purposes,
Evades them, with a bombast circumstance
Horribly stuffed with epithets of war;
And, in conclusion,   15
Nonsuits my mediators; for, 'Certes,' says he,
'I have already chosen my officer.'
And what was he?
Forsooth, a great arithmetician,
One Michael Cassio, a Florentine,   20
A fellow almost damned in a fair wife;
That never set a squadron in the field,
Nor the division of a battle knows
More than a spinster: unless the bookish theoric,
Wherein the toged consuls can propose   25
As masterly as he: mere prattle, without practice,
Is all his soldiership. But he, sir, had the election:
And I, of whom his eyes had seen the proof
At Rhodes, at Cyprus and on other grounds

1 Tush: *an expression of impatience*

3 this: *a reference to Othello and Desdemona eloping*

4 'Sblood: *By God's blood (a swear word)*

9 suit: *petition*

12 he: *Othello, unnamed, is verbally abused by Iago*
13 bombast circumstance: *pompous excuse*

16 Certes: *certainly*

19 arithmetician: *theorist*

20 Florentine: *Florence native*

25 toged consuls: *senators wearing the robes of peace*

27 had the election: *was chosen*

The rich fool *Roderigo, a rich Venetian in love with Desdemona, has been paying Iago handsomely to help win her love. He has now learned of Desdemona's marriage to Othello and is angry that Iago has not informed him of it: 'I take it much unkindly'.*

Seething hatred *Iago explains why he hates Othello. He accuses him of boasting. Iago is an experienced soldier ('I know my price'). He is bitter that Othello has chosen to ignore requests by influential people on his behalf. To his dismay, Othello has chosen the youthful Michael Cassio as his lieutenant. Iago is now furious at Othello and envious of Cassio, whom he keeps ridiculing.*

Clever manipulation *This is the first time Iago is seen extricating himself skilfully from an awkward situation, diverting attention away from his debts to Roderigo by focusing on how Othello is their common enemy.*

Christian and heathen, must be be-lee'd and calmed	30	30 be-lee'd: *pacified*
By debitor and creditor: this counter-caster,		31 counter-caster: *accountant*
He, in good time, must his lieutenant be,		
And I – God bless the mark!– his Moorship's ancient.		33 ancient: *old adviser, ensign, standard bearer*

Roderigo: By heaven, I rather would have been his hangman.

Iago: Why, there's no remedy; 'tis the curse of service.   35
Preferment goes by letter and affection,
And not by old gradation, where each second
Stood heir to the first. Now, sir, be judge yourself,
Whether I in any just term am affined
To love the Moor.

36 Preferment: *promotion*
36 letter: *academic qualifications*
37 gradation: *army service*

39 affined: *bound*

Roderigo: I would not follow him then.   40

Iago: O, sir, content you;
I follow him to serve my turn upon him:
We cannot all be masters, nor all masters
Cannot be truly followed. You shall mark
Many a duteous and knee-crooking knave,   45
That, doting on his own obsequious bondage,
Wears out his time, much like his master's ass,
For nought but provender, and when he's old, cashiered.
Whip me such honest knaves. Others there are
Who, trimmed, in forms and visages of duty,   50
Keep their hearts attending on themselves,
And throwing but shows of service on their lords,
Do well thrive by them and when they have lined
their coats
Do themselves homage: these fellows have some soul
And such a one do I profess myself. For, sir,   55
It is as sure as you are Roderigo,
Were I the Moor, I would not be Iago:
In following him, I follow but myself;

45 duteous: *diligent*
45 knee-crooking: *excessively attentive*
45 knave: *serving man*
46 obsequious bondage: *slavish behaviour*
48 provender: *food and drink*
48 cashiered: *dismissed from service*

50 visages of duty: *appearances of loyalty*

54 homage: *respect*

57 Were I the Moor, I would not be Iago: *cryptic remark suggesting that if Iago were Othello, he would not have anything to do with such a person as Iago*

- **Unflattering image** *Iago presents a dishonourable picture of his rival, Cassio: 'this counter-caster'. Furiously, he tells Roderigo why he hates both Cassio and Othello – he has not been promoted. He is a mere ensign, or standard-bearer, despite the fact that Othello had 'seen the proof' of Iago's expertise on the battlefield. Meanwhile, Cassio only knows the theory of war.*
- **Ingratitude in service** *The gullible Roderigo is easily led by Iago, who explains the 'curse of service' to him. Promotion depends on connections and favouritism rather than seniority. Iago reveals his plan to deceive Othello and eventually take revenge: 'I follow him to serve my turn upon him'.*
- **The reality of service** *A disapproving Iago recounts how a loyal servant spends his life like his master's donkey, working for food, and then when he is old, he is coldly dismissed from service. In Iago's cynical view, such servile servants deserve to be beaten, not praised.*

Heaven is my judge, not I for love and duty,
But seeming so, for my peculiar end: 60
For when my outward action doth demonstrate
The native act and figure of my heart
In compliment extern, 'tis not long after   *63 compliment extern: outward show*
But I will wear my heart upon my sleeve
For daws to peck at: I am not what I am.   65

Roderigo: What a full fortune does the thick-lips owe   *66 owe: own*
      If he can carry't thus!

Iago: Call up her father,
      Rouse him: make after him, poison his delight,
      Proclaim him in the streets; incense her kinsmen,
      And, though he in a fertile climate dwell,   70
      Plague him with flies: though that his joy be joy,
      Yet throw such vexations on't
      As it may lose some colour.

Roderigo: Here is her father's house; I'll call aloud.

Iago: Do, with like timorous accent, and dire yell,   75   *75 timorous: frightening or fearful*
      As when, by night and negligence, the fire
      Is spied in populous cities.

Roderigo: What ho! Brabantio! Signior Brabantio, ho!

Iago: Awake! What ho, Brabantio! Thieves, thieves!
      Look to your house, your daughter, and your bags!   80
      Thieves! thieves!

Brabantio appears above, at a window

Brabantio: What is the reason of this terrible summons?
      What is the matter there?

Roderigo: Signior, is all your family within?

Iago: Are your doors locked?

Brabantio: Why, wherefore ask you this?   85   *85 wherefore: why*

A scheming hypocrite *Iago reveals that he has no intention of resigning, but will remain in Othello's service 'for my peculiar end'. He will pretend to be loyal: 'I am not what I am'.*

The cunning plan *With fiendish ingenuity, Iago suggests to the gullible Roderigo that he awaken Senator Brabantio and tell him the news of his daughter's elopement.*

Derogatory language *Othello is not named directly, but Roderigo clearly enjoys using abusive racist language to ridicule him as 'the thick-lips'.*

Shakespeare Focus: Othello

Iago:	'Zounds, sir, you're robbed; for shame, put on	
	your gown;	
	Your heart is burst, you have lost half your soul;	
	Even now, now, very now, an old black ram	
	Is tupping your white ewe. Arise, arise;	
	Awake the snorting citizens with the bell,	90
	Or else the devil will make a grandsire of you:	
	Arise, I say.	
Brabantio:	What, have you lost your wits?	
Roderigo:	Most reverend signior, do you know my voice?	
Brabantio:	Not I: what are you?	
Roderigo:	My name is Roderigo.	
Brabantio:	The worser welcome:	95
	I have charged thee not to haunt about my doors:	
	In honest plainness thou hast heard me say	
	My daughter is not for thee; and now, in madness,	
	Being full of supper and distempering draughts,	
	Upon malicious bravery, dost thou come	100
	To start my quiet.	
Roderigo:	Sir, sir, sir—	
Brabantio:	But thou must needs be sure	
	My spirit and my place have in them power	
	To make this bitter to thee.	
Roderigo:	Patience, good sir.	
Brabantio:	What tell'st thou me of robbing? This is Venice;	105
	My house is not a grange.	
Roderigo:	Most grave Brabantio,	
	In simple and in pure soul I come to you.	

86 'Zounds: *by God's wounds (a swear word)*

89 tupping: *mating with*
89 white ewe: *Desdemona*
90 snorting: *snoring*
91 devil: *devils were often portrayed as black in old church paintings*

99 distempering draughts: *alcohol*

101 start: *disturb*

103 place: *position*

106 grange: *remote country house*

Animal imagery *Iago continues to use offensive animal imagery. He delights in hurting Desdemona's father, referring to Othello as* 'an old black ram' *who will make a* 'grandsire' *of Brabantio. Iago's crudity is clearly evident.*

Declaration *Roderigo openly declares himself to Brabantio, unlike the wily Iago:* 'do you know my voice?' *Iago is trying to ensure that Brabantio will take the news of Dedemona's disappearance seriously and will act quickly on it.*

Misunderstanding *Brabantio thinks Roderigo is drunk (*'full of supper and distempering draughts'*) and has come to make mischief. He has already rejected Roderigo's marriage proposal for Desdemona:* 'My daughter is not for thee'.

Iago: 'Zounds, sir, you are one of those that will not
serve God, if the devil bid you. Because we come to
do you service and you think we are ruffians, you'll   110
have your daughter covered with a Barbary horse;
you'll have your nephews neigh to you; you'll have
coursers for cousins and gennets for germans.

Brabantio: What profane wretch art thou?

Iago: I am one, sir, that comes to tell you your daughter   115
and the Moor are now making the beast with two backs.

Brabantio: Thou art a villain.

Iago: Thou art a senator.

Brabantio: This thou shalt answer; I know thee, Roderigo.

Roderigo: Sir, I will answer any thing. But, I beseech you,   120
If it be your pleasure and most wise consent,
As partly I find it is, that your fair daughter,
At this odd-even and dull watch o' the night,
Transported, with no worse nor better guard
But with a knave of common hire, a gondolier,   125
To the gross clasps of a lascivious Moor –
If this be known to you, and your allowance,
We then have done you bold and saucy wrongs;
But if you know not this, my manners tell me
We have your wrong rebuke. Do not believe   130
That, from the sense of all civility,
I thus would play and trifle with your reverence:
Your daughter, if you have not given her leave,
I say again, hath made a gross revolt;
Tying her duty, beauty, wit and fortunes   135
In an extravagant and wheeling stranger
Of here and everywhere: straight satisfy yourself.

111 Barbary horse: *Arabic horse*

113 coursers: *greyhounds*
113 gennets: *agile animals similar to civets*
113 germans: *relatives*

116 making the beast with two backs: *having sexual intercourse*

123 odd-even: *just after midnight*

126 lascivious: *lewd, lusty*

134 gross revolt: *blatant act of rebellion*

136 wheeling: *of no fixed place*

Interjection *Iago interrupts impatiently. He is disgusted at Roderigo's politeness and soon reverts to gross animal comparisons:* 'your daughter covered with a Barbary horse'. *Once again, Iago resorts to speaking in prose. His lack of respect and refinement is clearly evident.*

An angry father *Brabantio is incensed at Iago's lewd suggestions and immediately confronts him:* 'Thou art a villain'. *Iago, under cover of anonymity, smartly responds,* 'Thou art a senator'.

Terrible news *Roderigo describes Desdemona's* 'gross revolt' *into the arm of the* 'lascivious Moor', *a man of no consequence,* 'an extravagant and wheeling stranger/Of here and everywhere'. *He is devastated that Desdemona has chosen, in his opinion, so poorly,* 'Tying her duty, beauty, wit and fortunes' *to one such as Othello.*

Shakespeare Focus: Othello

	If she be in her chamber or your house,	
	Let loose on me the justice of the state	
	For thus deluding you.	

Brabantio: Strike on the tinder, ho!   140

Give me a taper! Call up all my people!

This accident is not unlike my dream:

Belief of it oppresses me already.

Light, I say, light!

Exit

Iago: Farewell; for I must leave you:

It seems not meet, nor wholesome to my place,   145

To be produced as, if I stay, I shall

Against the Moor: for, I do know, the state,

However this may gall him with some cheque,

Cannot with safety cast him, for he's embarked

With such loud reason to the Cyprus wars,   150

Which even now stand in act, that, for their souls,

Another of his fathom they have none,

To lead their business: in which regard,

Though I do hate him as I do hell-pains.

Yet, for necessity of present life,   155

I must show out a flag and sign of love,

Which is indeed but sign. That you shall surely find him,

Lead to the Sagittary the raised search;

And there will I be with him. So farewell.

Exit
Enter Brabantio and Servants with torches

Brabantio: It is too true an evil. Gone she is;   160

And what's to come of my despised time

Is nought but bitterness. Now, Roderigo,

Where didst thou see her? O unhappy girl!

The reaction *Brabantio calls for light:* ('Strike on the tinder'), *and a search party* ('call up all my people'). *He also reveals his superstitious nature,* 'This accident is not unlike my dream'. *Brabantio, just like Othello later in the play, condemns on hearsay without looking for evidence.*

Slippery knave *Iago explains to Roderigo that he cannot be seen to be associating with the search party, as his loyalty to Othello may be questioned. He reiterates his hatred for Othello as he exits:* 'Though I do hate him as I do hell-pains'.

With the Moor, say'st thou? Who would be a father!
How didst thou know 'twas she? O she deceives me   165
Past thought! What said she to you? Get more tapers:
Raise all my kindred. Are they married, think you?

Roderigo: Truly, I think they are.

Brabantio: O heaven! How got she out? O treason of the blood!
Fathers, from hence trust not your daughters' minds   170
By what you see them act. Is there not charms
By which the property of youth and maidhood
May be abused? Have you not read, Roderigo,
Of some such thing?

Roderigo: Yes, sir, I have indeed.   175

Brabantio: Call up my brother. O, would you had had her!
Some one way, some another. Do you know
Where we may apprehend her and the Moor?

Roderigo: I think I can discover him, if you please,
To get good guard and go along with me.   180

Brabantio: Pray you, lead on. At every house I'll call;
I may command at most. Get weapons, ho!
And raise some special officers of night.
On, good Roderigo; I'll deserve your pains.

Exeunt

171 charms: *spells, love potion*

184 deserve your pains: *reward you for your trouble*

Self-pitying father Brabantio complains, 'Who would be a father!' *He wonders if his daughter is really married and his broken speech vividly conveys his shattered state, as he is torn between love for his daughter and his anguish at her deception.*

The search party Desdemona's father vacillates between anger ('O treason of the blood') *and superstition* ('Is there not charms') *as he wishes all could be undone and that even Roderigo, whom he had despised, had married her:* 'O, would you had had her!'

Sure of support The distraught father starts to rally support from his friends and neighbours, confident that he is well-regarded in Venice. Brabantio thinks he can 'command at most'.

Key Points

- Shakespeare has created a dark night setting, with hushed, conspiratorial conversations adding to the mood of intrigue and dark practices.
- The playwright introduces the central conflict between Iago and Othello and establishes an atmosphere of deception.
- Iago embodies the blurred distinction between appearance and reality.
- The theme of love is introduced through Roderigo's disappointed hopes of romance and the elopement of Desdemona and Othello.
- Racism is clearly evident in the frequent belittling references to Othello's colour and background.
- The audience is poised in anticipation of meeting the Moor, a man both hated and loved.
- Othello is also the focus of Roderigo's jealousy and Brabantio's fury as well as Iago's evil scheming.

Act 1

SCENE 2 – *Venice: Outside the Sagittary Inn*

In this highly charged scene, Iago seeks out Othello. He warns him against both Roderigo and Brabantio. However, Othello remains calm, saying that he is respected in Venice. The search parties arrive, led by Cassio, who explains that Othello has been urgently summoned to the senate because of the Turkish invasion of Cyprus, a Venetian colony. Othello tries to pacify an angry Brabantio.

Enter Othello, Iago and attendants with torches

Iago:	Though in the trade of war I have slain men,	
	Yet do I hold it very stuff o' the conscience	2 stuff: *essence*
	To do no contrived murder: I lack iniquity	3 I lack iniquity: *sometimes*
	Sometimes to do me service: nine or ten times	*I'm too pleasant for my own good*
	I had thought to have yerked him here under the ribs. 5	5 yerked: *stabbed*
Othello:	'Tis better as it is.	
Iago:	Nay, but he prated,	
	And spoke such scurvy and provoking terms	
	Against your honour	
	That, with the little godliness I have,	
	I did full hard forbear him. But, I pray you, sir, 10	
	Are you fast married? Be assured of this,	
	That the magnifico is much beloved,	12 magnifico: *nobleman (referring to Brabantio)*
	And hath in his effect a voice potential	
	As double as the duke's. He will divorce you,	
	Or put upon you what restraint and grievance 15	
	The law, with all his might to enforce it on,	
	Will give him cable.	17 give him cable: *allow him*
Othello:	Let him do his spite:	
	My services which I have done the signiory	18 signiory: *Ventian government*
	Shall out-tongue his complaints. 'Tis yet to know –	
	Which, when I know that boasting is an honour, 20	

Dignified Othello *A very different Othello from what we were led to expect by Iago now emerges in this scene. Here is a man confident of his worth to the Venetian state:* 'My services ... Shall out-tongue his complaints'. *He is also proud of his family heritage:* 'men of royal siege'.

I shall provulgate – I fetch my life and being
From men of royal siege, and my demerits
May speak unbonneted to as proud a fortune
As this that I have reached. For know, Iago,
But that I love the gentle Desdemona,   25
I would not my unhoused free condition
Put into circumscription and confine
For the sea's worth. But look what lights come yond!

Iago: Those are the raised father and his friends:
You were best go in.

Othello: Not I; I must be found.   30
My parts, my title and my perfect soul
Shall manifest me rightly. Is it they?

Iago: By Janus, I think no.

Enter Cassio and certain officers with torches

Othello: The servants of the duke, and my lieutenant!
The goodness of the night upon you, friends.   35
What is the news?

Cassio: The duke does greet you, general,
And he requires your haste-post-haste appearance,
Even on the instant.

Othello: What is the matter, think you?   40

Cassio: Something from Cyprus as I may divine.
It is a business of some heat. The galleys
Have sent a dozen sequent messengers
This very night at one another's heels;
And many of the consuls, raised and met,   45
Are at the duke's already. You have been
hotly called for,
When, being not at your lodging to be found,

Glossary (right margin):

21 provulgate: *make public*

22 siege: *rank*
22 demerits: *traits*
23 unbonneted: *respectfully*

26 my unhoused free condition: *my status as a bachelor*
27 circumscription: *restriction*

28 raised: *alarmed and indignant*

33 Janus: *two-faced Roman god the month of January is named after, as it faces both winter and summer at the same time*

41 divine: *guess*

43 sequent: *one after the other*

Double-dealing *Iago simulates loyalty, pretending to be angry with Roderigo and offering to save Othello from the coming search party:* 'Those are the raised father and his friends: /You were best go in'.

Standing firm *Othello, confident of his worth, feels he can answer for his actions:* 'My services ... Shall out-tongue his complaints'. *He makes a genuine declaration of love* ('I love the gentle Desdemona') *and he forcefully declares that he would not have given up his freedom – his* 'unhoused free condition' *– otherwise.*

Heated news *Cassio brings urgent news from the Senate that the Turks have captured Cyprus. Othello is* 'hotly called for'. *This indicates that Othello is right in his estimation of his importance to the senate.*

The senate hath sent about three several quests
To search you out.

Othello: 'Tis well I am found by you.
I will but spend a word here in the house,
And go with you.

Exit

Cassio: Ancient, what makes he here?

Iago: 'Faith, he to-night hath boarded a land carrack: 50
If it prove lawful prize, he's made for ever.

Cassio: I do not understand.

Iago: He's married.

Cassio: To who?

Re-enter Othello

Iago: Marry, to – Come, captain, will you go?

Othello: Have with you.

Cassio: Here comes another troop to seek for you.

Iago: It is Brabantio. General, be advised,   55
He comes to bad intent.

*Enter Brabantio, Roderigo and officers
with torches and weapons*

Othello: Holla, stand there!

Roderigo: Signior, it is the Moor.

Brabantio: Down with him, thief!

They draw on both sides

Iago: You, Roderigo! Come, sir, I am for you.

50 land carrack: *treasure ship*
(Desdemona)
51 lawful prize: *legal capture*

Cynicism and loyalty *Othello's sincere declaration of love for Desdemona is twisted by the sceptical sneers of Iago, who can only see the relationship in terms of material gain to Othello. He refers to her in sea-faring terms as 'a land carrack' and 'lawful prize'. Cassio, a genuine friend, protects Othello by feigning ignorance of the marriage.*

'you shall more command with years'

Othello: Keep up your bright swords, for the dew will rust them.   59 Keep up: *put away*
Good signior, you shall more command with years   60
Than with your weapons.

Brabantio: O thou foul thief, where hast thou stowed my daughter?
Damned as thou art, thou hast enchanted her;
For I'll refer me to all things of sense,   64 refer me ... sense: *appeal*
If she in chains of magic were not bound,   65   *to common sense*

A calm leader *Othello firmly assumes authority over an increasingly tense situation as Brabantio and his followers arrive and draw their weapons:* 'Keep up your bright swords, for the dew will rust them'.

Whether a maid so tender, fair and happy,
So opposite to marriage that she shunned
The wealthy curled darlings of our nation,
Would ever have, to incur a general mock,
Run from her guardage to the sooty bosom   70
Of such a thing as thou – to fear, not to delight.
Judge me the world, if 'tis not gross in sense
That thou hast practised on her with foul charms,
Abused her delicate youth with drugs or minerals
That weaken motion: I'll have it disputed on;   75
'Tis probable and palpable to thinking.
I therefore apprehend and do attach thee
For an abuser of the world, a practiser
Of arts inhibited and out of warrant.
Lay hold upon him: if he do resist,   80
Subdue him at his peril.

Othello: Hold your hands,
Both you of my inclining, and the rest.
Were it my cue to fight, I should have known it
Without a prompter. Where will you that I go
To answer this your charge?

Brabantio: To prison, till fit time   85
Of law and course of direct session
Call thee to answer.

Othello: What if I do obey?
How may the duke be therewith satisfied,
Whose messengers are here about my side,
Upon some present business of the state   90
To bring me to him?

First Officer: 'Tis true, most worthy signior;
The duke's in council and your noble self,
I am sure, is sent for.

70 guardage: *guardianship*	
70 sooty bosom: *derogatory reference to Othello's colour*	
72 gross in sense: *quite obvious*	
79 out of warrant: *against the law*	
82 of my inclining: *my supporters*	

A hysterical father *Brabantio launches into a diatribe and charges Othello with using the dark arts ('in chains of magic') and drugs ('drugs or minerals') to win Desdemona. She has already refused many suitors: 'The wealthy curled darlings of our nation'. He insults Othello, dehumanising him as 'a thing', and is blatantly racist.*

Impressive composure *Othello confidently states, 'Were it my cue to fight, I should have known it/ Without a prompter'. The audience admires the self-control of this commanding figure.*

Righteous anger *Brabantio insists that the law try Othello in 'direct session'. He believes that the justice of his cause will vindicate him: 'the duke himself ... Cannot but feel this wrong as 'twere their own'. The audience is also likely to feel some sympathy for the wronged father.*

Brabantio: How! the duke in council!
In this time of the night! Bring him away:
Mine's not an idle cause: the duke himself,   95
Or any of my brothers of the state,
Cannot but feel this wrong as 'twere their own;
For if such actions may have passage free,
Bond-slaves and pagans shall our statesmen be.

Exeunt

96 brothers of the state: *fellow senators*

Key Points

Act 1, Scene 2

- A hypocritical Iago pretends to be outraged at Roderigo.
- A composed Othello refuses to be provoked.
- A furious father seeks redress while a nervous senate looks for its champion in an hour of crisis.

Act 1

SCENE 3 – *Venice: A council-chamber*

The Duke and senators hope that Othello will deal with the Turkish enemies. When Brabantio accuses Othello of using magic to win Desdemona, the couple explain how their love developed. The Duke is sympathetic, but is more concerned with the possible crisis in Cyprus and the security of the Venetian state. Othello agrees to leave immediately for Cyprus, requesting that Desdemona accompany him. Iago comes up with a plan to make Othello jealous by suggesting that Desdemona and Cassio are secret lovers.

The Duke and Senators sitting at a table with lights. Officers attending.

Duke of Venice:	There is no composition in these news
	That gives them credit.
First Senator:	Indeed, they are disproportioned.
	My letters say a hundred and seven galleys.
Duke of Venice:	And mine, a hundred and forty.
Second Senator:	And mine, two hundred:
	But though they jump not on a just account
	As in these cases, where the aim reports,
	'Tis oft with difference – yet do they all confirm
	A Turkish fleet, and bearing up to Cyprus.
Duke of Venice:	Nay, it is possible enough to judgment:
	I do not so secure me in the error,
	But the main article I do approve
	In fearful sense.
Sailor:	[*Within*] What, ho! What, ho! What, ho!
First Officer:	A messenger from the galleys.

Enter a Sailor

Line numbers and glosses:

5

10

1 composition: *agreement*

2 disproportioned: *inconsistent*

5 jump not on a just account: *do not agree precisely*

8 bearing up: *sailing towards*

10 secure me: *feel confident*

11 approve: *accept*

12 In fearful sense: *as a cause for alarm*

Crisis *This scene marks a change from private family concerns to public affairs of state. Venice had a vast commercial empire that relied on trade through the Mediterranean. Conflicting reports of danger are arriving thick and fast ('disproportioned').*

Duke of Venice: Now, what's the business?

Sailor: The Turkish preparation makes for Rhodes;
So was I bid report here to the state   15
By Signior Angelo.

Duke of Venice: How say you by this change?

First Senator: This cannot be,
By no assay of reason: 'tis a pageant,
To keep us in false gaze. When we consider
The importancy of Cyprus to the Turk,   20
And let ourselves again but understand,
That as it more concerns the Turk than Rhodes,
So may he with more facile question bear it,
For that it stands not in such warlike brace,
But altogether lacks the abilities   25
That Rhodes is dressed in: if we make thought of this,
We must not think the Turk is so unskilful
To leave that latest which concerns him first,
Neglecting an attempt of ease and gain,
To wake and wage a danger profitless.   30

Duke of Venice: Nay, in all confidence, he's not for Rhodes.

First Officer: Here is more news.

Enter a Messenger

Messenger: The Ottomites, reverend and gracious,
Steering with due course towards the isle of Rhodes,
Have there injointed them with an after fleet.   35

First Senator: Ay, so I thought. How many, as you guess?

Messenger: Of thirty sail: and now they do restem
Their backward course, bearing with frank appearance
Their purposes toward Cyprus. Signior Montano,
Your trusty and most valiant servitor,   40
With his free duty recommends you thus,
And prays you to believe him.

Margin glosses:
18 assay: *test*
18 pageant: *show, diversion*
24 brace: *readiness*
30 wage: *risk*
33 Ottomites: *Turks (from the Ottoman Empire)*
35 injointed: *linked up*
41 free duty: *respect*

Rumours of war *In great anxiety, the senate debates whether the Turks are pretending to go to Rhodes:* 'a pageant/To keep us in false gaze'. *Reports then arrive that the Turkish ships have joined up with another fleet and are doubling back:* 'Their purposes towards Cyprus'. *The Venetians frequently employed mercenaries to safeguard their empire, which depended on trade and safe sea routes for transporting goods.*

Duke of Venice:	'Tis certain, then, for Cyprus.
	Marcus Luccicos, is not he in town?
First Senator:	He's now in Florence.
Duke of Venice:	Write from us to him; post-post-haste dispatch. 45
First Senator:	Here comes Brabantio and the valiant Moor.

Enter Brabantio, Othello, Iago, Roderigo and Officers

Duke of Venice:	Valiant Othello, we must straight employe you
	Against the general enemy Ottoman.
	[*To Brabantio*]
	I did not see you; welcome, gentle signior; 50
	We lacked your counsel and your help tonight.
Brabantio:	So did I yours. Good your grace, pardon me;
	Neither my place nor aught I heard of business
	Hath raised me from my bed, nor doth the general care
	Take hold on me, for my particular grief 55
	Is of so flood-gate and o'erbearing nature
	That it engluts and swallows other sorrows
	And it is still itself.
Duke of Venice:	Why, what's the matter?
Brabantio:	My daughter! O, my daughter!
Senators:	Dead?
Brabantio:	Ay, to me;
	She is abused, stolen from me and corrupted 60
	By spells and medicines bought of mountebanks;
	For nature so preposterously to err,
	Sans witchcraft could not.

47 straight: *straight away*

57 engluts: *engulfs, overwhelms*

61 mountebanks: *dubious dealers*

63 Sans: *without*

High esteem *The Duke greets the arrival of Othello, Brabantio and the others by immediately appointing Othello as Venetian commander in charge of the defence of the state:* 'Valiant Othello, we must straight employ you/Against the general enemy Ottoman'. *In marked contrast, Brabantio is greeted by the remark,* 'I did not see you'. *However, he is assuaged by the comment* 'We lacked your counsel ... tonight'.

The broken father *Brabantio, out of control, makes wild, extravagant accusations against Othello, as he believes his daughter would never have acted this way unless she was* 'corrupted/By spells and medicines bought of mountebanks'.

Duke of Venice: Whoe'er he be that in this foul proceeding
Hath thus beguiled your daughter of herself   65
And you of her, the bloody book of law
You shall yourself read in the bitter letter
After your own sense, yea, though our proper son
Stood in your action.

Brabantio: Humbly I thank your grace.   70
Here is the man, this Moor, whom now, it seems,
Your special mandate for the state-affairs
Hath hither brought.

Duke of Venice: Senators: We are very sorry for it.

Duke of Venice: [*To Othello*] What, in your own part, can you say to this?

Brabantio: Nothing, but this is so.   75

Othello: Most potent, grave, and reverend signiors,
My very noble and approved good masters,
That I have taken away this old man's daughter,
It is most true; true, I have married her:
The very head and front of my offending   80
Hath this extent, no more. Rude am I in my speech,
And little blessed with the soft phrase of peace:
For since these arms of mine had seven years' pith,
Till now some nine moons wasted, they have used
Their dearest action in the tented field,   85
And little of this great world can I speak,
More than pertains to feats of broil and battle,
And therefore little shall I grace my cause
In speaking for myself. Yet, by your gracious patience,
I will a round unvarnish'd tale deliver   90
Of my whole course of love: what drugs, what charms,
What conjuration and what mighty magic –
For such proceeding I am charged withal –
I won his daughter.

---

68 After your own sense: *however you want*

83 pith: *strength*

85 field: *battlefield*

92 conjuration: *spells*

First reaction *On hearing the charges* ('foul proceeding'), *the Duke is outraged and promises swift justice:* 'the bloody book of law'.

Identified *Brabantio points to the offender:* 'Here is the man, this Moor'.

A magnificent defence *With quiet and solemn sincerity, Othello responds to the Duke's invitation to tell his* 'part'. *He admits,* 'I have married her', *and explains that he has little education:* 'Rude am I in my speech'. *He did not have time for such a luxury, as he had been on the battlefield continuously for seven years until nine months ago. The Moor is concerned that he will not help his cause by speaking for himself.*

Act 1, Scene 3   19

Brabantio: A maiden never bold;
Of spirit so still and quiet, that her motion   95   95 motion: *emotion, desires*
Blushed at herself; and she, in spite of nature,
Of years, of country, credit, everything,   97 credit: *reputation*
To fall in love with what she feared to look on?
It is a judgment maimed and most imperfect
That will confess perfection so could err   100
Against all rules of nature, and must be driven
To find out practices of cunning hell,
Why this should be. I therefore vouch again
That with some mixtures powerful o'er the blood
Or with some dram conjured to this effect   105   105 dram: *potion*
He wrought upon her.

Duke of Venice: To vouch this is no proof,   106 vouch: *assert*
Without more wider and more overt test
Than these thin habits and poor likelihoods   108 thin habits: *outward appearances*
Of modern seeming do prefer against him.   109 modern seeming: *common beliefs*

First Senator: But, Othello, speak:
Did you by indirect and forced courses   110
Subdue and poison this young maid's affections?
Or came it by request and such fair question
As soul to soul affordeth?

Othello: I do beseech you,
Send for the lady to the Sagittary,   115
If you do find me foul in her report,   116 foul: *wicked*
The trust, the office I do hold of you,
Not only take away, but let your sentence
Even fall upon my life.

Duke of Venice: Fetch Desdemona hither.   120

Answering the accusation *Othello continues his story (*'a round unvarnish'd tale'*) of how he won Brabantio's daughter by fair means, not foul.*

An incredulous father *Brabantio cannot accept that* 'A maiden never bold' *should fall in love* 'with what she feared to look on' – *another racist slur. Her father is insisting that this union of mixed race is so unnatural that Othello must have used* 'some mixtures powerful o'er the blood' *to win her.*

The Duke's reply *The careful voice of law is heard as the Duke reminds the grieving father that to simply say something is not to prove it:* 'To vouch this is no proof'.

A request *Othello asks that Desdemona is sent for to let her speak before her father. He wants her to corroborate his evidence and is completely confident of her response. He offers the Duke to* 'let your sentence/Even fall upon my life' *if she speaks badly of him.*

Othello: Ancient, conduct them: you best know the place.

Exeunt Iago and Attendants

And, till she come, as truly as to heaven
I do confess the vices of my blood,
So justly to your grave ears I'll present
How I did thrive in this fair lady's love,   125
And she in mine.

Duke of Venice: Say it, Othello.

Othello: Her father loved me; oft invited me;
Still questioned me the story of my life,
From year to year, the battles, sieges, fortunes,
That I have passed.   130
I ran it through, even from my boyish days,
To the very moment that he bade me tell it;
Wherein I spake of most disastrous chances, | 133 chances: *events*
Of moving accidents by flood and field of me | 134 by flood and field: *on sea and on land*
Of hair-breadth scapes i' the imminent deadly breach,   135
Of being taken by the insolent foe
And sold to slavery, of my redemption thence
And portance in my travels' history:
Wherein of antres vast and deserts idle, | 139 antres: *caves*
Rough quarries, rocks and hills whose heads touch heaven 140
It was my hint to speak – such was the process
And of the Cannibals that each other eat,
The Anthropophagi and men whose heads | 143 Anthropophagi: *man-eaters, cannibals*
Do grow beneath their shoulders. This to hear
Would Desdemona seriously incline;   145
But still the house-affairs would draw her thence:
Which ever as she could with haste dispatch,
She'd come again, and with a greedy ear
Devour up my discourse; which I observing,
Took once a pliant hour, and found good means   150 | 150 pliant: *favourable*

An heroic story *Now Othello recounts how he was frequently an invited guest in Brabantio's house. 'Her father loved me, oft invited me' to tell the dramatic story of his adventures, 'my travels' history'. A different picture is again emerging of Othello. His relationship with Brabantio was formerly warm and cordial, which is in direct contrast to the recent accusations levelled at him by the outraged father.*

The listener *As Othello spoke of the strange places and people he met, such as the 'Anthropophagi', Desdemona would come to listen 'seriously incline'.*

To draw from her a prayer of earnest heart
That I would all my pilgrimage dilate,
Whereof by parcels she had something heard,
But not intentively: I did consent,
And often did beguile her of her tears   155
When I did speak of some distressful stroke
That my youth suffered. My story being done,
She gave me for my pains a world of sighs:
She swore, in faith, 'twas strange,
'twas passing strange,
'Twas pitiful, 'twas wondrous pitiful: 160
She wished she had not heard it, yet she wished
That heaven had made her such a man. She
thanked me,
And bade me, if I had a friend that loved her,
I should but teach him how to tell my story,
And that would woo her. Upon this hint I spake: 165
She loved me for the dangers I had passed,
And I loved her that she did pity them.
This only is the witchcraft I have used:
Here comes the lady; let her witness it.

Enter Desdemona, Iago, and Attendants

Duke of Venice: I think this tale would win my daughter too.   170
Good Brabantio, take up this mangled matter at the best:
Men do their broken weapons rather use
Than their bare hands.

Brabantio: I pray you, hear her speak:
If she confess that she was half the wooer,
Destruction on my head, if my bad blame   175
Light on the man! Come hither, gentle mistress:
Do you perceive in all this noble company
Where most you owe obedience?

---

154 intentively: *altogether*

159 passing: *exceedingly*

169 witness: *give evidence about*

176 Light: *fall*

The reaction *Desdemona told Othello that if he had a* 'friend that loved her,/I should but teach him how to tell my story,/And that would woo her'. *Desdemona had freely initiated the relationship:* 'Upon this hint I spake'.

The judgement *The Duke advises Brabantio to make the best of a difficult situation. Is he thinking as a father or as a politician?*

The disbeliever *Brabantio still cannot believe that Desdemona was* 'half the wooer'. *He changes course, now demanding to know from his daughter* 'Where most you owe obedience?'.

Desdemona: My noble father,
I do perceive here a divided duty: 180
To you I am bound for life and education;
My life and education both do learn me   *182 learn me: teach me*
How to respect you; you are the lord of duty;
I am hitherto your daughter. But here's my husband,
And so much duty as my mother showed
To you, preferring you before her father,   185
So much I challenge that I may profess   *186 challenge: claim*
Due to the Moor my lord.

Brabantio: God bu'y! I have done.   *187 God bu'y: God be with you (goodbye)*
Please it your grace, on to the state-affairs.
I had rather to adopt a child than get it.
Come hither, Moor: 190
I here do give thee that with all my heart
Which, but thou hast already, with all my heart
I would keep from thee. For your sake, jewel,
I am glad at soul I have no other child,
For thy escape would teach me tyranny   195
To hang clogs on them. I have done, my lord.   *196 clogs: blocks of wood tied to horses' legs to stop them escaping*

Duke of Venice: Let me speak like yourself, and lay a sentence
Which as a grise or step may help these lovers   *198 grise: step on a staircase*
Into your favour.
When remedies are past, the griefs are ended   200
By seeing the worst which late on hopes depended.
To mourn a mischief that is past and gone
Is the next way to draw new mischief on.
What cannot be preserved when fortune takes,
Patience her injury a mockery makes.   205
The robbed that smiles steals something from the thief;
He robs himself that spends a bootless grief.   *207 bootless: useless*

Divided duty *Speaking quietly but forthrightly, Desdemona acknowledges the debt she owes her father for 'life and education', but just as her mother left her father for Brabantio, she too will do likewise.*

Denied *The distraught father erupts in angry frustration, declaring, 'I had rather to adopt a child than get it'. He advises the Duke to attend instead to the matters of state.*

Pragmatic advice *The Duke, with admirable common sense, advises Brabantio not to 'mourn a mischief that is past and gone'. This will simply invite other bad things to happen. Brabantio is not convinced and throws the Duke's words back at him, suggesting that if this is so, then Venetians will not lose Cyprus 'so long as we can smile'. Is Brabantio highlighting a flaw in the Duke's advice?*

Brabantio: So let the Turk of Cyprus us beguile;
We lose it not, so long as we can smile.
He bears the sentence well that nothing bears   210
But the free comfort which from thence he hears,
But he bears both the sentence and the sorrow
That, to pay grief, must of poor patience borrow.
These sentences, to sugar, or to gall,   214 gall: *bitterness*
Being strong on both sides, are equivocal: 215
But words are words; I never yet did hear
That the bruised heart was pierced through the ear.
I humbly beseech you, proceed to the affairs of state.

Duke of Venice: The Turk with a most mighty preparation makes for
Cyprus. Othello, the fortitude of the place is best
known to you; and though we have there a substitute   220
of most allowed sufficiency, yet opinion, a
sovereign mistress of effects, throws a more safer
voice on you: you must therefore be content to
slubber the gloss of your new fortunes with this   224 slubber: *spoil*
more stubborn and boisterous expedition.   225

Othello: The tyrant custom, most grave senators,
Hath made the flinty and steel couch of war
My thrice-driven bed of down: I do agnise   228: thrice-driven bed of
A natural and prompt alacrity   down: *a feather bed of the very finest quality*
I find in hardness, and do undertake   230   228 agnise: *acknowledge*
These present wars against the Ottomites.   231 Ottomites: *Turks*
Most humbly therefore bending to your state,
I crave fit disposition for my wife.   233 disposition: *arrangements*
Due reference of place and exhibition,   234 exhibition: *financial support*
With such accommodation and besort   235   235 besort: *servants*
As levels with her breeding.

Duke of Venice: If you please,
Be it at her father's.

Brabantio: I'll not have it so.

Othello: Nor I.

Desdemona: Nor I; I would not there reside,
To put my father in impatient thoughts

Pressing matters *Othello is clearly informed by the Duke of his importance in this time of national emergency:* 'opinion ... throws a more safer voice on you'. *He is the consummate professional soldier and eagerly agrees to undertake* 'These present wars against the Ottomites'.

<table>
<tr><td></td><td>By being in his eye. Most gracious duke,</td><td>240</td><td></td></tr>
</table>

By being in his eye. Most gracious duke,   240
To my unfolding lend your prosperous ear;
And let me find a charter in your voice,   242 let me find a charter in
To assist my simpleness.   your voice: *let me hear you*
                                                  allow me

Duke of Venice: What would you, Desdemona?

Desdemona: That I did love the Moor to live with him,
My downright violence and storm of fortunes   245   245 downright violence: *open*
May trumpet to the world: my heart's subdued   *rebellion*
Even to the very quality of my lord:
I saw Othello's visage in his mind,
And to his honour and his valiant parts
Did I my soul and fortunes consecrate.   250
So that, dear lords, if I be left behind,
A moth of peace, and he go to the war,
The rites for which I love him are bereft me,
And I a heavy interim shall support
By his dear absence. Let me go with him.   255

Othello: Let her have your voices.
Vouch with me, heaven, I therefore beg it not,
To please the palate of my appetite,
Nor to comply with heat the young affects
In me defunct and proper satisfaction,   260
But to be free and bounteous to her mind:
And heaven defend your good souls, that you think
I will your serious and great business scant   263 scant: *neglect*
For she is with me: no, when light-wing'd toys
Of feathered Cupid seal with wanton dullness   265   265 seal: *close up*
My speculative and officed instruments,
That my disports corrupt and taint my business,   267 disports: *sexual pleasures*
Let housewives make a skillet of my helm,
And all indign and base adversities   269 indign: *unworthy*
Make head against my estimation!   270

Desdemona asserts herself Brabantio, Othello and Desdemona refuse the Duke's suggestion that Desdemona stay at her father's house during Othello's absence. Instead, Desdemona eloquently pleads her case to accompany Othello on his campaign: 'I did love the Moor to live with him'. *Is Desdemona being selfish? Surely all partners of serving soldiers must endure separation? Is she putting her interests above that of the state? Or is she just totally in love with her new husband and does not mind sharing his dangerous mission so long as she can be with him?*

Romantic love Othello agrees with Desdemona and swears he will not neglect his duty if she accompanies him: 'your serious and great business scant'.

Act 1, Scene 3   25

Duke of Venice:	Be it as you shall privately determine,
	Either for her stay or going: the affair cries haste,
	And speed must answer it.
First Senator:	You must away to-night.
Othello:	With all my heart.
Duke of Venice:	At nine in the morning here we'll meet again.
	Othello, leave some officer behind,
	And he shall our commission bring to you;
	With such things else of quality and respect
	As doth import you.
Othello:	So please your grace, my ancient;
	A man he is of honest and trust:
	To his conveyance I assign my wife,
	With what else needful your good grace shall think
	To be sent after me.
Duke of Venice:	Let it be so.
	Good night to everyone.
	To Brabantio
	And, noble signior,
	If virtue no delighted beauty lack,
	Your son-in-law is far more fair than black.
First Senator:	Adieu, brave Moor, use Desdemona well.
Brabantio:	Look to her, Moor, if thou hast eyes to see:
	She has deceived her father, and may thee.
Othello:	My life upon her faith!

275

279 import: *concern*

280

285

285 delighted: *outstanding*

287 use: *treat*

290

Haste *The Duke agrees that whatever agreement they reach shall be as they* 'privately determine'. *He reiterates that speed is needed to repel the danger to the state:* 'the affair cries haste'. *The audience will wonder if he is genuinely concerned with the private family issue when he tells Brabantio that his* 'son-in-law is far more fair than black'. *Does his comment indicate the underlying racism within Venice? Is Othello's value only the military service he can bring to the state in a national emergency?*

A parting shot *Brabantio advises Othello to watch Desdemona:* 'She has deceived her father, and may thee'. *Is the father now losing the sympathy of the audience through this cruel remark? Could this comment come between the couple at a later stage in the play? Will Othello's dramatic declaration of love (*'My life upon her faith'*) prove true?*

Trust *Othello has complete faith in Iago:* 'A man he is of honest and trust'. *He has no hesitation in placing Desdemona in his care. The audience already knows the real Iago, of course, and that now Desdemona is at the mercy of this unscrupulous villain. The tension builds.*

Exeunt Duke, Brabantio, Cassio, Senators and Attendants

Othello: Honest Iago,
My Desdemona must I leave to thee:
I prithee, let thy wife attend on her:
And bring them after in the best advantage.   293 best advantage: *first opportunity*
Come, Desdemona: I have but an hour
Of love, of worldly matters and direction,   295
To spend with thee: we must obey the time.

Exeunt Othello and Desdemona

Roderigo: Iago.

Iago: What say'st thou, noble heart?

Roderigo: What will I do, thinkest thou?

Iago: Why, go to bed, and sleep.   300

Roderigo: I will incontinently drown myself.   301 incontinently: *immediately*

Iago: If thou dost, I shall never love thee after. Why, thou silly gentleman?

Roderigo: It is silliness to live when to live is torment: and then have we a prescription to die when death   305 is our physician.

Iago: O villainous! I have looked upon the world for four times seven years; and since I could distinguish betwixt a benefit and an injury, I never found man that knew how to love himself. Ere I would say, I would drown myself for the love of a guinea-hen, I would change my humanity with a baboon.   310

Roderigo: What should I do? I confess it is my shame to be so fond, but it is not in my virtue to amend it.

Iago: Virtue! A fig! 'Tis in ourselves that we are thus or thus. Our bodies are our gardens, to the which our wills are gardeners. So that if we will plant nettles, or sow lettuce, set hyssop and weed up   315   315 hyssop, thyme: *aromatic herbs*

A gullible character *Roderigo's response is to announce his intention of committing suicide because he has lost the love of his life, Desdemona: 'I will incontinently drown myself'.*

thyme, supply it with one gender of herbs or
distract it with many, either to have it sterile
with idleness, or manured with industry, why, the
power and corrigible authority of this lies in our
wills. If the balance of our lives had not one
scale of reason to poise another of sensuality, the 320
blood and baseness of our natures would conduct us
to most preposterous conclusions. But we have
reason to cool our raging motions, our carnal
stings, our unbitted lusts, whereof I take this that
you call love to be a sect or scion.

Roderigo: It cannot be. 325

Iago: It is merely a lust of the blood and a permission of
the will. Come, be a man. Drown thyself? Drown
cats and blind puppies. I have professed me thy
friend, and I confess me knit to thy deserving with
cables of perdurable toughness; I could never
better stead thee than now. Put money in thy 330
purse. Follow thou these wars; defeat thy favour with
an usurped beard. I say, put money in thy purse. It
cannot be that Desdemona should long continue her
love to the Moor – put money in thy purse – nor he
his to her. It was a violent commencement, and thou
shalt see an answerable sequestration – put but 335
money in thy purse. These Moors are changeable in
their wills – fill thy purse with money. The food
that to him now is as luscious as locusts, shall be

316 gender: *type*

318 corrigible authority:
ability to control

320 poise: *counterbalance*

322 carnal strings: *sexual
urges*
323 unbitted: *unbridled*

329 perdurable: *long-lasting*

330 stead: *help*

335 sequestration: *separation*

337 locusts: *fruit of the carob
tree*

A contemptuous villain *Iago cannot afford to lose Roderigo, as he is dependent on him for money. He
sets out his philosophy of life to the foolish Venetian. He believes in our* 'wills' *as the dominant force
that controls our destiny. This is in stark contrast to the outpourings of emotion of Othello, Desdemona
and now, Roderigo. Iago believes in head over heart:* 'we have reason to cool our raging motions, our
carnal stings, our unbitted lusts'. *Is Iago suggesting that the other characters have allowed themselves
to become out of control? Would the audience agree with his philosophy that reason must cool desire?*

A master of improvisation *Not only is Iago an astute judge of character, he can also quickly turn a
situation to his advantage. He now advises his dupe Roderigo to go to war with Othello and the Venetian
forces (*'Follow thou these wars'*) and most importantly, he counsels Roderigo to* 'put money in thy
purse'. *Iago intends to bleed him dry.*

A cynical predator *Iago has no concept of real emotions. He becomes repulsive to the audience as he
outlines how Desdemona* 'will find the error of her choice' *as soon as she gets bored with Othello. The
racist ensign also speaks disparagingly of Othello, saying,* 'These Moors are changeable in their wills'
*and cannot be faithful. Othello has already referred to the fact that he is older than his wife and Iago
repeats this:* 'She must change for youth'.

to him shortly as bitter as coloquintida. She must
change for youth; when she is sated with his body,
she will find the error of her choice. Therefore put   340
money in thy purse. If thou wilt needs damn thyself,
do it a more delicate way than drowning.
Make all the money thou canst.
If sanctimony and a frail vow betwixt an erring
barbarian and a super-subtle Venetian not too hard for
my wits and all the tribe of hell,
thou shalt enjoy her – therefore make money. A pox of   345
drowning thyself! It is clean out of the way. Seek
thou rather to be hanged in compassing thy joy than
to be drowned and go without her.

Roderigo: Wilt thou be fast to my hopes, if I depend on
the issue?

Iago: Thou art sure of me. Go, make money. I have told
thee often, and I retell thee again and again, I
hate the Moor. My cause is hearted: thine hath no   350
less reason. Let us be conjunctive in our revenge
against him. If thou canst cuckold him, thou dost
thyself a pleasure, me a sport. There are many
events in the womb of time which will be delivered.
Traverse! Go, provide thy money. We will have more
of this to-morrow. Adieu.   355

Roderigo: Where shall we meet in the morning?

Iago: At my lodging.

Roderigo: I'll be with thee betimes.

Iago: Go to; farewell. Do you hear, Roderigo?

Roderigo: What say you?   360

Iago: No more of drowning, do you hear?

Roderigo: I am changed.

Iago: Go to; farewell. Put money enough in your purse.

---

338 coloquintida: *bitter apple*

339 sated with: *tired of*

343 super-subtle: *refined*

345 pox: *plague*

351 conjunctive: *allied*

352 cuckold: *make him think his wife has committed adultery*

354 Traverse: *about turn*

A convincing motive *Iago continues to voice his feelings about Othello:* 'My cause is hearted'. *He bluntly states,* 'I hate the Moor'. *Again, his base nature is displayed as he suggests that Roderigo should* 'cuckold him' *and it will give both of them pleasure. The audience is likely to be increasingly appalled at the depth of Iago's depravity. However, Roderigo is easily convinced:* 'I am changed'.

Roderigo: I'll sell all my land.

Exit

Iago:	Thus do I ever make my fool my purse:	365

For I mine own gained knowledge should profane,
If I would time expend with such a snipe.
But for my sport and profit. I hate the Moor:
And it is thought abroad, that 'twixt my sheets
He has done my office. I know not if it be true
Yet I, for mere suspicion in that kind,
Will do as if for surety. He holds me well:
The better shall my purpose work on him.
Cassio's a proper man: let me see now:
To get his place and to plume up my will
In double knavery. How, how? Let's see.
After some time, to abuse Othello's ear
That he is too familiar with his wife;
He hath a person and a smooth dispose
To be suspected, framed to make women false.
The Moor is of a free and open nature,
That thinks men honest that but seem to be so,
And will as tenderly be led by the nose
As asses are.
I have't. It is engender'd. Hell and night
Must bring this monstrous birth to the world's light.

Exit

Marginal glosses:
367 snipe: *long-beaked bird; also a derogatory term*
369 abroad: *generously*
370 done my office: *slept with my wife*
374 proper: *handsome*
375 plume up my will: *have a bit of fun, glorify myself*
379 smooth dispose: *refined manner*
385 engender'd: *formed, created*

Line numbers: 370, 375, 380, 385

Photocopy (for later) [handwritten]

> **Iago's soliloquy** *Shakespeare allows the audience to hear Iago's thoughts as he considers each character's qualities. He despises Roderigo as a 'fool', 'purse' and 'snipe'. He emphasises his deep distaste for the Moor, now adding another reason: 'it is thought abroad, that 'twixt my sheets/He has done my office', presuming that his wife and Othello have been lovers. Iago has a realistic knowledge of the characters. He is aware that Othello 'holds me well'. He knows Cassio is a 'proper man' whose refinement and polished manners would appear attractive to any woman. Although Iago's hatred runs high, he is tempering it with reason. He decides to pollute Othello's mind with the suggestion that Cassio is 'too familiar' with Desdemona. He understands that Othello ('a free and open nature') takes everything on face value. By contrast, Iago's own despicable character is clearly revealed as he plots to lead Othello 'by the nose/As asses are'. The plan is in place: 'It is engender'd'. Will this villain be successful in destroying his enemies? Will he be able to exploit and corrupt the weaknesses and insecurities of others? And what is the audience's response to this 'monstrous birth' of evil?*

Key Points

Act 1, Scene 3

- The scene moves back and forth from the state's danger to the personal dilemmas of the characters as the practical Duke seeks to protect Venice's interests.
- Brabantio's distress gives way to an ominous warning against his daughter.
- Othello is admired and respected as the saviour of Venetian interests. He is at the height of his powers, a strong, reliable commander and a loving husband.
- Desdemona is captivated by romantic stories and idealistic ideas about love. Is she blindly romantic? Has she allowed her sudden feelings to cloud her judgement?
- Iago displays his duplicity as he appears 'honest' to both Othello and Roderigo.
- Desdemona reveals different facets of her character. She is respectful towards the Duke, defiant yet tactful towards her father and extremely loving towards her husband.
- Roderigo is shown as foolish, obviously exploited by the fiendish Iago for money and as a pawn in his plot of revenge against the Moor.
- There are ominous signs of tragedy ahead. The Turkish threat looms, Iago plots, Brabantio warns and love is blinded by excess. At the end of the Exposition, the audience is poised for the story to unfold, as all the significant facts of character and plot have been revealed.

Act 2

SCENE 1 – A quayside in Cyprus

There is news that a severe storm has destroyed the Turkish fleet. Iago continues to plot against Othello. He persuades Roderigo to provoke a fight with Cassio so that Cassio will lose his position as lieutenant. Iago also suspects that his own wife, Emilia, has been unfaithful to him.

Enter Montano and two Gentlemen

Montano: What from the cape can you discern at sea?

First Gentleman: Nothing at all; it is a high-wrought flood.
I cannot, 'twixt the heaven and the main,
Descry a sail.

Montano: Methinks the wind does speak aloud at land,   5
A fuller blast ne'er shook our battlements.
If it hath ruffianed so upon the sea,
What ribs of oak, when mountains melt on them,
Can hold the mortise? What shall we hear of this?

Second Gentleman: A segregation of the Turkish fleet: 10
For do but stand upon the banning shore,
The chidden billow seems to pelt the clouds;
The wind-shaked surge, with high and monstrous mane,
seems to cast water on the burning Bear,
And quench the guards of the ever-fixed Pole: 15
I never did like molestation view
On the enchafed flood.

Montano: If that the Turkish fleet
Be not ensheltered and embayed, they are drowned:
It is impossible they bear it out.

Glossary (right margin):

2 high-wrought: *rough*

4 Descry: *make out, see*

7 ruffianed: *raged*

8 ribs of oak: *wooden structure of a boat*
9 hold the mortise: *hold their joints together*

11 banning: *foaming*

12 chidden billow: *waves hurled back*

14, 15 Bear, Pole: *stars that guided sailors*

16 molestation: *disturbance*

19 bear it out: *survive*

New setting *The drama has moved to an open quayside location on the island of Cyprus, a disputed outpost on the edges of Venetian rule. Cosmopolitan Venice was the epitome of thriving capitalism and conscript soldiers were often hired to protect colonies, such as Cyprus.*

The storm *The great tempest scatters the Turkish fleet and Venice is no longer under threat. Shakespeare uses the storm to create suspense while the arrival of Othello is anxiously anticipated. The chaotic weather has the dramatic purpose of ominously foreshadowing the emotional tumult that will soon engulf Othello.*

Third Gentleman: News, lads! Our wars are done: 20
The desperate tempest hath so banged the Turks,
That their designment halts. A noble ship of Venice
Hath seen a grievous wreck and sufferance
On most part of their fleet.

Montano: How! Is this true?

Third Gentleman: The ship is here put in,   25
A Veronesa; Michael Cassio,
Lieutenant to the warlike Moor Othello,
Is come on shore; the Moor himself at sea,
And is in full commission here for Cyprus.

Montano: I am glad on't; 'tis a worthy governor.   30

Third Gentleman: But this same Cassio, though he speak of comfort
Touching the Turkish loss, yet he looks sadly,
And prays the Moor be safe; for they were parted
With foul and violent tempest.

Montano: Pray heavens he be;
For I have served him, and the man commands   35
Like a full soldier. Let's to the seaside, ho!
As well to see the vessel that's come in
As to throw out our eyes for brave Othello,
Even till we make the main and the aerial blue
An indistinct regard.

Third Gentleman: Come, let's do so: 40
For every minute is expectancy
Of more arrivance.

Enter Cassio

Cassio: Thanks, you the valiant of this warlike isle,
That so approve the Moor! O, let the heavens

---

22 designment: *plan*
22 halts: *fails*

26 Veronesa: *Italian ship*

32 Touching: *concerning*

38 main: *sea*
38 aerial blue: *sky*

A worthy governor *Those awaiting the arrival of Othello are full of praise for the* 'warlike Moor'. *First to arrive from Venice is the polished and courteous Cassio, who lives up to Iago's character analysis in the previous scene. There is a growing sense of tension. Cassio prays for Othello's safe arrival ('O, let the heavens/Give him defence against the elements'), as the sea and sky are blurred due to the storm's ferocity.*

	Give him defence against the elements,	45
	For I have lost us him on a dangerous sea.	
Montano:	Is he well shipped?	
Cassio:	His bark is stoutly timbered, his pilot	
	Of very expert and approved allowance;	
	Therefore my hopes, not surfeited to death,	50
	Stand in bold cure.	

A cry within: 'A sail, a sail, a sail!'
Enter a fourth Gentleman

Cassio:	What noise?	
Fourth Gentleman:	The town is empty; on the brow o' the sea	
	Stand ranks of people, and they cry 'A sail!'	
Cassio:	My hopes do shape him for the governor.	55

Guns heard

Second Gentlemen:	They do discharge their shot of courtesy:	
	Our friends at least.	
Cassio:	I pray you, sir, go forth,	
	And give us truth who 'tis that is arrived.	
Second Gentleman:	I shall.	

Exit

Montano:	But, good lieutenant, is your general wived?	60
Cassio:	Most fortunately: he hath achieved a maid	
	That paragons description and wild fame;	
	One that excels the quirks of blazoning pens,	
	And in the essential vesture of creation	
	Does tire the ingener.	

Re-enter second Gentleman

| | How now! who has put in? | 65 |

Side notes:

50 surfeited to death: *excessive*
51 in bold cure: *healthy*

60 wived: *married*

61 paragons: *excels*
62 blazoning: *praising*
63 essential vesture: *perfect beauty*
64 ingener: *designer*

Growing excitement *The crowd on the quayside in Cyprus waits in tense expectation for the safe arrival of their new 'governor', Othello.*

The new wife *Cassio eloquently praises Desdemona: 'a maid/That paragons description and wild fame'. His refined language is in direct contrast to Iago's vulgarity.*

Second Gentleman: 'Tis one Iago, ancient to the general.

Cassio: Has had most favourable and happy speed:
Tempests themselves, high seas, and howling winds,
The guttered rocks and congregated sands,
Traitors ensteeped to clog the guiltless keel,   70
As having sense of beauty, do omit
Their mortal natures, letting go safely by
The divine Desdemona.

Montano: What is she?

Cassio: She that I spake of, our great captain's captain,
Left in the conduct of the bold Iago,   75
Whose footing here anticipates our thoughts
A se'nnight's speed. Great Jove, Othello guard,
And swell his sail with thine own powerful breath,
That he may bless this bay with his tall ship,
Make love's quick pants in Desdemona's arms,   80
Give renewed fire to our extincted spirits
And bring all Cyprus comfort!

70 ensteeped: *built*

76 footing: *landing*
77 se'nnight's: *week's*

'our great captain's captain'

Suggestive imagery *Othello's dangerous position in relation to Iago is pointedly highlighted by the reference to the dangerous rocks and sands: 'Traitors ensteeped'. Meanwhile, Cassio's friendship with Othello seems strong.*

Enter Desdemona, Emilia, Iago, Roderigo, and Attendants

O, behold,
The riches of the ship is come on shore!
Ye men of Cyprus, let her have your knees.
Hail to thee, lady! And the grace of heaven,   85
Before, behind thee, and on every hand,
Enwheel thee round!

Desdemona: I thank you, valiant Cassio.
What tidings can you tell me of my lord?

Cassio: He is not yet arrived: nor know I aught
But that he's well and will be shortly here.   90

Desdemona: O, but I fear – how lost you company?

Cassio: The great contention of the sea and skies
Parted our fellowship. But, hark, a sail!

Second Gentleman: They give their greeting to the citadel;
This likewise is a friend.

Cassio: See for the news.   95

Exit Gentleman

Good ancient, you are welcome.

To Emilia

Welcome, mistress.
Let it not gall your patience, good Iago,
That I extend my manners; 'tis my breeding
That gives me this bold show of courtesy.

Kissing her

84 let her have your knees: *kneel to her*

87 Enwheel: *encircle*

97 gall: *annoy*

A gallant gentleman *Cassio's courteous manner is evident. He describes Desdemona as 'our great captain's captain'. He also demands that due respect should be paid to the new governor's wife: 'let her have your knees'. Cassio is obviously a charmer, but is there anything false about his behaviour? Meanwhile, Cassio continues to be a ladies' man, greeting Emilia with a kiss.*

Shakespeare Focus: Othello

Iago:	Sir, would she give you so much of her lips	100	
	As of her tongue she oft bestows on me,		
	You'll have enough.		

Desdemona: Alas, she has no speech.

Iago:	In faith, too much;		
	I find it still, when I have list to sleep:		104 have list: *wish*
	Marry, before your ladyship, I grant,	105	
	She puts her tongue a little in her heart,		
	And chides with thinking.		107 chides with thinking: *keeps her thoughts to herself*

Emilia: You have little cause to say so.

Iago:	Come on, come on; you are pictures out of doors,		109 pictures: *silent*
	Bells in your parlours, wild-cats in your kitchens,	110	110 Bells: *noisy*
	Saints in your injuries, devils being offended,		
	Players in your housewifery, and housewives in your beds.		112 Players: *pretenders* 112 housewifery: *complaining*

Desdemona: O, fie upon thee, slanderer!

| **Iago:** | Nay, it is true, or else I am a Turk: | | |
| | You rise to play and go to bed to work. | 115 | |

Emilia: You shall not write my praise.

Iago: No, let me not.

| **Desdemona:** | What wouldst thou write of me, if thou shouldst | | |
| | praise me? | | |

| **Iago:** | O gentle lady, do not put me to't; | | |
| | For I am nothing, if not critical. | | |

Desdemona: Come on, assay. There's one gone to the harbour?   120   120 assay: *try*

Iago: Aye, madam.

Desdemona:	I am not merry; but I do beguile		122 beguile: *divert attention from*
	The thing I am, by seeming otherwise.		
	Come, how wouldst thou praise me?		

| **Iago:** | I am about it; but indeed my invention | 125 | 126 birdlime: *sticky substance used to catch birds* |
| | Comes from my pate as birdlime does from frieze; | | 126 frieze: *woollen cloth* |

Puzzling banter *Desdemona indulges in clever word-play with Iago as they await the arrival of Othello. Are there signs that she is not quite as innocent as she first seemed? She hides her feelings of anxiety, saying, 'I am not merry; but I do beguile/The thing I am'. Is this in keeping with our impression of the Desdemona who defied her father and who anxiously pleaded her case for accompanying Othello to Cyprus?*

	It plucks out brains and all: but my muse labours,		127 muse: *poetic inspiration*
	And thus she is delivered.		
	If she be fair and wise, fairness and wit,		
	The one's for use, the other useth it.	130	

Desdemona: Well praised! How if she be black and witty?

Iago: If she be black, and thereto have a wit,
She'll find a white that shall her blackness fit.

Desdemona: Worse and worse.

Emilia: How if fair and foolish?   135

Iago: She never yet was foolish that was fair;
For even her folly helped her to an heir.

Desdemona: These are old fond paradoxes to make fools laugh i'   138 fond: *foolish*
the alehouse. What miserable praise hast thou for
her that's foul and foolish?   140

Iago: There's none so foul and foolish thereunto,
But does foul pranks which fair and wise ones do.

Desdemona: O heavy ignorance! thou praisest the worst best.
But what praise couldst thou bestow on a deserving
woman indeed, one that, in the authority of her   145   145 one that ... itself: *a good woman that even malice could praise*
merit, did justly put on the vouch of very malice itself?

Iago: She that was ever fair and never proud,
Had tongue at will and yet was never loud,
Never lacked gold and yet went never gay,
Fled from her wish and yet said 'Now I may',   150
She that being angered, her revenge being nigh,
Bade her wrong stay and her displeasure fly,
She that in wisdom never was so frail
To change the cod's head for the salmon's tail;
She that could think and ne'er disclose her mind,   155
See suitors following and not look behind,
She was a wight, if ever such wight were—   157 wight: *lover*

Class conflict *Iago's contempt for women is in marked contrast to Cassio's gracious behaviour. The audience listening to Iago's coarse banter can begin to see why Cassio has been chosen as Othello's second in command.*

Elizabethan humour *Verbal wit was widely enjoyed and revered by Elizabethan audiences. Iago gives a clever display using puns (word-play), paradoxes (riddles) and epigrams (short humorous poems and one-liners).*

Desdemona: To do what?

Iago: To suckle fools and chronicle small beer.

Desdemona: O most lame and impotent conclusion! Do not learn   160
of him, Emilia, though he be thy husband. How say
you, Cassio? is he not a most profane and liberal
counsellor?

Cassio: He speaks home, madam: You may relish him more in
the soldier than in the scholar.   165

Iago: [*Aside*] He takes her by the palm: ay, well said,
whisper: with as little a web as this will I
ensnare as great a fly as Cassio. Ay, smile upon
her, do; I will catch you in your own courtesies.
You say true; 'tis so, indeed: if such tricks as   170
these strip you out of your lieutenantry, it had
been better you had not kissed your three fingers so
oft, which now again you are most apt to play the
sir in. Very good; well kissed! An excellent
courtesy! 'Tis so, indeed. Yet again your fingers   175
to your lips? Would they were clyster-pipes for your sake!

Trumpet within

The Moor! I know his trumpet.

Cassio: 'Tis truly so.

Desdemona: Let's meet him and receive him.

Cassio: Lo, where he comes!   180

Enter Othello and Attendants

Othello: O my fair warrior!

Desdemona: My dear Othello!

Othello: It gives me wonder great as my content
To see you here before me. O my soul's joy!

Weaving a web *Iago stands aside, noting Cassio's mannerly behaviour towards Desdemona:* 'He takes her by the palm'. *The ensign is adept at using situations to his own advantage and he can now see how he will use Cassio's displays of chivalry against him. Shakespeare is again involving the audience in the drama; all the focus is on Iago's malicious ingenuity.*

'O, you are well tuned now!'

If after every tempest come such calms,   185
May the winds blow till they have wakened death!
And let the labouring bark climb hills of seas
Olympus-high and duck again as low
As hell's from heaven! If it were now to die,
'Twere now to be most happy; for, I fear,   190
My soul hath her content so absolute
That not another comfort like to this
Succeeds in unknown fate.

187 bark: *ship*

188 Olympus: *mountain home of the gods in classical Greek mythology*

A rapturous reunion *Othello arrives at last. There is genuine affection between the newlyweds.*

Dramatic irony *This is not the calm after the storm, as Othello thinks: 'If after every tempest come such calms'. Instead, it is the calm before the storm that Iago is about to unleash. The audience is caught between several responses – relief at the safe arrival of Othello, delight at the lovers' reunion and anxiety about Iago's malicious schemes.*

Desdemona: The heavens forbid
But that our loves and comforts should increase,
Even as our days do grow!

Othello: Amen to that, sweet powers!   195
I cannot speak enough of this content;
It stops me here; it is too much of joy:
And this, and this, the greatest discords be [*Kissing her*]
That e'er our hearts shall make!

Iago: [*Aside*] O, you are well tuned now!
But I'll set down the pegs that make this music,   200   200: set down the pegs:
As honest as I am.   *loosen the strings to cause*
                                                                                                              disharmony

Othello: Come, let us to the castle.
News, friends; our wars are done, the Turks are drowned.
How does my old acquaintance of this isle?
Honey, you shall be well desired in Cyprus;
I have found great love amongst them. O my sweet,   205
I prattle out of fashion, and I dote   206 I dote: *I'm not making*
In mine own comforts. I prithee, good Iago,   *sense*
Go to the bay and disembark my coffers: 208 coffers: *luggage*
Bring thou the master to the citadel;   209 master: *captain of the*
He is a good one, and his worthiness   210   *ship*
Does challenge much respect. Come, Desdemona,
Once more, well met at Cyprus.

Exeunt Othello, Desdemona, and Attendants

Iago: Do thou meet me presently at the harbour. Come
hither. If thou be'st valiant – as, they say, base
men being in love have then a nobility in their   215
natures more than is native to them – list me. The   216 list me: *listen to me*
lieutenant tonight watches on the court of
guard: – first, I must tell thee this – Desdemona is
directly in love with him.

Roderigo: With him! why, 'tis not possible.

Iago: Lay thy finger thus, and let thy soul be instructed.   220   220 Lay thy finger thus: *put*
Mark me with what violence she first loved the Moor,   *your finger to your lips (be*
                                                                                                              quiet

---

The plot thickens *Iago and Roderigo are left alone together as all the others proceed to the castle. Iago immediately insults Desdemona's good name by suggesting that she is having a secret love affair with Cassio: 'directly in love'.*

but for bragging and telling her fantastical lies:
and will she love him still for prating? let not
thy discreet heart think it. Her eye must be fed;
and what delight shall she have to look on the 225
devil? When the blood is made dull with the act of
sport, there should be, again to inflame it and to
give satiety a fresh appetite, loveliness in favour,
sympathy in years, manners and beauties; all which
the Moor is defective in: now, for want of these 230
required conveniences, her delicate tenderness will
find itself abused, begin to heave the gorge,
disrelish and abhor the Moor; very nature will
instruct her in it and compel her to some second
choice. Now, sir, this granted – as it is a most pregnant 235
and unforced position – who stands so eminently in the
degree of this fortune as Cassio does? a knave very voluble;
no further conscionable than in putting on the mere form
of civil and humane seeming, for the better compassing
of his salt and most hidden loose affection?
why, none; why, none: a subtle slippery knave, 240
a finder of occasions, that has an eye can stamp and
counterfeit advantages, though true advantage never
present itself; a devilish knave. Besides, the knave is
handsome, young and hath all those requisites in him that
folly and green minds look after: a pestilent complete knave; 245
and the woman hath found him already.

Roderigo: I cannot believe that in her; she's full of most blessed
condition.

Iago: Blessed fig's-end! The wine she drinks is made of
grapes: if she had been blessed, she would never
have loved the Moor. Blessed pudding! Didst thou not see 250
Her paddle with the palm of his hand? Didst not mark that?

Roderigo: Yes, that I did; but that was but courtesy.

Iago: Lechery, by this hand; an index and obscure prologue
to the history of lust and foul thoughts. They met
so near with their lips that their breaths embraced 255

238 compassing: *achieving*

239 salt: *lecherous*

240 subtle slippery: *smoothly treacherous*
241 stamp and counterfeit: *make a forgery of*

248 fig's end: *rubbish*

Duplicity *Iago convinces the credulous Roderigo that Cassio's gallantry had an ulterior motive, a* 'prologue
to the history of lust and foul thoughts'. *He inveigles Roderigo to provoke Cassio, who is prone to
outbursts of anger:* 'very sudden in choler'. *Roderigo worships Desdemona and cannot believe this. Yet
again, he is easily persuaded by Iago's clever, insinuating arguments.*

together. Villainous thoughts, Roderigo! When these
mutualities so marshal the way, hard at hand comes
the master and main exercise, the incorporate
conclusion, Pish! But, sir, be you ruled by me: I
have brought you from Venice. Watch you to-night;   260
for the command, I'll lay it upon you. Cassio knows
you not. I'll not be far from you: do you find
some occasion to anger Cassio, either by speaking
too loud, or tainting his discipline; or from what
other course you please, which the time shall more   265
favourably minister.

Roderigo: Well.

Iago: Sir, he is rash and very sudden in choler, and haply
may strike at you: provoke him, that he may; for
even out of that will I cause these of Cyprus to
mutiny; whose qualification shall come into no true   270
taste again but by the displanting of Cassio. So
shall you have a shorter journey to your desires by
the means I shall then have to prefer them; and the
impediment most profitably removed, without the
which there were no expectation of our prosperity.   275

Roderigo: I will do this, if I can bring it to any opportunity.

Iago: I warrant thee. Meet me by and by at the citadel:
I must fetch his necessaries ashore. Farewell.

Roderigo: Adieu.

Exit

Iago: That Cassio loves her, I do well believe it;   280
That she loves him, 'tis apt and of great credit:
The Moor, howbeit that I endure him not,
Is of a constant, loving, noble nature,
And I dare think he'll prove to Desdemona
A most dear husband. Now, I do love her too;   285

257 mutualities: *intimate exchanges*

267 in choler: *when angry*

270 qualification: *pacifying*

271 displanting: *displacement*

282 howbeit: *even though*

The master planner *Once again, an important scene concludes with a revealing soliloquy from Iago. He can clearly see Othello's qualities ('*constant, loving, noble nature'*) and he knows that the Moor will be a good husband to Desdemona. Iago's motives for his diabolical scheme are that he suspects both Othello and Cassio of being his own wife's lovers. But there is no real evidence at all that Emilia has been unfaithful. Iago's contempt for other people is illustrated in his reference to Roderigo as '*poor trash of Venice' and his decision to make Othello an '*ass' by making him jealous.*

Not out of absolute lust, though peradventure
I stand accountant for as great a sin,
But partly led to diet my revenge,
For that I do suspect the lusty Moor
Hath leaped into my seat; the thought whereof   290
Doth, like a poisonous mineral, gnaw my inwards;
And nothing can or shall content my soul
Till I am evened with him, wife for wife,
Or failing so, yet that I put the Moor
At least into a jealousy so strong   295
That judgment cannot cure. Which thing to do,
If this poor trash of Venice, whom I trace
For his quick hunting, stand the putting on,
I'll have our Michael Cassio on the hip,
Abuse him to the Moor in the rank garb –   300
For I fear Cassio with my night-cap too –
Make the Moor thank me, love me and reward me.
For making him egregiously an ass
And practising upon his peace and quiet
Even to madness. 'Tis here, but yet confused: 305
Knavery's plain face is never seen, till used.

Exit

286 peradventure: *perhaps*

290 leaped into my seat: *made love to my wife*
291 inwards: *innards, guts*

297 trace: *follow after*

299 on the hip: *at my mercy*
300 rank garb: *foul manner*

303 egregiously: *outstandingly*
304 practising upon: *plotting against*

Key Points

Act 2, Scene 1

- Shakespeare makes effective use of contrasting atmospheres, including unease, relief, joy and deception, to create dramatic tension in this scene.
- Once again, the thread of racism is evident in the witticisms exchanged between Iago and Desdemona: 'if she be black'.
- The reunion of Othello and Desdemona marks their happiest time together. Othello is acutely aware of this, but the intense feelings he has for his wife seem strangely obsessive.
- Iago's warped character is further revealed through his paranoid behaviour and hatred for almost everybody around him, especially Othello. He respects no one and his abusive language is a telling feature of his true nature.

Act 2

SCENE 2 – A street

Othello's spokesman announces a night of merrymaking to celebrate both the military victory over the Turks and Othello's recent marriage to Desdemona.

Enter a Herald with a proclamation. People following.

Herald: It is Othello's pleasure, our noble and valiant
general, that, upon certain tidings now arrived,
importing the mere perdition of the Turkish fleet,
every man put himself into triumph; some to dance,
some to make bonfires, each man to what sport and   5
revels his addiction leads him: for, besides these
beneficial news, it is the celebration of his
nuptial. So much was his pleasure should be
proclaimed. All offices are open, and there is full
liberty of feasting from this present hour of five   10
till the bell have told eleven. Heaven bless the
isle of Cyprus and our noble general Othello!

Exeunt

3 importing: *making known*
3 mere perdition: *total destruction*
4 put himself into triumph: *get ready to celebrate*

9 offices: *kitchens, food stores*
9 full liberty of: *free*

- Cyprus is established as the setting.
- Othello is the latest governor of Cyprus.
- New events provide Iago with opportunities to act out his plans.
- This joyful scene provides a pause before evil takes over.

Act 2

SCENE 3 – *A hall in the castle*

Five hours after the proclamation, Cyprus celebrates. Cassio is in charge of the guard and Othello and Desdemona retire. Meanwhile, Iago initiates his plan to dreadful effect.

Enter Othello, Desdemona, Cassio, and Attendants

Othello: Good Michael, look you to the guard to-night:
Let's teach ourselves that honourable stop,
Not to outsport discretion.

Cassio: Iago hath direction what to do;
But, notwithstanding, with my personal eye   5
Will I look to it.

Othello: Iago is most honest.
Michael, good night: to-morrow with your earliest
Let me have speech with you.

To Desdemona

Come, my dear love,
The purchase made, the fruits are to ensue;
That profit's yet to come 'tween me and you.   10
Good night.

Exeunt Othello, Desdemona, and Attendants
Enter Iago

2 stop: *self-control*

3 outsport discretion: *celebrate to excess*

9 the fruits are to ensue: *the joys of married love*

The warning *Five hours after the proclamation, Othello reminds Cassio, who is now in charge of the watch, not to allow the soldiers to drink to excess: 'Let's teach ourselves that honourable stop'. Otherwise, there is a danger that there might be a brawl, which would frighten the inhabitants of the island or even turn them against the newly arrived forces from Venice. Othello and Desdemona retire and Iago joins Cassio.*

Duty calls *Cassio wishes to organise the guard: 'we must to the watch'. Iago disagrees: 'Not this hour'.*

Cassio: Welcome, Iago; we must to the watch.

Iago: Not this hour, lieutenant; 'tis not yet ten o' the
clock. Our general cast us thus early for the love
of his Desdemona; who let us not therefore blame: 15
he hath not yet made wanton the night with her; and
she is sport for Jove.

14 cast us: *dismissed us*

17 Jove: *king of the gods, a lover of many women*

Cassio: She's a most exquisite lady.

Iago: And, I'll warrant her, full of game.

19 game: *love-making*

Cassio: Indeed, she's a most fresh and delicate creature. 20

Iago: What an eye she has! Methinks it sounds a parley of
provocation.

21 parley: *summons, invitation*

Cassio: An inviting eye; and yet methinks right modest.

Iago: And when she speaks, is it not an alarm to love?

Cassio: It is indeed perfection. 25

Iago: Well, happiness to their sheets! Come, lieutenant, I
have a stoup of wine; and here without are a brace of
Cyprus gallants that would fain have a measure to
the health of black Othello.

27 stoup: *jug, tankard*

28 a brace of Cyprus gallants: *a couple of fashionable Cypriot men*

Cassio: Not to-night, good Iago: I have very poor and 30
unhappy brains for drinking: I could well wish
courtesy would invent some other custom of
entertainment.

Iago: O, they are our friends; but one cup: I'll drink for you.

Cassio: I have drunk but one cup to-night, and that was 35
craftily qualified too, and, behold, what innovation
it makes here: I am unfortunate in the infirmity,
and dare not task my weakness with any more.

36 craftily qualified: *carefully diluted*
36 innovation: *agitation*

Iago: What, man! 'Tis a night of revels: the gallants
desire it. 40

A marked contrast *Iago's methods start to become clear. His vulgarity, referring to Desdemona as* 'sport' *and* 'full of game', *is very different to the chivalrous Cassio, who regards her as an* 'exquisite lady' *and a* 'delicate creature'.

The invitation *Iago proposes that he and Cassio share a drink to Othello's health with* 'a brace of Cyprus gallants'. *Cassio declines, explaining that he does not have a good head for drinking. He is* 'unfortunate in the infirmity'. *He has already drunk one diluted cup. Iago insists, exploiting Cassio's desire to be sociable:* ''Tis a night of revels: the gallants desire it'.

Cassio: Where are they?

Iago: Here at the door; I pray you, call them in.

Cassio: I'll do it; but it dislikes me.

43 dislikes: *displeases*

Exit

Iago: If I can fasten but one cup upon him,
With that which he hath drunk to-night already,   45
He'll be as full of quarrel and offence
As my young mistress' dog. Now, my sick fool Roderigo,
Whom love hath turned almost the wrong side out,
To Desdemona hath to-night caroused
Potations pottle-deep; and he's to watch: 50
Three lads of Cyprus, noble swelling spirits,
That hold their honours in a wary distance,
The very elements of this warlike isle,
Have I to-night flustered with flowing cups,
And they watch too. Now, amongst this flock of drunkards, 55
Am I to put our Cassio in some action
That may offend the isle. But here they come:
If consequence do but approve my dream,
My boat sails freely, both with wind and stream.

50 Potations pottle-deep: *many mugs of tankards of drink*

52 That hold their honours in a wary distance: *are quick to protect their honour*

54 flustered: *confused*

58 If consequence: *if events to come*

Re-enter Cassio; with him Montano and Gentlemen; servants following with wine

Cassio: 'Fore God, they have given me a rouse already.   60

60 rouse: *drink*

Montano: Good faith, a little one, not past a pint,
As I am a soldier.

Iago: Some wine, ho!

Sings

A weakness for drink *Cassio likes being popular and his easy-going nature means that he is too easily persuaded. He knows he should not drink too much. Othello has just warned him of the dire consequences if the watch do not behave. Yet he agrees reluctantly: 'I'll do it; but it dislikes me.' This will prove to be his undoing.*

Party time *Iago uses every chance he gets to further his cunning schemes. He understands Cassio's weakness for becoming angry when drinking. Roderigo is already drunk with 'Potations pottle-deep'. Iago relishes the mayhem he is about to unleash: 'If consequence do but approve my dream,/My boat sails freely'. Tension continues to build when Cassio enters on cue, complaining that he has already had another drink.*

And let me the canakin clink, clink;
And let me the canakin clink   65
A soldier's a man;
A life's but a span;
Why, then, let a soldier drink.
Some wine, boys!

Cassio: 'Fore God, an excellent song.   70

Iago: I learned it in England, where, indeed, they are
most potent in potting: your Dane, your German, and
your swag-bellied Hollander – Drink, ho! – are nothing
to your English.

Cassio: Is your Englishman so expert in his drinking?   75

Iago: Why, he drinks you, with facility, your Dane dead
drunk; he sweats not to overthrow your Almain; he
gives your Hollander a vomit, ere the next pottle
can be filled.

Cassio: To the health of our general!   80

Montano: I am for it, lieutenant; and I'll do you justice.

Iago: O sweet England!
King Stephen was a worthy peer,
His breeches cost him but a crown;
He held them sixpence all too dear,   85
With that he called the tailor lown.
He was a wight of high renown
And thou art but of low degree:
'Tis pride that pulls the country down;
Then take thine auld cloak about thee.   90
Some wine, ho!

Cassio: Why, this is a more exquisite song than the other.

Iago: Will you hear it again?

Cassio: No; for I hold him to be unworthy of his place that   95
does those things. Well, God's above all; and there
be souls must be saved, and there be souls
must not be saved.

64 cannikin: *drinking can, tankard*

72 potent in potting: *heavy drinkers*

77 Almain: *German*

86 lown: *lout*
87 wight: *man*
88 degree: *status*

The life and soul *In a riotous scene, Iago calls for more wine and performs two rousing drinking songs. He comments on the drinking capabilities of different nations, concluding that the English are the best drinkers. Cassio is becoming drunk very quickly and praises the songs as 'excellent' and 'exquisite'. The audience watches uneasily as Iago's plan begins to work.*

Iago: It's true, good lieutenant.

Cassio: For mine own part – no offence to the general, nor   100
any man of quality – I hope to be saved.

Iago: And so do I too, lieutenant.

Cassio: Ay, but, by your leave, not before me; the
lieutenant is to be saved before the ancient. Let's
have no more of this, let's to our affairs. Forgive   105
us our sins! Gentlemen, let's look to our business.
Do not think, gentlemen, I am drunk, this is my
ancient, this is my right hand, and this is my left:
I am not drunk now, I can stand well enough, and
speak well enough.   110

All: Excellent well.

Cassio: Why, very well then; you must not think then that I am drunk.

Exit

Montano: To the platform, masters; come, let's set the watch.

Iago: You see this fellow that is gone before;
He is a soldier fit to stand by Caesar   115
And give direction: and do but see his vice;
'Tis to his virtue a just equinox,
The one as long as the other: 'tis pity of him.
I fear the trust Othello puts him in.
On some odd time of his infirmity,   120
Will shake this island.

Montano: But is he often thus?

Iago: 'Tis evermore the prologue to his sleep:
He'll watch the horologe a double set,
If drink rock not his cradle.

113 platform: *gun ramparts*
113 set the watch: *mount the guard*

117 just equinox: *exact equivalent*

123 horologe a double set: *twice round the clock*

Drunk *Shakespeare cleverly catches the rhythm of Cassio's drunken speech:* 'Do not think, gentlemen, I am drunk ... this is my right hand, and this is my left'. *Foolishly, the lieutenant leaves his post and Montano has to take charge of the watch.*

Always the opportunist *Iago skilfully seizes the opportunity presented to condemn Cassio as he praises him to Montano. Pityingly, he refers to* 'his vice' *and how he* 'fears the trust Othello puts him in' *in case it has terrible consequences for the safety of Cyprus.*

 Shakespeare Focus: Othello

Montano: It were well
The general were put in mind of it.   125
Perhaps he sees it not; or his good nature
Prizes the virtue that appears in Cassio,
And looks not on his evils: is not this true?

Enter Roderigo

Iago: [*Aside to him*] How now, Roderigo!
I pray you, after the lieutenant; go.   130

Exit Roderigo

Montano: And 'tis great pity that the noble Moor
Should hazard such a place as his own second
With one of an ingraft infirmity:
It were an honest action to say
So to the Moor.

Iago: Not I, for this fair island: 135
I do love Cassio well; and would do much
To cure him of this evil. But, hark! What noise?

Cry within: 'Help! help!'
Re-enter Cassio, driving in Roderigo

Cassio: You rogue! You rascal!

Montano: What's the matter, lieutenant?

Cassio: A knave teach me my duty!   140
I'll beat the knave into a twiggen bottle.

Roderigo: Beat me!

Cassio: Dost thou prate, rogue?

Striking Roderigo

125 put in mind: *informed*

132 hazard: *risk*
133 ingraft: *deep-rooted*

141 twiggen bottle: *bottle covered in wicker work*

Responsible *Montano is a conscientious foil to Cassio. He is sociable but does not lose control of himself. He clearly understands the dangerous consequences of Cassio's 'evils' and he is concerned for Othello's position. Iago disagrees, pleading loyalty to Cassio.*

A chaotic situation *Roderigo is quickly dispatched by Iago to follow Cassio. A rumpus is heard and Cassio enters, shouting as he drives Roderigo before him with his sword.*

'A knave teach me my duty!'

Montano: Nay, good lieutenant;

Staying him

I pray you, sir, hold your hand.

Cassio: Let me go, sir,   145
Or I'll knock you over the mazzard.

145 mazzard: *head, skull*

Montano: Come, come, you're drunk.

Cassio: Drunk!

They fight

Iago: [*Aside to Roderigo*] Away, I say; go out, and cry a mutiny.

148 cry a mutiny: *call out that there is a riot*

Exit Roderigo

Iago's plan works *Just as Iago predicted, Cassio has become quarrelsome with drink and starts to fight with Roderigo. Montano attempts to intervene but Cassio rounds on him, threatening, 'I'll knock you over the mazzard'. Iago directs the action by getting Roderigo to run away and 'cry a mutiny', precisely what Othello had not wanted to happen. He pretends to try to calm the commotion as the alarm bell rings and Othello enters as Iago tells Cassio, 'You will be shamed for ever'.*

Shakespeare Focus: Othello

Nay, good lieutenant – alas, gentlemen –
Help, ho! Lieutenant. Sir. Montano.
Help, masters! Here's a goodly watch indeed!

Bell rings

Who's that which rings the bell? Diablo, ho!
The town will rise: God's will, lieutenant, hold!
You will be shamed for ever.

150

152 Diablo: *the devil*

154 shamed: *disgraced*

'hold, for shame'

Enter Othello, and gentlemen with weapons

Othello: What is the matter here?

Montano: 'Zounds, I bleed still; I am hurt to the death.   155

Othello: Hold for your lives!

Iago: Hold, ho! Lieutenant, sir, Montano, gentlemen,
Have you forgot all sense of place and duty?
Hold! The general speaks to you; hold, hold, for shame!

Othello: Why, how now, ho! From whence ariseth this? 160
Are we turned Turks, and to ourselves do that
Which heaven hath forbid the Ottomites?
For Christian shame, put by this barbarous brawl:
He that stirs next to carve for his own rage
Holds his soul light; he dies upon his motion. 165
Silence that dreadful bell: it frights the isle
From her propriety. What is the matter, masters?
Honest Iago, that looks dead with grieving,
Speak, who began this? on thy love, I charge thee.

Iago: I do not know: friends all but now, even now, 170
In quarter, and in terms like bride and groom
Devesting them for bed; and then, but now –
As if some planet had unwitted men –
Swords out, and tilting one at other's breast,
In opposition bloody. I cannot speak 175
Any beginning to this peevish odds;
And would in action glorious I had lost
Those legs that brought me to a part of it!

Othello: How comes it, Michael, you are thus forgot?

Cassio: I pray you, pardon me; I cannot speak. 180

Othello: Worthy Montano, you were wont be civil;
The gravity and stillness of your youth
The world hath noted, and your name is great
In mouths of wisest censure: what's the matter,
That you unlace your reputation thus 185
And spend your rich opinion for the name
Of a night-brawler? Give me answer to it.

Montano: Worthy Othello, I am hurt to danger:
Your officer, Iago, can inform you,
While I spare speech, which something now
offends me, 190
Of all that I do know: nor know I aught
By me that's said or done amiss this night;

161 Are we turned Turks: *Are we going to kill and so do to ourselves what Heaven has prevented the Turks from doing to us?*

164 carve for his own rage: *stab someone in anger*

165 Holds his soul light: *doesn't value his life*

167 propriety: *natural peace*

171 quarter: *on*

184 censure: *judgement*

Incensed *An angry Othello demands to know 'What is the matter here?' Ironically, he asks 'Honest Iago' for an explanation. In response, the ensign pretends to be the peace-maker. Cassio comes to his senses – but it is too late.*

Cassio's shame *The young lieutenant is so embarrassed that he is lost for words. Will the audience have any sympathy for him?*

	Unless self-charity be sometimes a vice,	
	And to defend ourselves it be a sin	
	When violence assails us.	

Othello: Now, by heaven,   195
My blood begins my safer guides to rule;
And passion, having my best judgment collied,
Assays to lead the way: if I once stir,
Or do but lift this arm, the best of you
Shall sink in my rebuke. Give me to know   200
How this foul rout began, who set it on;
And he that is approved in this offence,
Though he had twinned with me, both at a birth,
Shall lose me. What! In a town of war,
Yet wild, the people's hearts brimful of fear,   205
To manage private and domestic quarrel,
In night, and on the court and guard of safety!
'Tis monstrous. Iago, who began it?

Montano: If partially affined, or leagued in office,
Thou dost deliver more or less than truth,   210
Thou art no soldier.

Iago: Touch me not so near:
I had rather have this tongue cut from my mouth
Than it should do offence to Michael Cassio;
Yet, I persuade myself, to speak the truth
Shall nothing wrong him. Thus it is, general.   215
Montano and myself being in speech,
There comes a fellow crying out for help:
And Cassio following him with determined sword,
To execute upon him. Sir, this gentleman
Steps in to Cassio, and entreats his pause: 220
Myself the crying fellow did pursue,
Lest by his clamour – as it so fell out –
The town might fall in fright: he, swift of foot,
Outran my purpose; and I returned the rather
For that I heard the clink and fall of swords,   225
And Cassio high in oath; which till to-night

Glosses (right margin):

193 self-charity: *self-defence*

197 collied: *darkened*
198 Assays: *tries*

209 partially affined: *taking sides*
209 leagued in office: *frightened by being of inferior rank*

212 Touch me not: *do not remind me*

220 entreats his pause: *begs him to stop*

224 I returned...: *I thought it best to turn back because...*

Confusion *Montano leaves Iago to inform Othello about the disturbance. This further incenses the general, who is concerned that a drunken brawl has broken out in a 'town of war'. Iago gives the impression that he is reluctant to name Cassio in his version of what happened: 'I had rather have this tongue cut from my mouth'.*

I ne'er might say before. When I came back –
For this was brief – I found them close together,
At blow and thrust; even as again they were
When you yourself did part them.   230
More of this matter cannot I report:
But men are men; the best sometimes forget:
Though Cassio did some little wrong to him,
As men in rage strike those that wish them best,
Yet surely Cassio, I believe, received   235
From him that fled some strange indignity,
Which patience could not pass.

Othello: I know, Iago,
Thy honesty and love doth mince this matter,
Making it light to Cassio. Cassio, I love thee
But never more be officer of mine.   240

Re-enter Desdemona, attended

Look, if my gentle love be not raised up!
I'll make thee an example.

Desdemona: What's the matter?

Othello: All's well now, sweeting; come away to bed.
Sir, for your hurts, myself will be your surgeon: 245
Lead him off.

To Montano, who is led off

Iago, look with care about the town,
And silence those whom this vile brawl distracted.
Come, Desdemona: 'tis the soldier's life
To have their balmy slumbers waked with strife.   250

Exeunt all but Iago and Cassio

Iago: What, are you hurt, lieutenant?

Cassio: Ay, past all surgery.

Duty calls *Iago, in his guise as the general's obedient officer, continues his story of the brawl and succeeds in damning Cassio by pretending to excuse him: 'the best sometimes forget'. Othello angrily dismisses the young lieutenant from his post: 'never more be officer of mine'. He also calms a concerned Desdemona and leaves Iago in charge of quietening the disturbed town.*

 Shakespeare Focus: Othello

Iago: Marry, heaven forbid!

Cassio: Reputation, reputation, reputation! O, I have lost
my reputation! I have lost the immortal part of   255
myself, and what remains is bestial. My reputation,
Iago, my reputation!

Iago: As I am an honest man, I thought you had received
some bodily wound; there is more sense in that than
in reputation. Reputation is an idle and most false   260
imposition: oft got without merit, and lost without
deserving: you have lost no reputation at all,
unless you repute yourself such a loser. What, man!
There are ways to recover the general again: you
are but now cast in his mood, a punishment more in   265
policy than in malice, even so as one would beat his
offenceless dog to affright an imperious lion: sue
to him again, and he's yours.

Cassio: I will rather sue to be despised than to deceive so
good a commander with so slight, so drunken, and so   270
indiscreet an officer. Drunk? and speak parrot?
and squabble? swagger? swear? and discourse
fustian with one's own shadow? O thou invisible
spirit of wine, if thou hast no name to be known by,
let us call thee devil!   275

Iago: What was he that you followed with your sword? What
had he done to you?

Cassio: I know not.

Iago: Is't possible?

Cassio: I remember a mass of things, but nothing distinctly;   280
a quarrel, but nothing wherefore. O God, that men
should put an enemy in their mouths to steal away
their brains! That we should, with joy, pleasance
revel and applause, transform ourselves into beasts!

Iago: Why, but you are now well enough: how came you   285
thus recovered?

253 Marry: *indeed*

260 an idle and most
false imposition: *a useless,
deceptive thing placed on
people from outside*

265 cast in his mood:
dismissed in anger

267 sue: *appeal*

272 discourse fustian: *speak
rubbish*

281 nothing wherefore: *not
what it was about*

Reputation *Cassio bitterly surveys his reputation, which now lies in tatters. He realises he has* 'lost the
immortal part of myself'. *Is he exaggerating? Filled with self-pity? Iago, the consummate pragmatist,
puts forward the cynical argument that reputation is* 'oft got without merit, and lost without deserving'.

Cassio: It hath pleased the devil drunkenness to give place
to the devil wrath; one unperfectness shows me
another, to make me frankly despise myself.

Iago: Come, you are too severe a moraler: as the time,
the place, and the condition of this country
stands, I could heartily wish this had not befallen;
but, since it is as it is, mend it for your own good.

Cassio: I will ask him for my place again; he shall tell me
I am a drunkard! Had I as many mouths as Hydra,
such an answer would stop them all. To be now a
sensible man, by and by a fool, and presently a
beast! O strange! Every inordinate cup is
unblessed and the ingredient is a devil.

Iago: Come, come, good wine is a good familiar creature
if it be well used: exclaim no more against it.
And, good lieutenant, I think you think I love you.

Cassio: I have well approved it, sir. I drunk!

Iago: You or any man living may be drunk! at a time, man.
I'll tell you what you shall do. Our general's wife
is now the general: may say so in this respect, for
that he hath devoted and given up himself to the
contemplation, mark, and denotement of her parts and
graces: confess yourself freely to her; importune
her help to put you in your place again: she is of
so free, so kind, so apt, so blessed a disposition,
she holds it a vice in her goodness not to do more
than she is requested: this broken joint between
you and her husband entreat her to splinter; and, my
fortunes against any lay worth naming, this
crack of your love shall grow stronger
than it was before.

Cassio: You advise me well.

Iago: I protest, in the sincerity of love and honest kindness.

Cassio: I think it freely; and betimes in the morning I will
beseech the virtuous Desdemona to undertake for me:
I am desperate of my fortunes if they check me here.

Line	Note
290	
295	Hydra: *mythological snake that grew two heads where one was cut off*
	298 inordinate: *superfluous, of no use*
300	300 familiar creature: *friendly spirit*
	303 approved it: *tested it out*
305	
	308 denotement: *description*
310	
	314 splinter: *mend (apply a splint)*
315	
320	320 betimes: *early*

Iago offers advice *Cassio berates himself for his weakness, calling himself* 'a beast'. *Iago seizes another opportunity and advises him to ask Desdemona for help. After all, not only does she love doing good, but she now commands Othello:* 'now the general'. *Cassio gratefully agrees.*

Iago: You are in the right. Good night, lieutenant; I
must to the watch. 325

Cassio: Good night, honest Iago.

Exit

Iago: And what's he then that says I play the villain?
When this advice is free I give and honest,
Probal to thinking and indeed the course   329 Probal: *reasonable*
To win the Moor again? For 'tis most easy   330
The inclining Desdemona to subdue   331 inclining: *sympathetic*
In any honest suit: she's framed as fruitful
As the free elements. And then for her
To win the Moor – were it to renounce his baptism,   334 baptism: *Christian faith*
All seals and symbols of redeemed sin,   335   335 seals and symbols: *the sign of the cross, etc.*
His soul is so enfettered to her love,
That she may make, unmake, do what she list,
Even as her appetite shall play the god
With his weak function. How am I then a villain
To counsel Cassio to this parallel course,   340
Directly to his good? Divinity of hell!   341 Divinity: *study of religion*
When devils will the blackest sins put on,
They do suggest at first with heavenly shows,   343 suggest: *tempt*
As I do now: for whiles this honest fool
Plies Desdemona to repair his fortunes   345
And she for him pleads strongly to the Moor,
I'll pour this pestilence into his ear,
That she repeals him for her body's lust;   348 repeals him: *tries to get him reinstated*
And by how much she strives to do him good,
She shall undo her credit with the Moor.   350
So will I turn her virtue into pitch,
And out of her own goodness make the net
That shall enmesh them all.   353 enmesh: *trap*

Re-enter Roderigo

How now, Roderigo!

Appearance and reality *The ensign has now convinced both Othello and Cassio that he is 'honest Iago'. A repelled yet engrossed audience watches as Iago spins his web of deceit to ensnare the 'inclining Desdemona'. Unlike the other characters, he is acutely aware that appearances can be deceptive. Iago plans to use her appeal for Cassio's reinstatement to drive a wedge between herself and Othello. He will suggest that her motive for this request is 'her body's lust' for Cassio.*

Roderigo:	I do follow here in the chase, not like a hound that hunts, but one that fills up the cry. My money is almost spent; I have been to-night exceedingly well cudgelled; and I think the issue will be, I shall have so much experience for my pains, and so, with no money at all and a little more wit, return again to Venice.	355
Iago:	How poor are they that have not patience! What wound did ever heal but by degrees? Thou know'st we work by wit, and not by witchcraft; And wit depends on dilatory time. Does it not go well? Cassio hath beaten thee. And thou, by that small hurt, hast cashiered Cassio: Though other things grow fair against the sun, Yet fruits that blossom first will first be ripe: Content thyself awhile. By the mass, 'tis morning; Pleasure and action make the hours seem short. Retire thee; go where thou art billeted: Away, I say; thou shalt know more hereafter: Nay, get thee gone.	360 365 370

Exit Roderigo

Two things are to be done:
My wife must move for Cassio to her mistress;
I'll set her on;
Myself the while to draw the Moor apart,   375
And bring him jump when he may Cassio find
Soliciting his wife: ay, that's the way:
Dull not device by coldness and delay.

Exit

Marginal glosses:

355 one that fills up the cry: *on who is taking part in the main action (hunting term)*

357 cudgelled: *beaten*

363 dilatory: *slowly dragging*

365 cashiered Cassio: *got Cassio dismissed*

373 move: *plead*

375 the while: *at the same time*
376 jump: *at the very moment*

378 device: *plot*

Iago in control *Roderigo is dissatisfied that he has wasted his money for little return. However, Iago points out what Roderigo has achieved – he has succeeded in getting Cassio dismissed. His soliloquy leaves the audience with the impression that he is in total control of the unfolding events. He becomes more confident in his scheming, now resolving to get his own wife, Emilia, to speak to Desdemona on Cassio's behalf: 'My wife must move for Cassio to her mistress'. He also decides to position Othello so that he can see Cassio pleading with Desdemona.*

Shakespeare Focus: Othello

Key Points

- This scene presents the first clear victory of evil over good.
- Out of a sense of duty, an impulsive Othello dismisses Cassio.
- Much is revealed about Cassio's character. He is easily led, good-natured and a little too eager to please. His inability to hold his drink and his preoccupation with his personal reputation are turned against him by Iago.
- Roderigo stupidly persists in his self-delusion.
- Iago is a man of many parts: a lively drinking partner, a concerned friend, a wise observer, a dutiful officer, a scheming manipulator. Yet it is ironic that he succeeds in holding an untarnished reputation for being honest.
- Desdemona's goodness leaves her open to exploitation.

Act 3

SCENE 1 – Before the castle

Cassio's musicians, who are performing a greeting for the newlyweds, are dismissed by Othello's clown.

Enter Cassio and some Musicians

Cassio: Masters, play here; I will content your pains;
Something that's brief; and bid 'Good morrow, general.'

Music. Enter Clown

Clown: Why masters, have your instruments been in Naples,
that they speak i' the nose thus?

First Musician: How, sir, how!   5

Clown: Are these, I pray you, wind-instruments?

First Musician: Ay, marry, are they, sir.

Clown: O, thereby hangs a tail.

First Musician: Whereby hangs a tale, sir?

Clown: Marry, sir, by many a wind-instrument that I know.   10
But, masters, here's money for you: and the general
so likes your music, that he desires you, for love's
sake, to make no more noise with it.

First Musician: Well, sir, we will not.

Clown: If you have any music that may not be heard, to it   15
again: but, as they say to hear music the general
does not greatly care.

First Musician: We have none such, sir.

Clown: Then put up your pipes in your bag, for I'll away:
go; vanish into air; away!   20

1 **content your pains:** *pay you for your trouble*

4 **i' the nose:** *a pun on the nasal accent of Naples and the sound quality of the music*

Elizabethan customs *It was the tradition to wake newlyweds with music outside their bedchamber. Shakespeare's audiences also enjoyed the use of clever word-play and puns, which were used in comic scenes to alleviate tension.*

Exeunt Musicians

Cassio: Dost thou hear, my honest friend?

Clown: No, I hear not your honest friend; I hear you.

Cassio: Prithee, keep up thy quillets. There's a poor piece
of gold for thee: if the gentlewoman that attends
the general's wife be stirring, tell her there's   25
one Cassio entreats her a little favour of speech:
wilt thou do this?

Clown: She is stirring, sir: if she will stir hither, I
shall seem to notify unto her.

Cassio: Do, good my friend.

Exit Clown
Enter Iago

In happy time, Iago.   30

Iago: You have not been abed then?

Cassio: Why, no; the day had broke
Before we parted. I have made bold, Iago,
To send in to your wife: my suit to her
Is, that she will to virtuous Desdemona   35
Procure me some access.

Iago: I'll send her to you presently;
And I'll devise a mean to draw the Moor
Out of the way, that your converse and business
May be more free.

Cassio: I humbly thank you for it.   40

Exit Iago

I never knew
A Florentine more kind and honest.

Enter Emilia

23 quillets: *puns*

37 presently: *at once*

39 more free: *less restricted*

Timescale *It is the morning after the drunken party. Iago's comment, 'You have not been abed then?',
suggests that Cassio has been too upset to sleep. It also illustrates how well Iago can tune in to a
character's mood – something that helps him to manipulate people.*

Emilia: Good morrow, good Lieutenant: I am sorry
For your displeasure; but all will sure be well.
The general and his wife are talking of it;
And she speaks for you stoutly: the Moor replies, 45
That he you hurt is of great fame in Cyprus,
And great affinity, and that in wholesome wisdom
He might not but refuse you; but he protests he loves you
And needs no other suitor but his likings
To take the safest occasion by the front 50
To bring you in again.

Cassio: Yet, I beseech you,
If you think fit, or that it may be done,
Give me advantage of some brief discourse
With Desdemona alone.

Emilia: Pray you, come in;
I will bestow you where you shall have time 55
To speak your bosom freely.

Cassio: I am much bound to you.

Exeunt

43 your displeasure: *your being out of favour*

45 stoutly: *loyally*

47 great affinity: *important relations*
48 refuse: *dismiss*

56 bosom: *feelings*

Emilia's role in the drama As Iago's wife and Desdemona's companion, Emilia becomes an increasingly important character in the play. She is streetwise and cynical, in striking contrast to her mistress. She also moves the plot forward, as she provides an opportunity for Cassio and Desdemona to meet – with catastrophic consequences: 'I will bestow you where you shall have time/To speak your bosom freely'.

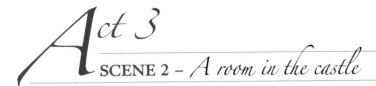

Act 3

SCENE 2 – *A room in the castle*

Othello, the busy military leader, inspects the defences of the town against possible military attack.

Enter Othello, Iago and Gentlemen

Othello: These letters give, Iago, to the pilot,
And by him do my duties to the senate.
That done, I will be walking on the works,   3 works: *fortifications*
Repair there to me.   4 Repair: *go*

Iago: Well, my good lord, I'll do it.

Othello: This fortification, gentlemen, shall we see it?   5

Gentleman: We'll wait upon your lordship.

Exeunt

Changed times *It is Iago who now accompanies Othello on business, not the disgraced Cassio, whom he has successfully displaced.*

Key Points

- Two short scenes show the aftermath of Cassio's fight and prepare the audience for Act 3, Scene 3. Tension increases with the success of Iago's plan.

- Scene 1 provides comic relief and reveals that Othello still holds Cassio in esteem despite his behaviour at the drunken brawl. Emilia is further drawn into the plot, while Cassio is unwilling to wait for Othello's forgiveness.

- Scene 2 shows Othello returning to military matters. He asks Iago to pay his respects to the council and then joins him as he inspects the island's fortifications. This allows time for Desdemona and Cassio to meet in private.

Act 3

SCENE 3 – *The garden of the the castle*

In the 'temptation scene', Desdemona attempts to reassure Cassio of her efforts to have him reinstated as lieutenant. Othello returns with Iago, who makes a seemingly casual remark about Cassio's hurried departure. He insinuates wrongdoing and draws Othello into his web by playing on the Moor's jealousy. Iago becomes increasingly influential, persuading Othello that his young wife is unfaithful.

Enter Desdemona, Cassio, and Emilia

Desdemona:	Be thou assured, good Cassio, I will do All my abilities in thy behalf.
Emilia:	Good madam, do, I warrant it grieves my husband, As if the case were his.
Desdemona:	O, that's an honest fellow. Do not doubt, Cassio, 5 But I will have my lord and you again As friendly as you were.
Cassio:	Bounteous madam, Whatever shall become of Michael Cassio, He's never anything but your true servant.
Desdemona:	I know it. I thank you. You do love my lord, 10 You have known him long, and be you well assured, He shall in strangeness stand no further off Than in a polite distance.
Cassio:	Ay, but, lady, That policy may either last so long, Or feed upon such nice and waterish diet, 15 Or breed itself so out of circumstance, That I being absent, and my place supplied, My general will forget my love and service.

3 warrant: *promise*

12 He shall in strangeness ... polite distance: *he will distance himself from you only while it is politically necessary*

15 nice: *trivial*

17 my place supplied: *my position filled*

The fateful meeting *Desdemona, Cassio and Emilia meet in the garden of the castle, where Desdemona pledges her support for his case for reinstatement, vowing to use 'All my abilities in thy behalf'. Cassio is impatient, fearing Othello 'will forget my love and service'. Is this yet another example of the underlying conflict between pubic and private life that is a mark of Desdemona's relationship with Othello?*

Desdemona: Do not doubt that: before Emilia here
I give thee warrant of thy place: assure thee 20
If I do vow a friendship, I'll perform it
To the last article; my lord shall never rest,
I'll watch him tame, and talk him out of patience;
His bed shall seem a school, his board a shrift,
I'll intermingle every thing he does 25
With Cassio's suit; therefore be merry, Cassio,
For thy solicitor shall rather die
Than give thy cause away.

Emilia: Madam, here comes my lord.

Cassio: Madam, I'll take my leave. 30

Desdemona: Why, stay, and hear me speak.

Cassio: Madam, not now, I am very ill at ease,
Unfit for mine own purposes.

Desdemona: Well, do your discretion.

Exit Cassio
Enter Othello and Iago

Iago: Ha! I like not that. 35

Othello: What dost thou say?

Iago: Nothing, my lord, or if – I know not what.

Othello: Was not that Cassio parted from my wife?

Iago: Cassio, my lord! No, sure, I cannot think it,
That he would steal away so guilty-like, 40
Seeing you coming.

Othello: I do believe 'twas he.

Desdemona: How now, my lord!
I have been talking with a suitor here,
A man that languishes in your displeasure. 45
Why, your lieutenant, Cassio. Good my lord,
If I have any grace or power to move you,

---

23 watch him tame: *keep him awake to wear down his resistance (used for taming hawks)*
24 board a shrift: *dining table will be like a confessional, a place for penance*

27 solicitor: *one who pleads your case*

45 languishes: *stagnates*

A hurried exit *As Othello enters, Cassio hurries away, still unable to face his general. This provides Iago with the perfect opportunity to spread suspicion ('Ha! I like not that') and begin his temptation of Othello.*

Irony *Desdemona swears to 'die' rather than fail in her efforts to help Cassio's reappointment.*

His present reconciliation take;	**48** His present reconciliation take: *accept his apology*
For if he be not one that truly loves you,	
That errs in ignorance and not in cunning, 50	**50** That errs in ignorance: *he was unaware of what he was doing*
I have no judgment in an honest face:	
I prithee, call him back.	

Othello: Went he hence now?

Desdemona: Yes, faith, so humbled
That he has left part of his grief with me,
To suffer with him. Good love, call him back.   55

Othello: Not now, sweet Desdemona; some other time.

Desdemona: But shall it be shortly?

Othello: The sooner, sweet, for you.

Desdemona: Shall it be tonight at supper?

Othello: No, not to-night.

Desdemona: Tomorrow dinner, then?

Othello: I shall not dine at home;
I meet the captains at the citadel.   60

Desdemona: Why, then, tomorrow night, or Tuesday morn,
On Tuesday noon, or night, or Wednesday morn:
I prithee, name the time, but let it not
Exceed three days: in faith, he's penitent;
And yet his trespass, in our common reason –   65
Save that, they say, the wars must make examples
Out of their best – is not almost a fault
To incur a private check. When shall he come?
Tell me, Othello: I wonder in my soul,
What you would ask me, that I should deny,   70
Or stand so mammering on. What! Michael Cassio,
That came a-wooing with you, and so many a time,
When I have spoke of you dispraisingly,
Has taken your part; to have so much to do
To bring him in! Trust me, I could do much—   75

66 Save: *except*

71 mammering: *hesitating*

Othello's response *When Desdemona begins to plead Cassio's case, Othello is indulgent at first, promising* 'The sooner, sweet, for you'. *As she continues to plead, however, her husband's answers become shorter and he reminds her that he has military business to attend to:* 'I meet the captains at the citadel'. *Playfully, she continues to urge,* 'When shall he come?'

Othello: Prithee, no more, let him come when he will,
I will deny thee nothing.

Desdemona: Why, this is not a boon,
'Tis as I should entreat you wear your gloves,
Or feed on nourishing dishes, or keep you warm,
Or sue to you to do a peculiar profit   80
To your own person: nay, when I have a suit
Wherein I mean to touch your love indeed,
It shall be full of poise and difficult weight
And fearful to be granted.

Othello: I will deny thee nothing:
Whereon, I do beseech thee, grant me this,   85
To leave me but a little to myself.

Desdemona: Shall I deny you? No, farewell, my lord.

Othello: Farewell, my Desdemona: I'll come to thee straight.

Desdemona: Emilia, come. Be as your fancies teach you;
Whatever you be, I am obedient.   90

Exeunt Desdemona and Emilia

Othello: Excellent wretch! Perdition catch my soul,
But I do love thee! And when I love thee not,
Chaos is come again.

Iago: My noble lord—

Othello: What dost thou say, Iago?

Iago: Did Michael Cassio, when you wooed my lady,   95
Know of your love?

Othello: He did, from first to last. Why dost thou ask?

Iago: But for a satisfaction of my thought.
No further harm.

Othello: Why of thy thought, Iago?

Iago: I did not think he had been acquainted with her.   100

---

77 boon: *favour*

80 peculiar: *personal*
81 suit: *request*

83 poise: *confidence*

89 fancies: *wishes*

91 wretch: *used affectionately, apparently*
91 Perdition: *damnation*

93 Chaos: *the end of the world, total catastrophe*

Foreshadowing disaster *Desdemona also becomes impatient because Othello refuses to meet Cassio. The scene is filled with dramatic irony. The Moor becomes exasperated with his wife and admits that he will deny her nothing. His fateful declaration, 'when I love thee not,/Chaos is come again', foreshadows the personal catastrophe that lies ahead.*

Shakespeare Focus: Othello

'What dost thou say, Iago?'

Othello: O yes, and went between us very oft.

Iago: Indeed!

Othello: Indeed! Indeed: discernest thou aught in that?
Is he not honest?

Iago: Honest, my lord! 105

Othello: Honest! Ay, honest.

Iago: My lord, for aught I know.

Othello: What dost thou think?

Iago: Think, my lord!

103 discernest thou aught
in that?: *do you see any
significance in that?*

Seeds of doubt *Iago seizes the moment to insidiously spread confusion. He asks probing questions, yet his own answers are evasive. He succeeds in exasperating Othello, who demands to know what the ensign is hinting at.*

Othello: Think, my lord! By heaven, he echoes me,   110
As if there were some monster in his thought
Too hideous to be shown. Thou dost mean something:
I heard thee say even now, thou lik'st not that,
When Cassio left my wife: what didst not like?
And when I told thee he was of my counsel   115
In my whole course of wooing, thou cried'st 'Indeed!'
And didst contract and purse thy brow together,
As if thou then hadst shut up in thy brain
Some horrible conceit: if thou dost love me,
Show me thy thought.   120

Iago: My lord, you know I love you.

Othello: I think thou dost,
And, for I know thou art full of love and honesty,
And weighest thy words before thou givest them breath,
Therefore these stops of thine fright me the more:
For such things in a false disloyal knave   125
Are tricks of custom, but in a man that's just
They are close denotements, working from the heart
That passion cannot rule.

Iago: For Michael Cassio,
I dare be sworn I think that he is honest.

Othello: I think so too.

Iago: Men should be what they seem,   130
Or those that be not, would they might seem none!

Othello: Certain, men should be what they seem.

Iago: Why, then, I think Cassio's an honest man.

Othello: Nay, yet there's more in this:
I prithee, speak to me as to thy thinkings,   135
As thou dost ruminate, and give thy worst of thoughts
The worst of words.

---

115 of my counsel: *in my confidence*

119 conceit: *idea*

126 tricks of custom: *familiar deceptions*
127 close denotements: *hints suggesting that something is hidden*

136 ruminate: *think*

Breathtaking hypocrisy *For the first time in the play, Shakespeare introduces the idea of jealousy as a 'monster'. The more Iago hesitates to speak his mind, the more Othello's imagination begins to fear the worst. Before an incredulous audience, this master of deception declares that* 'Men should be what they seem'. *When pressed by Othello to* 'give thy worst of thoughts/The worst of words', *he replies that even slaves can keep their thoughts private. Honesty is very important to the Moor. He likes to be certain about everything.*

 Shakespeare Focus: Othello

Iago: Good my lord, pardon me:
Though I am bound to every act of duty,
I am not bound to that all slaves are free to.
Utter my thoughts? Why, say they are vile and false: 140
As where's that palace whereinto foul things
Sometimes intrude not? Who has a breast so pure,
But some uncleanly apprehensions
Keep leets and law-days and in session sit
With meditations lawful? 145

Othello: Thou dost conspire against thy friend, Iago,
If thou but thinkest him wronged and makest his ear
A stranger to thy thoughts.

Iago: I do beseech you –
Though I perchance am vicious in my guess,
As, I confess, it is my nature's plague 150
To spy into abuses, and oft my jealousy
Shapes faults that are not – that your wisdom yet,
From one that so imperfectly conceits,
You would take no notice, nor build yourself a trouble
Out of my scattering and unsure observance. 155
It were not for your quiet nor your good,
Nor for my manhood, honesty, or wisdom,
To let you know my thoughts.

Othello: What dost thou mean?

Iago: Good name in man and woman, dear my lord,
Is the immediate jewel of their souls: 160
Who steals my purse steals trash; 'tis something, nothing,
'Twas mine, 'tis his, and has been slave to thousands:
But he that filches from me my good name
Robs me of that which not enriches him
And makes me poor indeed. 165

Othello: By heaven, I'll know thy thoughts.

Iago: You cannot, if my heart were in your hand;
Nor shall not, whilst 'tis in my custody.

Othello: Ha!

141 whereinto: into which

144 leets: local courts
144 law-days: days on which courts are in session

150 it is my nature's plague: it is part of my character

153 conceits: imagines

155 scattering and unsure observance: random and uncertain insights
156 quiet: peace of mind

163 filches: steals

The skilled manipulator *Unlike Desdemona's simple methods of persuasion, Iago cleverly manipulates Othello by warning him against the very emotion that he wants to plant in the Moor's mind: 'jealousy'. Othello begins to slide into the trap where he will be consumed by the* 'green-eyed monster' *and is now reduced to short exclamations of angry self-pity.*

'I'll see before I doubt'

Iago: O, beware, my lord, of jealousy;
It is the green-eyed monster which doth mock 170
The meat it feeds on. That cuckold lives in bliss
Who, certain of his fate, loves not his wronger;
But, O, what damned minutes tells he o'er
Who dotes, yet doubts, suspects, yet strongly loves!

171 cuckold: *wronged husband*

174 dotes: *loves*

Othello: O misery! 175

Iago: Poor and content is rich and rich enough,
But riches, fineless, is as poor as winter
To him that ever fears he shall be poor.
Good heaven, the souls of all my tribe defend
From jealousy!

177 fineless: *endless*

Othello: Why, why is this? 180
Thinkest thou I would make a life of jealousy,
To follow still the changes of the moon
With fresh suspicions? No, to be once in doubt
Is once to be resolved: exchange me for a goat,
When I shall turn the business of my soul 185
To such exsufflicate and blown surmises,
Matching thy inference. 'Tis not to make me jealous

186 exsufflicate and blown surmises: *exaggerated suspicions*
187 Matching thy inference: *equal to your interpretation*

To say my wife is fair, feeds well, loves company,
Is free of speech, sings, plays and dances well;
Where virtue is, these are more virtuous: 190
Nor from mine own weak merits will I draw
The smallest fear or doubt of her revolt,
For she had eyes, and chose me. No, Iago,
I'll see before I doubt; when I doubt, prove,
And on the proof, there is no more but this –   195
Away at once with love or jealousy!

Iago: I am glad of it, for now I shall have reason
To show the love and duty that I bear you
With franker spirit. Therefore, as I am bound,
Receive it from me. I speak not yet of proof.   200
Look to your wife, observe her well with Cassio,
Wear your eye thus, not jealous nor secure.
I would not have your free and noble nature,
Out of self-bounty, be abused, look to it:
I know our country disposition well;   205
In Venice they do let heaven see the pranks
They dare not show their husbands: their best conscience
Is not to leave it undone, but keep unknown.

Othello: Dost thou say so?

Iago: She did deceive her father, marrying you;   210
And when she seem'd to shake and fear your looks,
She loved them most.

Othello: And so she did.

Iago: Why, go to then;
She that, so young, could give out such a seeming,
To seal her father's eyes up close as oak –
He thought 'twas witchcraft – but I am much to blame;   215

202 Wear your eye thus: *look at it this way*

204 self-bounty: *natural generosity and kindness*

206 pranks: *mischievous behaviour*

213 seeming: *pretence*

214 seal: *stitch up*
214 close as oak: *like the close grain of an oak tree*

A question of balance *Othello hardly knows what to think anymore. He recollects Desdemona's good qualities: she is 'fair, feeds well, loves company'. He decides he must have definite proof before he judges her: 'I'll see before I doubt'. Iago plays a trump card by using Othello's vulnerable position as an outsider of Venetian society to launch an attack: 'In Venice they do let heaven see the pranks/They dare not show their husbands'. Othello accepts Iago's assertions that Venetian women cheat on their husbands.*

The deceptive daughter *The Moor listens intently while Iago continues to undermine Desdemona's character by using her impetuous love for Othello as possible proof of her infidelity. He suggests that she was always deceptive, even to her own father: 'She did deceive her father, marrying you'.*

	I humbly do beseech you of your pardon For too much loving you.	
Othello:	I am bound to thee for ever.	217 bound: *indebted*
Iago:	I see this hath a little dashed your spirits.	
Othello:	Not a jot, not a jot.	
Iago:	I' faith, I fear it has. I hope you will consider what is spoke 220 Comes from my love. But I do see you're moved, I am to pray you not to strain my speech To grosser issues nor to larger reach Than to suspicion.	222 strain: *push further* 223 larger reach: *go beyond*
Othello:	I will not.	
Iago:	Should you do so, my lord, 225 My speech should fall into such vile success As my thoughts aim not at. Cassio's my worthy friend – My lord, I see you are moved.	226 success: *result*
Othello:	No, not much moved: I do not think but Desdemona's honest.	
Iago:	Long live she so! And long live you to think so! 230	
Othello:	And yet, how nature erring from itself—	
Iago:	Ay, there's the point: as - to be bold with you – Not to affect many proposed matches Of her own clime, complexion, and degree, Whereto we see in all things nature tends – 235 Fie! one may smell in such a will most rank, Foul disproportion, thoughts unnatural. But pardon me: I do not in position Distinctly speak of her, though I may fear Her will, recoiling to her better judgment, 240 May fall to match you with her country forms And happily repent.	233 affect: *like* 234 clime: *country* 237 disproportion: *improper behaviour* 241 fall to match: *come to compare* 241 country forms: *own countrymen* 242 happily: *perhaps*

Growing influence *Iago now apologises for upsetting Othello:* 'I humbly do beseech you of your pardon'. *But the Moor's fate has now become inextricably linked to his tormentor:* 'I am bound to thee for ever'. *Othello's simple nature struggles to contain his feelings, saying he is* 'not much moved'. *Yet it is obvious that he is torn apart in the face of Iago's cunning onslaught. The ensign is replacing Desdemona in Othello's affections.*

'Why did I marry?'

Othello: Farewell, farewell:
If more thou dost perceive, let me know more;
Set on thy wife to observe: leave me, Iago.

Iago: [*Going*] My lord, I take my leave.   245

Othello: Why did I marry? This honest creature doubtless
Sees and knows more, much more, than he unfolds.

Iago: [*Returning*] My lord, I would I might entreat
your honour
To scan this thing no further, leave it to time:
Though it be fit that Cassio have his place,   250
For sure, he fills it up with great ability,
Yet, if you please to hold him off awhile,
You shall by that perceive him and his means:

253 means: *method*

> **Mixed marriage** *Iago describes how Desdemona has already shown unnatural inclinations by refusing* 'many proposed matches/Of her own clime, complexion, and degree'. *Othello is increasingly suspicious and now wants Desdemona watched:* 'Set on thy wife to observe'. *Alone and heartbroken, he wonders,* 'Why did I marry?' *Is his self-pity understandable? Iago returns to suggest that Othello should hold Cassio* 'off awhile' *to see if Desdemona continues to plead his case.*

	Note, if your lady strain his entertainment	
	With any strong or vehement importunity,	255
	Much will be seen in that. In the meantime,	
	Let me be thought too busy in my fears –	
	As worthy cause I have to fear I am –	
	And hold her free, I do beseech your honour.	

Othello: Fear not my government. 260

Iago: I once more take my leave.

Exit

Othello: This fellow's of exceeding honesty,
And knows all qualities, with a learned spirit,
Of human dealings. If I do prove her haggard,
Though that her jesses were my dear heartstrings, 265
I'ld whistle her off and let her down the wind,
To pray at fortune. Haply, for I am black
And have not those soft parts of conversation
That chamberers have, or for I am declined
Into the vale of years – yet that's not much – 270
She's gone. I am abused, and my relief
Must be to loathe her. O curse of marriage,
That we can call these delicate creatures ours,
And not their appetites! I had rather be a toad,
And live upon the vapour of a dungeon, 275
Than keep a corner in the thing I love
For others' uses. Yet, 'tis the plague of great ones
Prerogatived are they less than the base,
'Tis destiny, unshunnable, like death:
Even then this forked plague is fated to us 280
When we do quicken. Desdemona comes:

Re-enter Desdemona and Emilia

If she be false, O, then heaven mocks itself!
I'll not believe it.

---

254 strain his entertainment: *urges his reinstatement*
255 importunity: *pleading*

260 government: *self-control*

265 jesses: *ties to me*

267 Haply, for: *perhaps because*

269 chamberers: *gallant young men*

278 Prerogatived: *privileged*

280 forked plague: *the sign for a deceived husband*
281 quicken: *are born*

Confusion reigns *Othello reiterates his belief in Iago's 'exceeding honesty'. He uses a hawking metaphor to express his feelings about Desdemona. He wants to release her and let her look after herself ('To pray at fortune'). He considers his own character defects: he is an outsider who lacks refinement and he is older than his wife. He curses marriage, preferring to live as a 'toad' in a dungeon than in a faithless marriage. Yet when he sees Desdemona again, he cannot believe she is false.*

Desdemona: How now, my dear Othello!
Your dinner, and the generous islanders
By you invited, do attend your presence. 285

Othello: I am to blame.

Desdemona: Why do you speak so faintly?
Are you not well?

Othello: I have a pain upon my forehead here.

Desdemona: 'Faith, that's with watching, 'twill away again:
Let me but bind it hard, within this hour 290
It will be well.

Othello: Your napkin is too little:

He puts the handkerchief from him, and it drops.

Let it alone. Come, I'll go in with you.

Desdemona: I am very sorry that you are not well.

Exeunt Othello and Desdemona

Emilia: I am glad I have found this napkin:
This was her first remembrance from the Moor: 295
My wayward husband hath a hundred times
Wooed me to steal it, but she so loves the token,
For he conjured her she should ever keep it,
That she reserves it ever more about her
To kiss and talk to. I'll have the work taken out, 300
And give it Iago: what he will do with it
Heaven knows, not I;
I nothing but to please his fantasy.

Re-enter Iago

Iago: How now! What do you here alone?

Emilia: Do not you chide, I have a thing for you. 305

---

289 watching: *being on duty without sleep*

295 remembrance: *keepsake, gift*
296 wayward: *unpredictable*

298 conjured her: *made her swear*

300 work taken out: *the embroidery copied*

303 fantasy: *whim*

305 chide: *scold*

The handkerchief plot *Desdemona tries to soothe Othello's forehead with her handkerchief after he complains of having a headache, but as he brushes her away, she drops it. Emilia retrieves it, remarking how it was Desdemona's treasured first gift from Othello. She also reveals how Iago has repeatedly asked her to steal it. She decides to have the embroidery copied and give the replica to her husband: 'I nothing but to please his fantasy'. Ironically, this symbol of love will soon become one of betrayal.*

Iago: A thing for me? It is a common thing—

Emilia: Ha!

Iago: To have a foolish wife.

Emilia: O, is that all? What will you give me now
For that same handkerchief?

Iago: What handkerchief?   310

Emilia: What handkerchief!
Why, that the Moor first gave to Desdemona,
That which so often you did bid me steal.

Iago: Hast stolen it from her?

Emilia: No, 'faith; she let it drop by negligence. 315
And, to the advantage, I, being here, took it up.
Look, here it is.

Iago: A good wench, give it me.

Emilia: What will you do with it, that you have been
So earnest to have me filch it?

Iago: [*Snatching it*] Why, what's that to you? 320

Emilia: If it be not for some purpose of import,
Give it me again: poor lady, she'll run mad
When she shall lack it.

Iago: Be not acknown on it. I have use for it.
Go, leave me.   325

Exit Emilia

I will in Cassio's lodging lose this napkin,
And let him find it. Trifles light as air
Are to the jealous confirmations strong
As proofs of holy writ: this may do something.
The Moor already changes with my poison: 330
Dangerous conceits are, in their natures, poisons,

315 negligence: *paying no attention*
316 to the advantage: *as luck would have it*

317 wench: *common woman*

319 filch: *steal*

321 purpose of some import: *some important use*

324 Be not acknown on: *do not admit*

327 Trifles: *seemingly unimportant things*

329 holy writ: *the Bible*

331 conceits: *imaginings*

The dutiful wife *In the face of Iago's patronising scolding, Emilia attempts to ingratiate herself by showing the lost handkerchief to her husband. Once again, Iago seizes every chance he can to destroy his sworn enemies. He plans to plant Desdemona's handkerchief in Cassio's lodgings, aware that 'Trifles light as air/Are to the jealous confirmations strong'. Will this be the proof Othello needs to convince him that his wife is cheating on him?*

Which at the first are scarce found to distaste,
But with a little act upon the blood.
Burn like the mines of sulphur. I did say so.
Look, where he comes!   335

334 sulphur: *combustible chemical*

Re-enter Othello

Not poppy, nor mandragora,
Nor all the drowsy syrups of the world,
Shall ever medicine thee to that sweet sleep
Which thou owedst yesterday.

336 poppy, nor mandragora: *sleep-inducing drugs*

339 thou owedst: *was yours*

Othello: Ha! ha! False to me?

Iago: Why, how now, general! No more of that.   340

Othello: Avaunt! Be gone! Thou hast set me on the rack:
I swear 'tis better to be much abused
Than but to know it a little.

341 rack: *instrument of torture*

Iago: How now, my lord!

Othello: What sense had I of her stolen hours of lust?
I saw it not, thought it not, it harmed not me: 345
I slept the next night well, was free and merry;
I found not Cassio's kisses on her lips:
He that is robbed, not wanting what is stolen,
Let him not know it, and he's not robbed at all.

Iago: I am sorry to hear this.   350

Othello: I had been happy, if the general camp,
Pioners and all, had tasted her sweet body,
So I had nothing known. O, now, for ever
Farewell the tranquil mind! Farewell content!
Farewell the plumed troop, and the big wars,   355
That make ambition virtue! O, farewell!
Farewell the neighing steed, and the shrill trump,
The spirit-stirring drum, the ear-piercing fife,
The royal banner, and all quality,
Pride, pomp and circumstance of glorious war!   360
And, O you mortal engines, whose rude throats

351 general camp: *whole army*
352 Pioners: *the lowest rank in the army*

357 trump: *trumpet*

360 circumstance: *ceremony*
361 engines: *cannons*

Farewell content *Othello seems to have abandoned all reason. He dismisses Iago and admits that he has been set* 'on the rack' *now that he knows of Desdemona's* 'stolen hours of lust'. *Until this moment, he was happy, but now his life has changed forever. Everything that was important to him (the* 'Pride, pomp and circumstance of glorious war') *is gone.*

	The immortal Jove's dead clamours counterfeit,	
	Farewell! Othello's occupation's gone!	
Iago:	Is it possible, my lord?	
Othello:	Villain, be sure thou prove my love a whore,	365
	Be sure of it, give me the ocular proof,	
	Or by the worth of man's eternal soul,	
	Thou hadst been better have been born a dog	
	Than answer my waked wrath!	
Iago:	Is it come to this?	
Othello:	Make me to see it; or, at the least, so prove it,	370
	That the probation bear no hinge nor loop	
	To hang a doubt on; or woe upon thy life!	
Iago:	My noble lord –	
Othello:	If thou dost slander her and torture me,	
	Never pray more, abandon all remorse.	375
	On horror's head horrors accumulate;	
	Do deeds to make heaven weep, all earth amazed;	
	For nothing canst thou to damnation add	
	Greater than that.	
Iago:	O grace! O heaven forgive me!	
	Are you a man? have you a soul or sense?	380
	God be wi' you; take mine office. O wretched fool,	
	That livest to make thine honesty a vice!	
	O monstrous world! Take note, take note, O world,	
	To be direct and honest is not safe.	
	I thank you for this profit; and from hence	385
	I'll love no friend, since love breeds such offence.	
Othello:	Nay, stay; thou shouldst be honest.	
Iago:	I should be wise, for honesty's a fool	
	And loses that it works for.	
Othello:	By the world,	
	I think my wife be honest and think she is not;	390
	I think that thou art just and think thou art not.	

Margin glosses:

362 clamours: *thunderous sound*
363 occupation's gone: *Othello's career is over*

366 ocular proof: *evidence Othello can actually see*

371 probation: *proof*

381 office: *job*

385 profit: *lesson*

A man of action *He warns the ensign that he requires 'ocular proof' of his wife's guilt, otherwise the consequences for Iago will be disastrous. In response, Iago pretends to be hurt and protests that he is not being appreciated. Caught in the web of Iago's insinuations, Othello struggles to comprehend the complex world of emotion by reverting to his army training.*

I'll have some proof. Her name, that was as fresh
As Dian's visage, is now begrimed and black
As mine own face. If there be cords, or knives,
Poison, or fire, or suffocating streams,   395
I'll not endure it. Would I were satisfied!

Iago: I see, sir, you are eaten up with passion:
I do repent me that I put it to you.
You would be satisfied?

Othello: Would! nay, I will.

Iago: And may: but, how? How satisfied, my lord?   400
Would you, the supervisor, grossly gape on –
Behold her topped?

Othello: Death and damnation! O!

Iago: It were a tedious difficulty, I think,
To bring them to that prospect: damn them then,
If ever mortal eyes do see them bolster   405
More than their own! What then? how then?
What shall I say? Where's satisfaction?
It is impossible you should see this,
Were they as prime as goats, as hot as monkeys,
As salt as wolves in pride, and fools as gross   410
As ignorance made drunk. But yet, I say,
If imputation and strong circumstances,
Which lead directly to the door of truth,
Will give you satisfaction, you may have it.

Othello: Give me a living reason she's disloyal.   415

Iago: I do not like the office:
But, since I am entered in this cause so far,
Pricked to it by foolish honesty and love,
I will go on. I lay with Cassio lately,
And, being troubled with a raging tooth,   420
I could not sleep.
There are a kind of men so loose of soul,
That in their sleeps will mutter their affairs.
One of this kind is Cassio.

393 Dian's visage: *the moon;
Diana is the goddess of the
moon and purity*

396 satisfied: *certain*

402 topped: *with a lover*

403 tedious difficulty: *hard
thing to arrange*

405 bolster: *share a pillow*

409 prime: *lecherous*
410 salt: *lusty*

416 office: *task*

Painting pictures *Using typically coarse language, Iago succeeds in inflaming Othello's rage before
presenting his so-called proof, an erotic dream which Cassio is supposed to have had where he reached
out for Desdemona in his sleep. Does Othello's immediate acceptance of Iago's story suggest that he is
predisposed to jealousy?*

In sleep I heard him say 'Sweet Desdemona,   425
Let us be wary, let us hide our loves!'
And then, sir, would he gripe and wring my hand,   427 gripe: *clutch*
Cry 'O sweet creature!' and then kiss me hard,
As if he plucked up kisses by the roots
That grew upon my lips: then laid his leg   430
Over my thigh, and sighed, and kissed; and then
Cried 'Cursed fate that gave thee to the Moor!'

Othello: O monstrous! Monstrous!

Iago: Nay, this was but his dream.

Othello: But this denoted a foregone conclusion: 434 But this denoted: *this shows something had already taken place*
'Tis a shrewd doubt, though it be but a dream.   435   435 shrewd doubt: *penetrating guess*
                                                                     436 thicken: *firm up*

Iago: And this may help to thicken other proofs
That do demonstrate thinly.

Othello: I'll tear her all to pieces.

Iago: Nay, but be wise, yet we see nothing done,
She may be honest yet. Tell me but this,   440
Have you not sometimes seen a handkerchief
Spotted with strawberries in your wife's hand?

Othello: I gave her such a one, 'twas my first gift.

Iago: I know not that, but such a handkerchief –
I am sure it was your wife's – did I today   445
See Cassio wipe his beard with.

Othello: If it be that—

Iago: If it be that, or any that was hers,
It speaks against her with the other proofs.

Othello: O, that the slave had forty thousand lives!
One is too poor, too weak for my revenge.   450
Now do I see 'tis true. Look here, Iago,
All my fond love thus do I blow to heaven.
'Tis gone.
Arise, black vengeance, from thy hollow cell!

Degradation *Othello descends to the level of a beast as he roars, 'I'll tear her all to pieces'. Iago calmly recounts a fictitious incident of the handkerchief being used by Cassio to 'wipe his beard with'. The furious husband now desires to wreak vengeance on Cassio, wishing 'the slave had forty thousand lives'. He craves 'blood, blood, blood' as he swears never to swerve from his set course of revenge. His violent language clearly reflects his loss of control.*

Yield up, O love, thy crown and hearted throne   455
To tyrannous hate! Swell, bosom, with thy fraught,
For 'tis of aspics' tongues!

456 fraught: *burden, cargo*
457 aspics: *poisonous snakes*

Iago: Yet be content.

Othello: O, blood, blood, blood!

Iago: Patience, I say; your mind perhaps may change.

Othello: Never, Iago. Like to the Pontic sea,   460
Whose icy current and compulsive course
Never feels retiring ebb, but keeps due on
To the Propontic and the Hellespont,
Even so my bloody thoughts, with violent pace,
Shall ne'er look back, ne'er ebb to humble love,   465
Till that a capable and wide revenge
Swallow them up. Now, by yond marble heaven,

460 Pontic Sea: *the Black Sea*

463 Propontic: *Sea of Marmora*
463 Hellespont: *Dardanelles*

466 capable: *ample*

Kneels

In the due reverence of a sacred vow
I here engage my words.

Iago: Do not rise yet.

Kneels

Witness, you ever-burning lights above,   470
You elements that clip us round about,
Witness that here Iago doth give up
The execution of his wit, hands, heart,
To wronged Othello's service! Let him command,
And to obey shall be in me remorse,   475
What bloody business ever.

471 clip: *encircle*

473 execution: *activities*

476 What bloody business ever: *however murderous it gets*

They rise

Othello: I greet thy love,
Not with vain thanks, but with acceptance bounteous,
And will upon the instant put thee to it:

477 acceptance bounteous: *generous reward*

The oath *In a chilling conclusion to the scene, Othello kneels to swear a 'sacred vow' of vengeance. Iago joins him, as he hypocritically promises to join the 'wronged Othello's service'. Interestingly, he asks for Desdemona's life to be spared. This demonic pact is sealed with Othello declaring, 'I greet thy love'. Iago has now become Othello's nemesis: 'I am your own for ever'.*

Within these three days let me hear thee say
That Cassio's not alive.

Iago: My friend is dead:
'Tis done at your request. But let her live. 480

Othello: Damn her, lewd minx! O, damn her!
Come, go with me apart. I will withdraw,
To furnish me with some swift means of death
For the fair devil. Now art thou my lieutenant.

Iago: I am your own for ever. 485

Exeunt

Key Points

Act 3, Scene 3

- Cassio's impatience for Othello's forgiveness is evident as he eagerly enlists Desdemona's assistance.
- Desdemona appears naive, continually pressurising her husband to reinstate the lieutenant. Her natural kindness is shown in her treatment of Othello's mood swings.
- Iago's evil cunning shocks the audience. He casts suspicion through doubtful evidence and succeeds in damaging Cassio and Desdemona's reputations.
- The terrible bond of vengeance is sworn by Othello and Iago. Othello instructs Iago to kill Cassio and he will kill Desdemona himself. Finally, Iago is appointed his lieutenant.
- Othello's roles as soldier and husband are in conflict throughout the scene. Iago understands this and displays ingenious skill in exploiting the Moor's weaknesses.
- The handkerchief is an important symbol that is central to Shakespeare's development of plot. It almost seems to possess magical powers for Othello, who becomes obsessed with it.
- Othello is corrupted from his earlier honourable self to become a confused and compulsive avenger blinded by jealousy, his essential flaw.
- In this crucial scene, Othello is transformed. Act 3, Scene 3 marks the turning point in the story and the audience can now sense that the play's tragic ending is inevitable.

Act 3

SCENE 4 – *Outside the castle*

Desdemona is confident that she has successfully persuaded Othello to reinstate Cassio. She is concerned over the loss of her special handkerchief and is unable to produce it at Othello's request. He informs her of its unique powers. Changing the conversation, she again pleads for Cassio. Othello abruptly departs and Emilia wryly comments on the behaviour of men. Cassio has an argument with a jealous Bianca, who feels neglected.

Enter Desdemona, Emilia, and Clown

Desdemona:	Do you know, sirrah, where Lieutenant Cassio lies?	1 lies: *lodges*
Clown:	I dare not say he lies any where.	
Desdemona:	Why, man?	
Clown:	He's a soldier, and for one to say a soldier lies, is stabbing. 5	
Desdemona:	Go to, where lodges he?	
Clown:	To tell you where he lodges, is to tell you where I lie.	
Desdemona:	Can any thing be made of this?	
Clown:	I know not where he lodges, and for me to devise a lodging and say he lies here or he lies there, were 10 to lie in mine own throat.	9 devise: *make up, invent*
Desdemona:	Can you inquire him out, and be edified by report?	12 edified: *instructed*
Clown:	I will catechise the world for him; that is, make questions and by them answer.	13 catechise: *a means of religious instruction*
Desdemona:	Seek him, bid him come hither: tell him I have 15 moved my lord on his behalf, and hope all will be well.	16 moved: *pleaded with*
Clown:	To do this is within the compass of man's wit, and therefore I will attempt the doing it.	17 compass: *scope*

Exit

Oblivious *Desdemona has no idea of Othello's suspicions and the imminent danger she faces. In complete contrast to the previous dark, tense scene, she engages in light-hearted banter as she sends the Clown to tell Cassio that he will be given his former position again: 'I have moved my lord on his behalf'.*

'Lend me thy handkerchief.'

Desdemona:	Where should I lose that handkerchief, Emilia?
Emilia:	I know not, madam.

20

Desdemona:	Believe me, I had rather have lost my purse
	Full of crusadoes: and, but my noble Moor
	Is true of mind and made of no such baseness
	As jealous creatures are, it were enough
	To put him to ill thinking.

22 crusadoes: *gold coins*

Emilia:	Is he not jealous?

25

Desdemona:	Who, he? I think the sun where he was born
	Drew all such humours from him.

27 humours: *moods*

Emilia:	Look, where he comes.
Desdemona:	I will not leave him now till Cassio
	Be called to him.

Enter Othello

How is it with you, my lord?

Concern and pretence *A troubled Desdemona confides her worry over the lost handkerchief to Emilia, who pretends to know nothing about it: 'I know not, madam.' Othello also engages in pretence, saying that he is well: 'Well, my good lady.'*

Othello:	Well, my good lady.	30
	[Aside]	
	O, hardness to dissemble! −	
	How do you, Desdemona?	

30 dissemble: *hide one's true feelings*

Desdemona: Well, my good lord.

Othello: Give me your hand: this hand is moist, my lady.

Desdemona: It yet hath felt no age nor known no sorrow.

Othello:	This argues fruitfulness and liberal heart;	
	Hot, hot, and moist, this hand of yours requires	35
	A sequester from liberty; fasting and prayer,	
	Much castigation, exercise devout;	
	For here's a young and sweating devil here,	
	That commonly rebels. 'Tis a good hand,	
	A frank one.	

36 sequester: *removal*

37 castigation: *discipline*

Desdemona:	You may indeed say so,	40
	For 'twas that hand that gave away my heart.	

Othello:	A liberal hand: the hearts of old gave hands,
	But our new heraldry is hands, not hearts.

Desdemona: I cannot speak of this. Come now, your promise.

Othello: What promise, chuck? 45

45 chuck: *dear (term of endearment)*

Desdemona: I have sent to bid Cassio come speak with you.

Othello:	I have a salt and sorry rheum offends me;
	Lend me thy handkerchief.

47 salt and sorry rheum: *running cold*

Desdemona: Here, my lord.

Othello: That which I gave you. 50

Desdemona: I have it not about me.

Othello: Not?

Desdemona: No, indeed, my lord.

A warm hand *Othello has taken Desdemona's hand and comments on how hot and moist it is, often regarded as a sign of lust: 'a young and sweating devil here'. However, Desdemona declares that this was the same hand that gave her heart away to Othello and proceeds again to question Othello about reinstating Cassio. Is this insistence by Desdemona rebelliousness and unwarranted interference in military business?*

Superstition *Othello, pretending to have a cold, requests the handkerchief he had given her. When she is unable to produce it, he informs Desdemona about its charmed origins.*

Othello:	That is a fault. That handkerchief		
	Did an Egyptian to my mother give;		
	She was a charmer, and could almost read	55	55 charmer: *witch*
	The thoughts of people: she told her, while		
	she kept it,		
	'Twould make her amiable and subdue my father		57 amiable: *beloved*
	Entirely to her love, but if she lost it		
	Or made gift of it, my father's eye		
	Should hold her loathed and his spirits should hunt	60	
	After new fancies: she, dying, gave it me,		61 fancies: *new loves*
	And bid me, when my fate would have me wive,		62 wive: *marry*
	To give it her. I did so: and take heed on it,		
	Make it a darling like your precious eye,		
	To lose it or give it away were such perdition	65	65 perdition: *damnation*
	As nothing else could match.		
Desdemona:	Is it possible?		
Othello:	'Tis true, there's magic in the web of it.		
	A sibyl, that had numbered in the world		68 sibyl: *prophetess*
	The sun to course two hundred compasses,		
	In her prophetic fury sewed the work;	70	
	The worms were hallowed that did breed the silk,		
	And it was dyed in mummy which the skilful		72 mummy: *embalming fluid*
	Conserved of maidens' hearts.		
Desdemona:	Indeed! Is it true?		
Othello:	Most veritable, therefore look to it well.		
Desdemona:	Then would to God that I had never seen it!	75	
Othello:	Ha! wherefore?		
Desdemona:	Why do you speak so startingly and rash?		
Othello:	Is it lost? Is it gone? Speak, is it out of the way?		
Desdemona:	Heaven bless us!		
Othello:	Say you?	80	

Another world *Othello recounts how his mother had told him that this handkerchief has magical properties. If treasured, it would ensure faithful love. Othello's exotic background, where belief in the supernatural is common, contrasts starkly with Desdemona's sophisticated upbringing in cosmopolitan Venice. She senses that the handkerchief is coming between them and complains, 'Then would to God that I had never seen it!' Outraged, Othello demands to know if she has lost it. Desdemona is still unaware of its importance and innocently asks, 'what and if it were?'*

Desdemona: It is not lost; but what and if it were?

Othello: How!

Desdemona: I say, it is not lost.

Othello: Fetch it, let me see it.

Desdemona: Why, so I can, sir, but I will not now.
This is a trick to put me from my suit,   85
Pray you, let Cassio be received again.

85 suit: *original purpose*

Othello: Fetch me the handkerchief, my mind misgives.

87 misgives: *is suspicious*

Desdemona: Come, come,
You'll never meet a more sufficient man.

88 sufficient: *competent*

Othello: The handkerchief!

Desdemona: I pray, talk me of Cassio.   90

Othello: The handkerchief!

Desdemona: A man that all his time
Hath founded his good fortunes on your love,
Shared dangers with you—

Othello: The handkerchief!

Desdemona: In faith, you are to blame.

Othello: 'Zounds!   95

95 'Zounds: *curse*

Exit

Emilia: Is not this man jealous?

Desdemona: I ne'er saw this before.
Sure, there's some wonder in this handkerchief:
I am most unhappy in the loss of it.

Emilia: 'Tis not a year or two shows us a man: 100
They are all but stomachs, and we all but food;
To eat us hungerly, and when they are full,
They belch us. Look you, Cassio and my husband!

Cross purposes *A sharp exchange takes place between the couple. Othello demands the handkerchief and Desdemona still insists on speaking on Cassio's behalf. Should Desdemona have lied? Should she have admitted the handkerchief was mislaid? The row culminates in Desdemona blaming Othello. His reaction is to storm off. The world-wise Emilia correctly deduces that Othello is jealous. Desdemona starts to consider whether 'there's some wonder in this handkerchief'.*

Enter Cassio and Iago

Iago: There is no other way, 'tis she must do it,
And, lo, the happiness! Go, and importune her. 105

Desdemona: How now, good Cassio! What's the news with you?

Cassio: Madam, my former suit. I do beseech you
That by your virtuous means I may again
Exist, and be a member of his love
Whom I with all the office of my heart 110
Entirely honour: I would not be delayed.
If my offence be of such mortal kind
That nor my service past, nor present sorrows,
Nor purposed merit in futurity,
Can ransom me into his love again, 115
But to know so must be my benefit;
So shall I clothe me in a forced content,
And shut myself up in some other course,
To fortune's alms.

Desdemona: Alas, thrice-gentle Cassio!
My advocation is not now in tune; 120
My lord is not my lord, nor should I know him,
Were he in favour as in humour altered.
So help me every spirit sanctified,
As I have spoken for you all my best
And stood within the blank of his displeasure 125
For my free speech! You must awhile be patient;
What I can do I will, and more I will
Than for myself I dare: let that suffice you.

Iago: Is my lord angry?

Emilia: He went hence but now,
And certainly in strange unquietness. 130

Iago: Can he be angry? I have seen the cannon,
When it hath blown his ranks into the air,
And, like the devil, from his very arm
Puffed his own brother: – and can he be angry?

---

110 office: *loyal service*

118 shut myself up: *confine myself to*
119 To fortune's alms: *to whatever Fate gives*

120 advocation: *the act of advocating or pleading*

122 favour: *appearance*

125 blank: *centre target*

The encircling web *While Emilia cynically remarks on how men treat women as a means of satisfying their desires, Iago directs Cassio to ask Desdemona to intervene on his behalf again. Cassio's refinement is in stark contrast to Othello's rudeness and Desdemona responds 'thrice-gentle Cassio', confiding in him how Othello is 'in humour altered'.*

Something of moment then: I will go meet him,   135
There's matter in it indeed, if he be angry.

Desdemona: I prithee, do so.

Exit Iago

Something, sure, of state,
Either from Venice, or some unhatched practice
Made demonstrable here in Cyprus to him,   140
Hath puddled his clear spirit: and in such cases
Men's natures wrangle with inferior things,
Though great ones are their object. 'Tis even so.
For let our finger ache, and it endues
Our other healthful members even to that sense   145
Of pain. Nay, we must think men are not gods,
Nor of them look for such observancy
As fit the bridal. Beshrew me much, Emilia,
I was, unhandsome warrior as I am,
Arraigning his unkindness with my soul;   150
But now I find I had suborned the witness,
And he's indicted falsely.

Emilia: Pray heaven it be state-matters, as you think,
And no conception nor no jealous toy
Concerning you.   155

Desdemona: Alas the day! I never gave him cause.

Emilia: But jealous souls will not be answered so;
They are not ever jealous for the cause,
But jealous for they are jealous: 'tis a monster
Begot upon itself, born on itself.   160

Desdemona: Heaven keep that monster from Othello's mind!

Emilia: Lady, amen.

Desdemona: I will go seek him. Cassio, walk hereabout:
If I do find him fit, I'll move your suit
And seek to effect it to my uttermost.   165

Cassio: I humbly thank your ladyship.

135 of moment: *of importance*

139 unhatched: *uncovered*

141 puddled: *muddied*

144 endues: *infects*

147 observancy: *loving attention*
148 bridal: *wedding night*
148 Beshrew: *Damn*

150 Arraigning: *accusing*
151 suborned the witness: *made the witness give false evidence*
152 indicted: *accused*

154 toy: *misgiving*

The cause *Iago remarks that it must be 'Something of moment' to make Othello angry. Desdemona speculates that it might be a matter of state, but the astute Emilia correctly suspects jealousy. The two women pray, in marked contrast to the men's hellish oath, that 'Heaven keep that monster from Othello's mind'.*

Exeunt Desdemona and Emilia
Enter Bianca

Bianca: Save you, friend Cassio!

167 Save you: *God save you*
(greeting)

Cassio: What make you from home?
How is it with you, my most fair Bianca?
I' faith, sweet love, I was coming to your house.

Bianca: And I was going to your lodging, Cassio.　　　　170
What, keep a week away? Seven days and nights?
Eight score eight hours? And lovers' absent hours,
More tedious than the dial eight score times?
O weary reckoning!

Cassio: Pardon me, Bianca:
I have this while with leaden thoughts been pressed:　175
But I shall, in a more continuate time,
Strike off this score of absence. Sweet Bianca,

176 continuate: *uninterrupted*

Giving her Desdemona's handkerchief

Take me this work out.

178 Take me this work out:
copy this embroidery for me

Bianca: O Cassio, whence came this?
This is some token from a newer friend:
To the felt absence now I feel a cause.　　　　　　180
Is it come to this? Well, well.

Cassio: Go to, woman!
Throw your vile guesses in the devil's teeth,
From whence you have them. You are jealous now
That this is from some mistress, some remembrance.
No, by my faith, Bianca.

Bianca: Why, whose is it?　　　　　　　　　　　　185

A lovers' quarrel *Bianca meets Cassio and bitterly complains about how he neglects her and takes her for granted. Cassio casually gives Bianca the handkerchief he has found in his lodging. He asks her to copy the embroidery. Bianca now feels she has good reason for her dissatisfaction with Cassio's behaviour: 'I feel a cause'.*

Contrast *Although Bianca is jealous, she does not descend to the extreme behaviour of Othello and is willing to be appeased as Cassio accompanies her for a short way before he stops to wait for Othello. The handkerchief is now becoming a potential weapon for Iago to use with deadly accuracy in his mission of destruction.*

Cassio: I know not, sweet. I found it in my chamber.
I like the work well: ere it be demanded –
As like enough it will – I'd have it copied.
Take it, and do it, and leave me for this time.

Bianca: Leave you! wherefore? 190

Cassio: I do attend here on the general;
And think it no addition, nor my wish,
To have him see me womaned.

193: womaned: *in the company of a woman*

Bianca: Why, I pray you?

Cassio: Not that I love you not.

Bianca: But that you do not love me.
I pray you, bring me on the way a little, 195
And say if I shall see you soon at night.

Cassio: 'Tis but a little way that I can bring you;
For I attend here: but I'll see you soon.

Bianca: 'Tis very good; I must be circumstanced.

199 be circumstanced: *indulged, put up with*

Exeunt

Key Points

Act 3, Scene 4

- Although she means no harm, Emilia's deceit, while showing her loyalty to her husband, places Desdemona in a precarious position.
- Desdemona's evasion about the loss of the handkerchief leaves her vulnerable to attack by Iago, who uses it as a device to seal her doom.
- Two cultures collide as Othello's former unsophisticated world of magic and superstition meets Venetian refinement.
- The Moor is torn between two conflicting passions: love and jealousy. His ability to function rationally rapidly declines as he slips into jealous rages.
- Iago's luck continues. He still controls events and delights in how well his plan is going.
- Bianca is a courtesan, and like the other women in this patriarchal society, she is submissive to men. Her mild jealousy contrasts with the dark depths of Othello's egotistical passion.

Act 4

SCENE 1 – *Cyprus. Before the castle*

Othello sinks to new depths, eavesdropping on Cassio and physically striking Desdemona in public. Iago gloats as Othello is no longer the noble Moor, but a base creature torn between extremes of love and jealousy for his wife.

Enter Othello and Iago

Iago: Will you think so?

Othello: Think so, Iago!

Iago: What,
To kiss in private?

Othello: An unauthorised kiss.

4 unauthorised: immoral

Iago: Or to be naked with her friend in bed   5
An hour or more, not meaning any harm?

Othello: Naked in bed, Iago, and not mean harm?
It is hypocrisy against the devil:
They that mean virtuously, and yet do so,
The devil their virtue tempts, and they tempt heaven.

Iago: So they do nothing, 'tis a venial slip.
But if I give my wife a handkerchief—   10

9 venial slip: trivial fault

Othello: What then?

Iago: Why, then, 'tis hers, my lord; and, being hers,
She may, I think, bestow it on any man.

Othello: She is protectress of her honour too,
May she give that?   15

Iago: Her honour is an essence that's not seen,
They have it very oft that have it not:
But, for the handkerchief—

Psychological insight *Iago accurately pinpoints Othello's weakness. Well aware of the jealous Moor's fixation, he mentions a handkerchief: 'if I give my wife a handkerchief'.*

96   *Shakespeare Focus: Othello*

Othello: By heaven, I would most gladly have forgot it!
Thou said'st – it comes o'er my memory,
As doth the raven o'er the infected house,
Boding to all – he had my handkerchief.   20

Iago: Ay, what of that?

Othello: That's not so good now.

Iago: What, if I had said I had seen him do you wrong?
Or heard him say – as knaves be such abroad,   25
Who having, by their own importunate suit,
Or voluntary dotage of some mistress,
Convinced or supplied them, cannot choose
But they must blab—

Othello: Hath he said any thing?

Iago: He hath, my lord, but be you well assured,   30
No more than he'll unswear.

Othello: What hath he said?

Iago: 'Faith, that he did – I know not what he did.

Othello: What? what?

Iago: Lie—

Othello: With her?   35

Iago: With her, on her; what you will.

Othello: Lie with her! lie on her! We say lie on her, when
they belie her. Lie with her! That's fulsome.
– Handkerchief – confessions – handkerchief! – To
confess, and be hanged for his labour – first, to be
hanged, and then to confess – I tremble at it.
Nature would not invest herself in such shadowing   40
passion without some instruction. It is not words
that shake me thus. Pish! Noses, ears, and lips.
– Is it possible? – Confess – handkerchief! – O devil!

Falls in a trance

25 abroad: *in the world*
26 importunate suit: *persistent chatting up, wooing*
27 voluntary dotage: *willing infatuation*
28 Convinced or supplied: *overpowered or seduced*

37 fulsome: *revolting, slander, foul*

40 shadowing: *overwhelming*
41 instruction: *reason*

Igniting the flame *Iago continues to harass Othello, indirectly suggesting that Cassio is boasting of his affair with Desdemona: 'But they must blab'. Firstly, he targets the Moor's immense pride. Then he pretends that he does not want to tell what was said, goading Othello to extract it from him detail by painful detail. The torture is evident, as Othello becomes totally illogical, incoherently muttering to himself and finally collapsing at Iago's feet. It is a powerfully symbolic moment.*

'savage madness'

Iago: Work on,
　　　My medicine, work! Thus credulous fools are caught,   45
　　　And many worthy and chaste dames even thus,
　　　All guiltless, meet reproach. What, ho! my lord!
　　　My lord, I say! Othello!
　　　How now, Cassio!

Cassio: What's the matter?

> **Glittering evil** *A delighted Iago towers in absolute triumph over the fallen Othello. He sadistically chants, 'Work on,/My medicine, work'. Iago dismisses those who believe too easily as mere fools. He easily removes Cassio, who wishes to assist Othello, with a lie. The Moor, once a noble leader, has become a savage follower. The language he and Iago use reflects the darkness of their vicious world, full of monsters and beasts.*

Iago: My lord is fallen into an epilepsy,   50
This is his second fit; he had one yesterday.

Cassio: Rub him about the temples.

Iago: No, forbear,
The lethargy must have his quiet course: 53 lethargy: *fit*
If not, he foams at mouth and by and by
Breaks out to savage madness. Look, he stirs: 55
Do you withdraw yourself a little while,
He will recover straight: when he is gone,
I would on great occasion speak with you.

Exit Cassio

How is it, general? Have you not hurt your head?

Othello: Dost thou mock me?

Iago: I mock you! No, by heaven.   60
Would you would bear your fortune like a man!

Othello: A horned man's a monster and a beast.   62 horned man: *cuckold*

Iago: There's many a beast then in a populous city,
And many a civil monster.   64 civil: *civilised*

Othello: Did he confess it?

Iago: Good sir, be a man,   65
Think every bearded fellow that's but yoked   66 yoked: *married*
May draw with you: there's millions now alive
That nightly lie in those unproper beds
Which they dare swear peculiar: your case is better.   69 peculiar: *their own*
O, 'tis the spite of hell, the fiend's arch-mock,   70
To lip a wanton in a secure couch,   71 lip: *kiss*
And to suppose her chaste! No, let me know,   71 wanton: *loose woman*
And knowing what I am, I know what she shall be.

Othello: O, thou art wise, 'tis certain.

Turning the screw *Not content with this humiliation of his enemy, Iago forces Othello to confront the full implications of what has actually happened to him:* 'To lip a wanton in a secure couch,/And to suppose her chaste'. *He proceeds to orchestrate a conversation between Cassio and himself in which he will get Cassio to tell the tale of his conquest of Desdemona once more. Othello will be placed so that he can observe the pair. Of course, he will only see them from a distance and will not realise that Cassio speaks of Bianca, not Desdemona.*

Iago: Stand you awhile apart;
Confine yourself but in a patient list. 75
Whilst you were here o'erwhelmed with your grief –
A passion most unsuiting such a man –
Cassio came hither: I shifted him away,
And laid good 'scuse upon your ecstasy,
Bade him anon return and here speak with me, 80
The which he promised. Do but encave yourself,
And mark the jeers, the gibes, and notable scorns,
That dwell in every region of his face;
For I will make him tell the tale anew,
Where, how, how oft, how long ago, and when 85
He hath, and is again to cope your wife:
I say, but mark his gesture. Marry, patience;
Or I shall say you are all in all in spleen,
And nothing of a man.

Othello: Dost thou hear, Iago?
I will be found most cunning in my patience; 90
But – dost thou hear? – most bloody.

Iago: That's not amiss;
But yet keep time in all. Will you withdraw?

Othello retires

Now will I question Cassio of Bianca,
A housewife that by selling her desires
Buys herself bread and clothes: it is a creature 95
That dotes on Cassio; as 'tis the strumpet's plague
To beguile many and be beguiled by one:
He, when he hears of her, cannot refrain
From the excess of laughter. Here he comes:

Re-enter Cassio

As he shall smile, Othello shall go mad, 100
And his unbookish jealousy must construe

75 a patient list: *the bounds of patience*

79 ecstasy: *fit*

86 cope: *meet with*

88 spleen: *anger*

101 unbookish: *ignorant*
101 construe: *interpret*

Masterful exploitation *Iago is contemptuous of Othello and refers to his lack of education in the phrase 'unbookish jealousy'. He knows Othello, who is unable to hear the conversation, will interpret Cassio's behaviour in the wrong way because he believes Cassio is discussing Desdemona, while he is actually mocking Bianca. Cassio enters, still mourning his lost position: 'Whose want even kills me'. Othello, who is now completely under Iago's control, actually applauding Iago's performance, is slowly being driven to the point of insanity.*

Shakespeare Focus: Othello

Poor Cassio's smiles, gestures and light behaviour,
Quite in the wrong. How do you now, lieutenant?

Cassio: The worser that you give me the addition
Whose want even kills me. 105

Iago: Ply Desdemona well, and you are sure on it.

Speaking lower

Now, if this suit lay in Bianca's power,
How quickly should you speed!

Cassio: Alas, poor caitiff!

Othello: Look, how he laughs already!

Iago: I never knew woman love man so. 110

Cassio: Alas, poor rogue! I think, in faith, she loves me.

Othello: Now he denies it faintly, and laughs it out.

Iago: Do you hear, Cassio?

Othello: Now he importunes him
To tell it o'er. Go to, well said, well said.

Iago: She gives it out that you shall marry her, 115
Do you intend it?

Casssio: Ha, ha, ha!

Othello: Do you triumph, Roman? Do you triumph?

Cassio: I marry her! What? A customer!
Prithee, bear some charity to my wit, 120
Do not think it so unwholesome.
Ha, ha, ha!

Othello: So, so, so, so: they laugh that win.

Iago: 'Faith, the cry goes that you shall marry her.

Cassio: Prithee, say true.

Iago: I am a very villain else. 125

Othello: Have you scored me? Well.

104 addition: *title*

105 Whose want: *the lack of which*

108 poor caitiff: *poor wretch*

118 Roman: *like a victorious Roman warrior*

119 customer: *prostitute*

120 bear some charity: *give some credit*

123 cry: *gossip*

126 scored: *wounded*

Misinterpretation *Iago tells Cassio about a widespread rumour that he is to marry Bianca. Cassio laughs derisively. Meanwhile, Othello is under the impression that Cassio is discussing Desdemona: 'Look, how he laughs already!'.*

Cassio: This is the monkey's own giving out: she is persuaded
I will marry her, out of her own love and flattery, not
out of my promise.

127 the monkey's own giving: *Bianca's version*

Othello: Iago beckons me, now he begins the story.   130

Cassio: She was here even now, she haunts me in every place.
I was the other day talking on the sea-bank with
certain Venetians; and thither comes the bauble,
and, by this hand, she falls me thus about my neck—

133 bauble: *pretty thing*

Othello: Crying 'O dear Cassio!' as it were; his gesture   135
imports it.

Cassio: So hangs, and lolls, and weeps upon me; so hales,
and pulls me. Ha, ha, ha!

136 hales: *tugs*

Othello: Now he tells how she plucked him to my chamber. O,
I see that nose of yours, but not that dog I shall   140
throw it to.

Cassio: Well, I must leave her company.

Iago: Before me! Look, where she comes.

Cassio: 'Tis such another fitchew! Marry, a perfumed one.

143 fitchew: *polecat*

Enter Bianca

What do you mean by this haunting of me?   145

Bianca: Let the devil and his dam haunt you! What did you
mean by that same handkerchief you gave me even now?
I was a fine fool to take it. I must take out the
work? – A likely piece of work, that you should find
it in your chamber, and not know who left it there!   150
This is some minx's token, and I must take out the
work? There; give it your hobby-horse: wheresoever
you had it, I'll take out no work on it.

146 dam: *mother*

151 minx: *flirt*

Cassio: How now, my sweet Bianca! How now! How now!

Othello: By heaven, that should be my handkerchief!   155

Male supremacy *Does the scene illustrate the way men think about women as possessions? Examine Cassio's language ('monkey', 'bauble') when he rejects Bianca's feelings for him.*

A woman scorned *Bianca angrily refuses Cassio's request to copy the embroidery because she believes it was a gift from another woman. Her role as lover and courtesan mirrors Othello's roles as husband and soldier.*

Bianca: An you'll come to supper to-night, you may; an you will not, come when you are next prepared for.

Exit

Iago: After her, after her.

Cassio: 'Faith, I must; she'll rail in the street else.

Iago: Will you sup there? 160

Cassio: 'Faith, I intend so.

Iago: Well, I may chance to see you, for I would very fain speak with you.

Cassio: Prithee, come; will you?

Iago: Go to; say no more. 165

Exit Cassio

Othello: [*Advancing*] How shall I murder him, Iago?

Iago: Did you perceive how he laughed at his vice?

Othello: O Iago!

Iago: And did you see the handkerchief?

Othello: Was that mine? 170

Iago: Yours by this hand: and to see how he prizes the foolish woman your wife! She gave it him, and he hath given it his whore.

Othello: I would have him nine years a-killing.
A fine woman! A fair woman! A sweet woman! 175

Iago: Nay, you must forget that.

Othello: Ay, let her rot, and perish, and be damned to-night, for she shall not live: no, my heart is turned to stone; I strike it, and it hurts my hand. O, the world has not

156 An: *if*

159 rail: *shout*

162 very fain: *like to*

171 by this hand: *I swear it*
171 prizes: *values*

174 a-killing: *dying a slow death*

A reversal of roles *Instead of commanding Iago, the Moor now depends on him, asking for advice about killing Cassio. The scene becomes even more tragic as Othello alternates between loving thoughts about Desdemona and utter hatred. Ironically, he is all too unaware of his own tragic blindness as he utters the heart-wrenching comment about his terrible dilemma: 'my heart is turned to stone'.*

	a sweeter creature: she might lie by an emperor's side and command him tasks.	180
Iago:	Nay, that's not your way.	
Othello:	Hang her! I do but say what she is: so delicate with her needle, an admirable musician. O! She will sing the savageness out of a bear! Of so high and plenteous wit and invention!	185 186 wit: *intelligence*
Iago:	She's the worse for all this.	
Othello:	A thousand thousand times: and then, of so gentle a condition!	
Iago:	Ay, too gentle.	190
Othello:	Nay, that's certain: but yet the pity of it, Iago! O Iago, the pity of it, Iago!	
Iago:	If you are so fond over her iniquity, give her patent to offend; for, if it touch not you, it comes near nobody.	195 193 fond over: *foolish about* 193 patent: *licence*
Othello:	I will chop her into messes. Cuckold me!	
Iago:	O, 'tis foul in her.	
Othello:	With mine officer!	
Iago:	That's fouler.	
Othello:	Get me some poison, Iago; this night: I'll not expostulate with her, lest her body and beauty unprovide my mind again, this night, Iago.	200 200 expostulate: *discuss* 201 unprovide: *weaken*
Iago:	Do it not with poison, strangle her in her bed, even the bed she hath contaminated.	
Othello:	Good, good. The justice of it pleases; very good.	205
Iago:	And for Cassio, let me be his undertaker: you shall hear more by midnight.	
Othello:	Excellent good.	

A trumpet within

What trumpet is that same?

Justice redefined Othello, now using the violent language of a soldier, agrees with Iago that killing Desdemona in her bed would be an appropriate punishment. He has redefined justice to suit himself.

 Shakespeare Focus: Othello

Iago: Something from Venice, sure. 'Tis Lodovico   210
Come from the duke: and, see, your wife is with him.

Enter Lodovico, Desdemona, and Attendants

Lodovico: Save you, worthy general!

Othello: With all my heart, sir.

Lodovico: The duke and senators of Venice greet you.

Gives him a letter

Othello: I kiss the instrument of their pleasures.

Opens the letter, and reads

Desdemona: And what's the news, good cousin Lodovico?   215

Iago: I am very glad to see you, signior.
Welcome to Cyprus.

Lodovico: I thank you. How does Lieutenant Cassio?

Iago: Lives, sir.

Desdemona: Cousin, there's fallen between him and my lord   220
An unkind breach, but you shall make all well.

Othello: Are you sure of that?

Desdemona: My lord?

Othello: [*Reads*] 'This fail you not to do, as you will—'

Lodovico: He did not call; he's busy in the paper.   225
Is there division between my lord and Cassio?

Desdemona: A most unhappy one: I would do much
To atone them, for the love I bear to Cassio.

Othello: Fire and brimstone!

214 pleasures: *wishes*

225 in the paper: *with the letter*

227 atone: *reconcile*

Another world *Lodovico, a close relative of Desdemona's, arrives with orders from the Duke. His appearance in this hellish scene is a reminder of the civilised Venetian world that Othello has left behind.*
Unkind divisions *Civilised behaviour is restored – for a time. Desdemona recounts to Lodovico how her husband and Cassio have fallen out despite her best efforts to 'atone them'. She reverts to the courtly speech of the city: 'for the love I bear to Cassio'. Othello misunderstands what she is saying and becomes enraged.*

Desdemona: My lord?

Othello: Are you wise?

Desdemona: What, is he angry?

Lodovico: Maybe the letter moved him;   230
For, as I think, they do command him home,
Deputing Cassio in his government.

Desdemona: Trust me, I am glad on it.

Othello: Indeed!

Desdemona: My lord?

Othello: I am glad to see you mad.

Desdemona: Why, sweet Othello?

Othello: [*Striking her*] Devil!   235

Desdemona: I have not deserved this.

Lodovico: My lord, this would not be believed in Venice,
Though I should swear I saw it: 'tis very much:
Make her amends, she weeps.

Othello: O devil, devil!
If that the earth could teem with woman's tears,   240
Each drop she falls would prove a crocodile.
Out of my sight!

Desdemona: I will not stay to offend you.

Going

Lodovico: Truly, an obedient lady:
I do beseech your lordship, call her back.

Othello: Mistress!   245

Desdemona: My lord?

Othello: What would you with her, sir?

---

241 prove a crocodile: *be hypocritical*

245 Mistress: *derogatory term*

Public humiliation *Lodovico thinks Othello is angry because the letter contains orders that he is being recalled to Venice and Cassio made Governor of Cyprus. Desdemona is delighted at the news. When Othello strikes her, Lodovico is alarmed at the Moor's transformation. A submissive Desdemona maintains what dignity she can, but Othello dismisses her cruelly. Audiences are likely to ask if Lodovico does enough to protect Desdemona.*

Lodovico: Who, I, my lord?

Othello: Ay; you did wish that I would make her turn:
Sir, she can turn, and turn, and yet go on,
And turn again, and she can weep, sir, weep;   250
And she's obedient, as you say, obedient,
Very obedient. Proceed you in your tears.
Concerning this, sir – O well-painted passion! –
I am commanded home. Get you away!
I'll send for you anon. Sir, I obey the mandate,   255
And will return to Venice. Hence, avaunt!

248 turn: *turn back; be false*

253 well-painted: *false*

255 mandate: *command*

256 avaunt: *get out of my sight*

'I have not deserved this.'

Exit Desdemona

Cassio shall have my place. And, sir, tonight,
I do entreat that we may sup together:
You are welcome, sir, to Cyprus. – Goats and monkeys!

259 Goats and monkeys: *supposedly lecherous animals*

Exit

Volatile behaviour *Even before he lost his position as governor, Othello had already lost his air of authority and his self-control. He momentarily turns his attention to business and agrees to obey the senate's command. However, he abruptly mimics Iago's coarse language: 'Goats and monkeys'.*

Lodovico:	Is this the noble Moor whom our full senate	260
	Call all in all sufficient? Is this the nature	**261** all in all sufficient: *fully competent*
	Whom passion could not shake? whose solid virtue	
	The shot of accident, nor dart of chance,	
	Could neither graze nor pierce?	
Iago:	He is much changed.	
Lodovico:	Are his wits safe? Is he not light of brain?	265
Iago:	He's that he is; I may not breathe my censure	**266** censure: *judgement*
	What he might be. If what he might he is not,	
	I would to heaven he were!	
Lodovico:	What, strike his wife!	
Iago:	'Faith, that was not so well; yet would I knew	
	That stroke would prove the worst!	
Lodovico:	Is it his use?	270	**270** use: *custom*
	Or did the letters work upon his blood,	**271** blood: *passions*
	And new-create this fault?	
Iago:	Alas, alas!	
	It is not honesty in me to speak	
	What I have seen and known. You shall observe him,	
	And his own courses will denote him so	275	**275** courses: *actions*
	That I may save my speech: do but go after,	
	And mark how he continues.	
Lodovico:	I am sorry that I am deceived in him.	

Exeunt

Deception *Lodovico is appalled by Othello's barbarity. Iago dishonestly says he cannot 'speak/What I have seen and known' and he suggests that Lodovico follow Othello to observe him. Iago manipulates everyone.*

Key Points

- Othello's jealousy has blinded him to reason.
- Iago never leaves the stage and completely controls Othello, as if he were a pawn.
- Luck favours Iago when the innocent Bianca arrives with the handkerchief.
- Othello's behaviour towards Desdemona shows how he has descended to the level of a beast.
- Lodovico, representing civilised behaviour, is shocked at Othello's transformation.

Act 4

SCENE 2 – A room in the castle

Emilia tries to convince Othello of his wife's innocence, but to no avail. Desdemona herself is confused and upset when Othello accuses her of infidelity. Emilia suspects that someone has been poisoning the Moor's mind with malicious gossip. Roderigo angrily attacks Iago, who soothes him with the promise that he can still win Desdemona.

Enter Othello and Emilia

Othello: You have seen nothing then?

Emilia: Nor ever heard, nor ever did suspect.

Othello: Yes, you have seen Cassio and she together.

Emilia: But then I saw no harm, and then I heard
Each syllable that breath made up between them.   5

> 5 that breath made up between them: *spoken*

Othello: What, did they never whisper?

Emilia: Never, my lord.

Othello: Nor send you out of the way?

Emilia: Never.

Othello: To fetch her fan, her gloves, her mask, nor nothing?

Emilia: Never, my lord.   10

Othello: That's strange.

Emilia: I durst, my lord, to wager she is honest,
Lay down my soul at stake: if you think other,
Remove your thought; it doth abuse your bosom.
If any wretch have put this in your head,   15
Let heaven requite it with the serpent's curse!
For, if she be not honest, chaste, and true,

> 12 durst: *dare*

> 16 requite: *repay*

Questions *Othello quizzes Emilia closely about Desdemona's behaviour. He is especially curious to know if his wife has ever been alone with Cassio. Emilia, in her attempts to convince Othello of Desdemona's innocence, ironically curses her own husband: 'If any wretch have put this in your head,/Let heaven requite it with the serpent's curse!'*

Shakespeare Focus: Othello

There's no man happy. The purest of their wives
Is foul as slander.

Othello: Bid her come hither: go.

Exit Emilia

She says enough, yet she's a simple bawd   20   20 bawd: *keeper of a brothel*
That cannot say as much. This is a subtle whore,
A closet lock and key of villainous secrets
And yet she'll kneel and pray; I have seen her do it.

Enter Desdemona with Emilia

Desdemona: My lord, what is your will?

Othello: Pray, chuck, come hither.

Desdemona: What is your pleasure?

Othello: Let me see your eyes;   25
Look in my face.

Desdemona: What horrible fancy's this?

Othello: [*To Emilia*] Some of your function, mistress;   27 Some of your function:
Leave procreants alone and shut the door;   *get on with your job*
Cough, or cry 'hem,' if any body come: 28 procreants: *lovers*
Your mystery, your mystery: nay, dispatch.   30   30 mystery: *get on with your
                                                                 trade*

Exit Emilia

Desdemona: Upon my knees, what doth your speech import?   31 import: *suggest*
I understand a fury in your words.
But not the words.

Othello: Why, what art thou?

Desdemona: Your wife, my lord; your true and loyal wife.   35

Othello: Come, swear it, damn thyself
Lest, being like one of heaven, the devils themselves
Should fear to seize thee: therefore be double damned:
Swear thou art honest.

Contempt *Othello sends Emilia to fetch Desdemona. He now doubts all women: 'This is a subtle whore'.
His insults echo Iago's misogyny. Although Desdemona kneels before him proclaiming her loyalty, he is
no longer able to believe anything she says.*

Desdemona: Heaven doth truly know it.

Othello: Heaven truly knows that thou art false as hell.   40

Desdemona: To whom, my lord? With whom? How am I false?

Othello: O Desdemona! Away! Away! Away!

Desdemona: Alas the heavy day! Why do you weep?
Am I the motive of these tears, my lord?
If haply you my father do suspect   45
An instrument of this your calling back,
Lay not your blame on me. If you have lost him,   *47 lost him: lost*
Why, I have lost him too.

Othello: Had it pleased heaven
To try me with affliction; had they rained
All kinds of sores and shames on my bare head.   50
Steeped me in poverty to the very lips,
Given to captivity me and my utmost hopes,
I should have found in some place of my soul
A drop of patience: but, alas, to make me
A fixed figure for the time of scorn   55
To point his slow unmoving finger at!
Yet could I bear that too; well, very well:
But there, where I have garnered up my heart,   *58 garnered: stored*
Where either I must live, or bear no life;
The fountain from the which my current runs,   60
Or else dries up, to be discarded thence,
Or keep it as a cistern for foul toads
To knot and gender in! Turn thy complexion there,   *63 gender: breed*
Patience, thou young and rose-lipped cherubin –   *64 cherubin: angel*
Ay, there, look grim as hell!   65

Desdemona: I hope my noble lord esteems me honest.

Othello: O, ay, as summer flies are in the shambles,   *67 shambles: slaughterhouse*
That quicken even with blowing.   *68 quicken even with blowing: hatch as soon as the eggs are laid*
O thou weed,
Who art so lovely fair and smellest so sweet   70

Wild accusations *Othello accuses a perplexed Desdemona:* 'Heaven truly knows that thou art false as hell'. *Desdemona thinks he is upset because perhaps Brabantio has been instrumental in getting her husband recalled from Cyprus. Loyally she declares,* 'If you have lost him,/Why, I have lost him too.'

Self-pity *Othello is fully engrossed in his own pain, likening himself to Job, who suffered much in the Bible story. His language becomes bestial (*'foul toads'*) as he descends ever lower.*

	That the sense aches at thee, would thou hadst never been born!	
Desdemona:	Alas, what ignorant sin have I committed?	72 ignorant: *unknowing*
Othello:	Was this fair paper, this most goodly book,	73 fair paper: *Desdemona*
	Made to write 'whore' upon? What committed!	
	Committed! O thou public commoner! 75	
	I should make very forges of my cheeks,	76 make very forges of my cheeks: *blush so much as if my cheeks were on fire*
	That would to cinders burn up modesty,	
	Did I but speak thy deeds. What committed!	
	Heaven stops the nose at it and the moon winks,	79 Heaven stops the nose at it: *the offence smells to Heaven*
	The bawdy wind that kisses all it meets 80	80 bawdy wind: *promiscuous wind*
	Is hushed within the hollow mine of earth,	
	And will not hear it. What committed?	
	Impudent strumpet!	
Desdemona:	By heaven, you do me wrong.	
Othello:	Are you not a strumpet?	
Desdemona:	No, as I am a Christian:	
	If to preserve this vessel for my lord 85	
	From any other foul unlawful touch	
	Be not to be a strumpet, I am none.	
Othello:	What, not a whore?	
Desdemona:	No, as I shall be saved.	
Othello:	Is't possible?	
Desdemona:	O, heaven forgive us!	
Othello:	I cry you mercy, then: 90	
	I took you for that cunning whore of Venice	
	That married with Othello. You, mistress	

Raising his voice

That have the office opposite to Saint Peter,	93 Saint Peter: *the saint who guards the entrance to Heaven*
And keep the gate of hell!	

Re-enter Emilia

Revulsion Othello, *in a storm of sexual jealousy, insults his wife by calling her an* 'impudent strumpet'. *He compares her to the wayward wind, which* 'kisses all it meets'. *Desdemona responds innocently,* 'No, as I am a Christian'.

You, you, ay, you!
We have done our course; there's money for your pains: 95
I pray you, turn the key and keep our counsel.

Exit

'I cannot weep'

Emilia:	Alas, what does this gentleman conceive?	97 conceive: *imagine*
	How do you, madam? How do you, my good lady?	
Desdemona:	'Faith, half asleep.	
Emilia:	Good madam, what's the matter with my lord? 100	
Desdemona:	With who?	
Emilia:	Why, with my lord, madam.	
Desdemona:	Who is thy lord?	
Emilia:	He that is yours, sweet lady.	

Disbelief Othello still will not believe his wife and again treats Emilia as a common prostitute. Emilia herself is amazed at what she sees. Desdemona, worn out ('I cannot weep'), decides not to fight but requests her wedding sheets for her bed and asks Emilia to contact Iago.

Desdemona: I have none: do not talk to me, Emilia;
I cannot weep; nor answer have I none, 105
But what should go by water. Prithee, tonight
Lay on my bed my wedding sheets: remember;
And call thy husband hither.

105 should go by water: *should be expressed in tears*

Emilia: Here's a change indeed!

Exit

Desdemona: 'Tis meet I should be used so, very meet.
How have I been behaved, that he might stick 110
The smallest opinion on my least misuse?

109 meet: *appropriate*

Re-enter Emilia with Iago

Iago: What is your pleasure, madam?
How is it with you?

Desdemona: I cannot tell. Those that do teach young babes
Do it with gentle means and easy tasks:
He might have chid me so; for, in good faith, 115
I am a child to chiding.

115 chid: *criticised*

116 a child to chiding: *not used to this verbal abuse*

Iago: What's the matter, lady?

Emilia: Alas, Iago, my lord hath so bewhored her.
Thrown such despite and heavy terms upon her,
As true hearts cannot bear.

117 bewhored her: *called her a whore*
118 despite: *abuse*

Desdemona: Am I that name, Iago?

Iago: What name, fair lady? 120

Desdemona: Such as she says my lord did say I was.

Emilia: He called her whore: a beggar in his drink
Could not have laid such terms upon his callat.

123 callat: *slut*

Iago: Why did he so?

Desdemona: I do not know; I am sure I am none such. 125

Iago: Do not weep, do not weep. Alas the day!

Weary acceptance *A dejected Desdemona wonders what she could possibly have done to merit such abuse from Othello. She tells Iago that she is not used to this type of treatment: 'I am a child to chiding'. Will the audience reaction be one of profound pity for her? Or is her utter submissiveness frustrating?*

Emilia: Hath she forsook so many noble matches,
Her father and her country and her friends,
To be called whore? Would it not make one weep?

'Fie, there is no such man'

Desdemona: It is my wretched fortune.

Iago: Beshrew him for it!   130
How comes this trick upon him?

Desdemona: Nay, heaven doth know.

Emilia: I will be hanged, if some eternal villain,
Some busy and insinuating rogue,
Some cogging, cozening slave, to get some office,
Have not devised this slander; I'll be hanged else.   135

Iago: Fie, there is no such man; it is impossible.

134 cogging, cozening:
cheating, deceiving
134 office: *job*

Guessing correctly *Intuitively, Emilia pinpoints precisely what has been happening. Someone has been poisoning Othello's mind to gain promotion: 'Some cogging, cozening slave'. Ironically, she never suspects her own husband. Iago attempts to quieten her, but Emilia will not be silenced.*

Shakespeare Focus: Othello

Desdemona: If any such there be, heaven pardon him!

Emilia: A halter pardon him! And hell gnaw his bones!
Why should he call her whore? Who keeps her company?
What place? What time? What form? What likelihood?   140
The Moor's abused by some most villainous knave,
Some base notorious knave, some scurvy fellow.
O heaven, that such companions thou'dst unfold,
And put in every honest hand a whip
To lash the rascals. Naked through the world   145
Even from the east to the west!

Iago: Speak within doors.

Emilia: O, fie upon them! Some such squire he was
That turned your wit the seamy side without,
And made you to suspect me with the Moor.

Iago: You are a fool; go to.

Desdemona: O good Iago,   150
What shall I do to win my lord again?
Good friend, go to him; for, by this light of heaven,
I know not how I lost him. Here I kneel:
If ever my will did trespass against his love,
Either in discourse of thought or actual deed,   155
Or that mine eyes, mine ears, or any sense,
Delighted them in any other form;
Or that I do not yet, and ever did.
And ever will – though he do shake me off
To beggarly divorcement – love him dearly,   160
Comfort forswear me! Unkindness may do much;
And his unkindness may defeat my life,
But never taint my love. I cannot say 'whore:'
It does abhor me now I speak the word;
To do the act that might the addition earn   165
Not the world's mass of vanity could make me.

Iago: I pray you, be content, 'tis but his humour,
The business of the state does him offence,
And he does chide with you.

---

138 halter: *noose*

146 within doors: *quietly*

148 seamy side without: *inside out*

161 Comfort forswear: *let joy forsake me*

164 abhor: *horrify*

169 chide with: *rebuke*

False explanations *Desdemona still proclaims her love, ironically stating that* 'his unkindness may defeat my life'. *She can barely say the word she is accused of. Iago's explanation for Othello's behaviour is a lie:* 'The business of the state'.

Desdemona: If 'twere no other—

Iago: 'Tis but so, I warrant.   170

Trumpets within

Hark, how these instruments summon to supper!
The messengers of Venice stay the meat;   172 stay the meat: *await*
Go in, and weep not; all things shall be well.   *dinner*

Exeunt Desdemona and Emilia
Enter Roderigo

How now, Roderigo!

Roderigo: I do not find that thou dealest justly with me.   175

Iago: What in the contrary?

Roderigo: Every day thou daffest me with some device, Iago;   177 daffest me: *fob me off*
and rather, as it seems to me now, keepest from me
all conveniency than suppliest me with the least   179 conveniency: *opportunity*
advantage of hope. I will indeed no longer endure   180
it, nor am I yet persuaded to put up in peace what
already I have foolishly suffered.

Iago: Will you hear me, Roderigo?

Roderigo: Faith, I have heard too much, for your words and
performances are no kin together.   185   185 no kin together: *do not*
match

Iago: You charge me most unjustly.

Roderigo: With nought but truth. I have wasted myself out of
my means. The jewels you have had from me to
deliver to Desdemona would half have corrupted a
votarist: you have told me she hath received them   190   190 votarist: *nun*
and returned me expectations and comforts of sudden
respect and acquaintance, but I find none.   191 sudden respect:
immediate attention

Iago: Well; go to; very well.

Turning the tables *Roderigo confronts Iago because his attempts to woo Desdemona have come to nothing. Roderigo threatens to reveal the truth and even challenges Iago to a duel. Ingeniously, Iago does not rise to the contest, but instead he praises Roderigo for his courage ('mettle'). As always, Iago displays a different persona to please whoever he is with.*

Roderigo: Very well! Go to! I cannot go to, man; nor 'tis
not very well: nay, I think it is scurvy, and begin   195
to find myself fopped in it.

196 fopped: *fooled*

Iago: Very well.

Roderigo: I tell you 'tis not very well. I will make myself known
to Desdemona: if she will return me my jewels, I will
give over my suit and repent my unlawful solicitation;   200
if not, assure yourself I will seek satisfaction of you.

201 seek satisfaction of you: *challenge you to a duel*

Iago: You have said now.

Roderigo: Ay, and said nothing but what I protest intendment
of doing.

Iago: Why, now I see there's mettle in thee, and even from   205
this instant to build on thee a better opinion than
ever before. Give me thy hand, thou hast
taken against me a most just exception; but yet, I
protest, I have dealt most directly in thy affair.

Roderigo: It hath not appeared.   210

Iago: I grant indeed it hath not appeared, and your
suspicion is not without wit and judgment. But,
Roderigo, if thou hast that in thee indeed, which I
have further reason to believe now than ever, I mean
purpose, courage and valour, this night show it: if   215
thou the next night following enjoy not Desdemona,
take me from this world with treachery and devise
engines for my life.

218 engines for: *plots against*

Roderigo: Well, what is it? Is it within reason and compass?

Iago: Sir, there is especial commission come from Venice   220
to depute Cassio in Othello's place.

Roderigo: Is that true? Why, then Othello and Desdemona
return again to Venice.

Iago: O, no, he goes into Mauritania and takes away with
him the fair Desdemona, unless his abode be lingered   225

224 Mauritania: *region of North Africa*
225 abode be lingered: *stay be prolonged*

Duped again *Iago again promises Desdemona to Roderigo. He explains that Othello is to depart to Mauritania with Desdemona and that Cassio will take his place in Cyprus. However, if Roderigo kills Cassio, this cannot happen. Not surprisingly, Iago easily manipulates Roderigo by a warped combination of flattery and false hope.*

here by some accident: wherein none can be
so determinate as the removing of Cassio.

Roderigo: How do you mean, removing of him?

Iago: Why, by making him uncapable of Othello's place;
knocking out his brains. 230

Roderigo: And that you would have me to do?

Iago: Ay, if you dare do yourself a profit and a right.
He sups to-night with a harlot, and thither will I   233 harlot: *prostitute*
go to him: he knows not yet of his honourable fortune.
If you will watch his going thence, which I will   235
fashion to fall out between twelve and one, you may
take him at your pleasure: I will be near to second   237 second: *support*
your attempt, and he shall fall between us. Come,
stand not amazed at it, but go along with me; I will
show you such a necessity in his death that you shall   240   240 necessity in: *need for*
think yourself bound to put it on him. It is now high   241 put it on him: *kill him*
suppertime, and the night grows to waste: about it.

Roderigo: I will hear further reason for this.

Iago: And you shall be satisfied.

Exeunt

Key Points

<table>
<tr><td>Act 4, Scene 2</td></tr>
</table>

- The scene is full of religious imagery, with both Othello and Desdemona associating themselves with Christianity. The Moor's language makes his wife's perceived betrayal take on a spiritual significance.
- Emilia loyally protects Desdemona against Othello's accusations.
- Othello's natural sense of justice has been perverted. In agony, he struggles to endure. He can stand all afflictions except the loss of his love.
- Desdemona bears no resentment towards Othello. Ironically, she turns to Iago for assistance.
- Roderigo's intervention sets off the plan to kill Cassio.

Act 4

SCENE 3 – *Another room in the castle*

This calm interlude takes place on the evening of the official banquet for the visitors from Venice. Othello bids goodnight to Lodovico and abruptly orders his wife to go to bed, where he will join her shortly. Desdemona speaks with Emilia of her love for Othello, of death and of Barbary, her mother's maid. The two women discuss their differing attitudes to marriage and fidelity.

Enter Othello, Lodovico, Desdemona, Emilia, and Attendants

Lodovico:	I do beseech you, sir, trouble yourself no further.
Othello:	O, pardon me, it shall do me good to walk.
Lodovico:	Madam, good night. I humbly thank your ladyship.
Desdemona:	Your honour is most welcome.
Othello:	Will you walk, sir? 5 O – Desdemona—
Desdemona:	My lord?
Othello:	Get you to bed on the instant. I will be returned forthwith: dismiss your attendant there. Look it be done.
Desdemona:	I will, my lord. 10

8 be returned: *return*

Exeunt Othello, Lodovico, and Attendants

Emilia:	How goes it now? He looks gentler than he did.
Desdemona:	He says he will return incontinent: He hath commanded me to go to bed, And bade me to dismiss you.
Emilia:	Dismiss me?

12 incontinent: *immediately*

Contrast *The world of Venetian refinement continues to be contrasted with the boorish behaviour of Othello, who rudely dismisses his wife: 'Get you to bed on the instant'. Desdemona is now anxious to appease him, but Emilia is becoming increasingly concerned.*

Desdemona: It was his bidding: therefore, good Emilia,   15
Give me my nightly wearing, and adieu:
We must not now displease him.

Emilia: I would you had never seen him!

Desdemona: So would not I my love doth so approve him,
That even his stubbornness, his checks, his frowns –   20
Prithee, unpin me – have grace and favour in them.

Emilia: I have laid those sheets you bade me on the bed.

Desdemona: All's one. Good faith, how foolish are our minds!
If I do die before thee prithee, shroud me
In one of those same sheets.

Emilia: Come, come you talk.   25

Desdemona: My mother had a maid called Barbary,
She was in love, and he she loved proved mad
And did forsake her: she had a song of 'willow',
An old thing 'twas, but it expressed her fortune,
And she died singing it: that song to-night   30
Will not go from my mind; I have much to do,
But to go hang my head all at one side,
And sing it like poor Barbary. Prithee, dispatch.

Emilia: Shall I go fetch your night-gown?

Desdemona: No, unpin me here.
This Lodovico is a proper man.   35

Emilia: A very handsome man.

Desdemona: He speaks well.

Emilia: I know a lady in Venice would have walked barefoot
to Palestine for a touch of his nether lip.

Desdemona: [*Singing*] *The poor soul sat sighing by a sycamore tree,*   40
Sing all a green willow:
Her hand on her bosom, her head on her knee,
Sing willow, willow, willow:

---

19 approve: *value*

20 checks: *insults*

28 willow: *willow trees are traditionally associated with deserted lovers*

33 Prithee, dispatch: *please, hurry up*

Omens of death *Desdemona asks Emilia to bury ('shroud') her in her wedding sheets, an obvious sign that she is now anticipating her own death.*

The 'willow' song *Shakespeare also foreshadows Desdemona's death through Barbary's tragic song. Just like the unfortunate maid who was rejected, Desdemona has lost her lover to jealousy and madness. As Desdemona prepares for bed, she confides in Emilia.*

The fresh streams ran by her, and murmured her moans;
Sing willow, willow, willow.   45
Her salt tears fell from her, and softened the stones;
Lay by these –

47 Lay by these: *put these (clothes) away*

[*Singing*] *Sing willow, willow, willow.*
Prithee, hie thee; he'll come anon –
[*Singing*] *Sing all a green willow must be my garland.*   50
Let nobody blame him; his scorn I approve –
ay, that's not next – Hark! Who is it that knocks?

Emilia: It's the wind.

Desdemona: [*Singing*] *I called my love false love; but what said he then?*
Sing willow, willow, willow.   55
If I court moe women, you'll couch with moe men!
So, get thee gone; good night. Mine eyes do itch,
Doth that bode weeping?

56 moe: *more*

58 bode: *foretell*

Emilia: 'Tis neither here nor there.

Desdemona: I have heard it said so. O, these men, these men!
Dost thou in conscience think – tell me, Emilia –   60
That there be women do abuse their husbands
In such gross kind?

60 in conscience: *honestly*

61 gross kind: *crudely*

Emilia: There be some such, no question.

Desdemona: Wouldst thou do such a deed for all the world?

Emilia: Why, would not you?

Desdemona: No, by this heavenly light!

Emilia: Nor I neither by this heavenly light,   65
I might do it as well in the dark.

Desdemona: Wouldst thou do such a deed for all the world?

Emilia: The world's a huge thing: it is a great price.
For a small vice.

Desdemona: In troth, I think thou wouldst not.

Emilia: In troth, I think I should; and undo it when I had   70
done. Marry, I would not do such a thing for a

Mood of sadness *Desdemona sings the 'willow' song in which love is cruelly betrayed. In her naivety, she is amazed that there could be women who would cheat on their husbands. Emilia is much more worldly than her idealistic mistress: 'it is a great price/For a small vice'.*

joint-ring, nor for measures of lawn, nor for
gowns, petticoats, nor caps, nor any petty
exhibition; but for the whole world – why, who would
not make her husband a cuckold to make him a 75
monarch? I should venture purgatory for it.

Desdemona: Beshrew me, if I would do such a wrong
For the whole world.

Emilia: Why the wrong is but a wrong in the world: and
having the world for your labour, 'tis a wrong in your 80
own world, and you might quickly make it right.

Desdemona: I do not think there is any such woman.

Emilia: Yes, a dozen; and as many to the vantage as would
store the world they played for.
But I do think it is their husbands' faults 85
If wives do fall: say that they slack their duties,
And pour our treasures into foreign laps,
Or else break out in peevish jealousies,
Throwing restraint upon us; or say they strike us,
Or scant our former having in despite 90
Why, we have galls, and though we have some grace,
Yet have we some revenge. Let husbands know
Their wives have sense like them: they see, and smell
And have their palates both for sweet and sour,
As husbands have. What is it that they do 95
When they change us for others? Is it sport?
I think it is: and doth affection breed it?
I think it doth. Is it frailty that thus errs?
It is so too. And have not we affections,
Desires for sport, and frailty, as men have? 100

---

72 joint-ring: *a cheap ring*
72 measures of lawn: *lengths of fabric*
74 exhibition: *amount of money*

76 venture purgatory: *risk being condemned to the torture of purgatory, a lesser form of Hell*

83 to the vantage: *in addition*

89 peevish jealousies: *petty resentments*

90 in despite: *out of spite*

91 galls: *grudges*

The ways of the world *Emilia remarks that she might be unfaithful if it would benefit her husband ('make him a monarch'). Ironically, her views reinforce the idea that wives are ultimately concerned with obeying their husbands. The audience will remember that she has still not told anyone about giving Iago the handkerchief. Nonetheless, Emilia also attempts to explain to Desdemona that women usually cheat because their men treat them badly.*

Revenge *Emilia claims that wives have desires similar to their husbands, so if men are unfaithful, the women will be too. They copy men's behaviour: 'The ills we do, their ills instruct us so'. Desdemona wishes Emilia goodnight, preferring to learn from her bad experiences rather than to seek vengeance.*

Gender issues *Some critics argue that Shakespeare challenges Elizabethan patriarchy in this scene. Emilia draws attention to the double standard between the sexes – men have affairs for 'sport' but wives are expected to remain faithful.*

Then let them use us well: else let them know,
The ills we do, their ills instruct us so.

Desdemona: Good night, good night. Heaven me such uses send,
Not to pick bad from bad, but by bad mend!

Exeunt

103 uses: *habits*

104 Not to pick bad from
bad: *not to grow worse
through bad luck, but to learn
from it*

Key Points

Act 4, Scene 3

- Desdemona is selfless, innocent and submissive. She is still in love with Othello despite his terrible treatment of her.
- The atmosphere of impending death is conveyed by the moving store of Barbary and the singing of the 'willow' song.
- The world-wise Emilia provides a contrast to the naive Desdemona, who has become a focus of pity.

Act 5

SCENE 1 – Cyprus: A street

Iago has convinced Roderigo to kill Cassio. They wait for him in the darkness outside Bianca's lodgings. During the attack, Roderigo is wounded and Cassio escapes. Othello, hearing the cries, mistakenly believes Iago has done what he promised. But Iago then pretends to help Cassio and kills Roderigo to prevent him talking.

Enter Iago and Roderigo

Iago: Here, stand behind this bulk; straight will he come:
Wear thy good rapier bare, and put it home:
Quick, quick; fear nothing; I'll be at thy elbow:
It makes us, or it mars us; think on that,
And fix most firm thy resolution.   5

Roderigo: Be near at hand, I may miscarry in it.

Iago: Here, at thy hand. Be bold, and take thy stand.

Retires

Roderigo: I have no great devotion to the deed;
And yet he hath given me satisfying reasons:
'Tis but a man gone. Forth, my sword: he dies.   10

Iago: I have rubbed this young quat almost to the sense,
And he grows angry. Now, whether he kill Cassio,
Or Cassio him, or each do kill the other,
Every way makes my gain: live Roderigo,
He calls me to a restitution large   15
Of gold and jewels that I bobbed from him,
As gifts to Desdemona;

1 bulk: *projecting wall*
1 straight: *immediately*
4 mars: *ruins*
11 quat: *pimple (referring to Roderigo)*
14 live Roderigo: *if Roderigo lives*
16 bobbed: *tricked*

The intrigue continues *Just as in the play's opening scene, Roderigo and Cassio hide in the dark. Roderigo is not enthusiastic about killing Cassio, but he accepts Iago's 'satisfying reasons'. The audience also hears Iago consider whether or not he should kill Roderigo. As always, his cynical calculations are chilling.*

The real Iago? *There are further indications of Iago's complex personality when he admits to feeling 'ugly' beside Cassio's 'daily beauty'. Is his evil, bitter behaviour caused by a basic sense of inferiority?*

 Shakespeare Focus: Othello

It must not be: if Cassio do remain,
He hath a daily beauty in his life
That makes me ugly; and, besides, the Moor   20
May unfold me to him; there stand I in much peril.

21 unfold me: *expose me*

No, he must die. But so, I hear him coming

Enter Cassio

Roderigo: I know his gait, 'tis he. – Villain, thou diest!

23 gait: *way of walking*

Makes a pass at Cassio

Cassio: That thrust had been mine enemy indeed,
But that my coat is better than thou knowest   25
I will make proof of thine.

25 coat is better: *armour is stronger*

Draws, and wounds Roderigo

Roderigo: O, I am slain!

Iago from behind wounds Cassio in the leg, and exit

Cassio: I am maimed for ever. Help, ho! Murder! Murder!

Falls
Enter Othello

Othello: The voice of Cassio; Iago keeps his word.

Roderigo: O, villain that I am!

Othello: It is even so.

Cassio: O, help, ho! Light! A surgeon!   30

Othello: 'Tis he. – O brave Iago, honest and just,
That hast such noble sense of thy friend's wrong!
Thou teachest me. Minion, your dear lies dead,
And your unblest fate hies: strumpet, I come.

33 Minion: *darling (spoken in contempt about Desdemona)*
34 hies: *approaches*

A dramatic turnabout *Amid the chaos, Roderigo attacks Cassio but is unsuccessful. Cassio retaliates and wounds Roderigo. Iago then stabs Cassio in the leg. Othello hears the cries and thinks that Iago has kept his word. He continues on his way to exact a terrible vengeance on the innocent Desdemona, whose 'unblest fate hies'.*

Forth of my heart those charms, thine eyes, are blotted.   35
Thy bed, lust-stained, shall with lust's blood be spotted.

Exit
Enter Lodovico and Gratiano

Cassio: What, ho! No watch? No passage? Murder! Murder!

Gratiano: 'Tis some mischance; the cry is very direful.

Cassio: O, help!

Lodovico: Hark!   40

Roderigo: O wretched villain!

Lodovico: Two or three groan: it is a heavy night:
These may be counterfeits: let's think it unsafe
To come in to the cry without more help.

Roderigo: Nobody come? Then shall I bleed to death.

Lodovico: Hark!

Re-enter Iago, with a light

Gratiano: Here's one comes in his shirt, with light and weapons.   45

Iago: Who's there? Whose noise is this that cries on murder?

Lodovico: We do not know.

Iago: Did not you hear a cry?

Cassio: Here, here! For heaven's sake, help me!

Iago: What's the matter?   50

Gratiano: This is Othello's ancient, as I take it.

Lodovico: The same indeed, a very valiant fellow.

Iago: What are you here that cry so grievously?

Cassio: Iago? O, I am spoiled, undone by villains!
Give me some help.   55

Iago: O me, lieutenant! What villains have done this?

> 35 blotted: *wiped out*
>
> 37 watch: *night patrol*
> 37 passage: *passers-by*
> 38 direful: *dreadful*
>
> 42 heavy: *dark*
>
> 43 counterfeits: *decoys*
>
> 53 What: *who*
>
> 54 spoiled: *wounded*

Unexpected arrivals Iago *adopts the role of the confused bystander, pretending not to know what has happened. His questions give the impression of genuine concern:* 'Whose noise is this that cries on murder?' *As a result, he receives widespread praise* ('valiant fellow'), *exactly the kind of attention he craves.*

Cassio: I think that one of them is hereabout,
And cannot make away.

58 make away: *escape*

Iago: O treacherous villains!
What are you there? Come in, and give some help.

To Lodovico and Gratiano

Roderigo: O, help me here!   60

Cassio: That's one of them.

Iago: O murderous slave! O villain!

Stabs Roderigo

'O treacherous villains!'

Roderigo: O damned Iago! O inhuman dog!

Iago: Kill men in the dark! – Where be these bloody thieves? –
How silent is this town! – Ho! Murder! Murder! –
What may you be? Are you of good or evil?   65

Iago improvises *Ever skilful at turning difficult situations to his advantage, Iago immediately goes to Cassio's aid, requesting the others' help. Roderigo calls out and Iago, once more seizing the moment, stabs him. Only now as he is about to die does the foolish Roderigo realise how he has been tricked by an 'inhuman dog'. He is the first character to see the true Iago.*

Lodovico:	As you shall prove us, praise us.	
Iago:	Signior Lodovico?	
Lodovico:	He, sir.	
Iago:	I cry you mercy. Here's Cassio hurt by villains.	69 cry you mercy: *beg your pardon*
Gratiano:	Cassio!	70
Iago:	How is it, brother!	
Cassio:	My leg is cut in two.	
Iago:	Marry, heaven forbid! Light, gentlemen; I'll bind it with my shirt.	

Enter Bianca

Bianca:	What is the matter, ho? Who is it that cried?	
Iago:	Who is it that cried!	75
Bianca:	O my dear Cassio! my sweet Cassio! O Cassio, Cassio, Cassio!	
Iago:	O notable strumpet! Cassio, may you suspect Who they should be that have thus mangled you?	78 notable: *well-known*
Cassio:	No.	80
Gratiano:	I am sorry to find you thus: I have been to seek you.	
Iago:	Lend me a garter. So. – O, for a chair, To bear him easily hence!	82 chair: *sedan chair*
Bianca:	Alas, he faints! O Cassio, Cassio, Cassio!	
Iago:	Gentlemen all, I do suspect this trash To be a party in this injury. Patience awhile, good Cassio. Come, come; Lend me a light. Know we this face or no? Alas my friend and my dear countryman Roderigo! No: – yes, sure. O heaven! Roderigo.	85 — 85 trash: *rubbish (referring to Bianca)* 86 To be a party in: *to have something to do with*

A practical man *The self-interested Iago has a pragmatic attitude to murder and doesn't care about who gets killed since he will benefit regardless.*

Acting the part *Iago acts the concerned friend and tries to bind Cassio's wounds with his shirt. Bianca becomes distraught at the sight of the wounded Cassio. To cast doubt, Iago takes advantage of her appearance and accuses Bianca of being 'a party in this injury'. He takes a light and pretends to look for Roderigo.*

Gratiano:	What, of Venice?	90	

Iago: Even he, sir; did you know him?

Gratiano: Know him! Ay.

Iago: Signior Gratiano? I cry you gentle pardon;
These bloody accidents must excuse my manners,
That so neglected you.

Gratiano: I am glad to see you.

Iago: How do you, Cassio? O, a chair, a chair! 95

Gratiano: Roderigo!

Iago: He, 'tis he.

A chair brought in

O, that's well said; the chair!

Gratiano: Some good man bear him carefully from hence;
I'll fetch the general's surgeon.

To Bianca

For you, mistress,
Save you your labour. He that lies slain here, Cassio, 100
Was my dear friend: what malice was between you?

Cassio: None in the world, nor do I know the man.

Iago: [*To Bianca*] What, look you pale? O, bear him out
o' the air.

Cassio and Roderigo are borne off

Stay you, good gentlemen. Look you pale, mistress?
Do you perceive the gastness of her eye? 105
Nay, if you stare, we shall hear more anon.
Behold her well; I pray you, look upon her:
Do you see, gentlemen? Nay, guiltiness will speak,
Though tongues were out of use.

The director of proceedings *Iago takes charge, greeting Gratiano and being solicitous to Cassio as he calls for 'a chair, a chair'. He dismisses Bianca's attempts to help and then questions Cassio on what 'malice' was between him and Iago's 'dear friend', Roderigo. He orders the removal of the wounded. Events are still going Iago's way, but will his luck hold out for much longer?*

Enter Emilia

Emilia: 'Las, what's the matter? What's the matter, husband?   110

Iago: Cassio hath here been set on in the dark
By Roderigo and fellows that are scaped:
He's almost slain, and Roderigo dead.

Emilia: Alas, good gentleman! Alas, good Cassio!

Iago: This is the fruit of whoring. Prithee, Emilia,   115
Go know of Cassio where he supped tonight.

To Bianca

What, do you shake at that?

Bianca: He supped at my house; but I therefore shake not.

Iago: O, did he so? I charge you, go with me.

Emilia: Fie, fie upon thee, strumpet!   120

Bianca: I am no strumpet; but of life as honest
As you that thus abuse me.

Emilia: As I! Foh! Fie upon thee!

Iago: Kind gentlemen, let's go see poor Cassio dressed.
Come, mistress, you must tell us another tale.
Emilia run you to the citadel,   125
And tell my lord and lady what hath happed.
Will you go on afore? I pray.

Aside

This is the night
That either makes me or fordoes me quite.

Exeunt

115 fruit: *result*

118: I therefore shake not:
I'm not afraid to say so

120 strumpet: *prostitute*

123 dressed: *wounds treated*

126 happed: *happened*

128 fordoes me: *ruins me*

Guilt and honesty *With typically clever insinuation, Iago continues to lay suspicion on Bianca. He is adept at diverting attention from himself and encourages his wife to criticise Bianca: 'This is the fruit of whoring.' Emilia immediately rounds on Bianca, calling her a 'strumpet', and the two women argue.*

Endgame *Iago knows that he is in a precarious position. His diabolical schemes are poised on the edge of success or failure: 'This is the night/That either makes me or fordoes me quite.' Everything has gone his way so far, apart from the one exception that Cassio is still alive. Is there a sense that he delights in the thrill of such life-and-death risk-taking?*

Key Points

Act 5, Scene 1

- Iago's villainy is now in full stride. He sets up the attack on Cassio, kills Roderigo, casts suspicion on Bianca and dupes Othello into thinking he has carried out their agreement.

- Othello's noble nature has been totally eclipsed and he now takes satisfaction in the cries of the injured Cassio.

- Roderigo only realises how evil Iago is when he is stabbed by him and lies dying.

- Bianca also questions Iago's sincerity when he claims to be as honest as he is.

- The more Iago gambles with people's lives, the more tension there is. But there are signs that his increasingly intricate plans are beginning to unravel. It could be argued that his downfall now seems inevitable.

Act 5

SCENE 2 – *A bedchamber in the castle*

Othello enters Desdemona's bedroom, where she is sleeping. He regards himself as an agent of justice. Desdemona awakes. He accuses her of unfaithfulness with Cassio. She pleads her innocence. But he refuses to listen and smothers her. Emilia discovers the dying Desdemona, who attempts to save Othello by taking the blame for her own death. Emilia calls for help, but it is too late. Othello finally discovers the tragic truth. He attacks Iago, who escapes, stabbing Emilia. Othello speaks of the service he has done the state of Venice and then commits suicide. Iago is caught, but will not give any explanation of his conduct. Lodovico leaves for Venice to report the sad news in full.

'Yet she must die'

Enter Othello

Othello: It is the cause, it is the cause, my soul –
Let me not name it to you, you chaste stars! –
It is the cause. Yet I'll not shed her blood;
Nor scar that whiter skin of hers than snow,
And smooth as monumental alabaster.   5
Yet she must die, else she'll betray more men.

1 cause: *reason*

5 alabaster: *smooth and pale plaster*

'thou flaming minister'

Put out the light, and then put out the light:
If I quench thee, thou flaming minister,
I can again thy former light restore,
Should I repent me: but once put out thy light,   10
Thou cunning pattern of excelling nature,
I know not where is that Promethean heat
That can thy light relume. When I have plucked the rose,
I cannot give it vital growth again.
It must needs wither; I'll smell it on the tree.   15

Kissing her

7 Put out the light: *he will put out the torch and also extinguish his wife's life*
8 flaming minister: *burning torch*

12 Promethean heat: *Prometheus stole fire from the gods and used it to give life to mortals (Greek myth)*
13 relume: *light again*

Justice Othello has persuaded himself that he is acting honourably. He is convinced that if he does not kill Desdemona, she will betray more men. He realises the enormity of what he is about to do. He cannot bring Desdemona back to life if he kills her: 'When I have plucked the rose,/I cannot give it vital growth again.' Paradoxically, he thinks that killing her is the only way to ensure that their love will survive.

Oh balmy breath, that dost almost persuade
Justice to break her sword! One more, one more.
Be thus when thou art dead, and I will kill thee,
And love thee after. One more, and this the last:
So sweet was ne'er so fatal. I must weep,   20
But they are cruel tears. This sorrow's heavenly,
It strikes where it doth love. She wakes.

17 sword: *justice was often depicted as a female figure with scales and a sword*

Desdemona: Who's there? Othello?

Othello: Ay, Desdemona.

Desdemona: Will you come to bed, my lord?

Othello: Have you prayed to-night, Desdemona?

Desdemona: Ay, my lord.   25

Othello: If you bethink yourself of any crime
Unreconciled as yet to heaven and grace,
Solicit for it straight.

28 Solicit for it straight: *pray for forgiveness at once*

Desdemona: Alas, my lord, what do you mean by that?

Othello: Well, do it, and be brief. I will walk by.   30
I would not kill thy unprepared spirit.
No, heaven forfend! I would not kill thy soul.

32 forfend: *forbid*

Desdemona: Talk you of killing?

Othello: Ay, I do.

Desdemona: Then heaven
Have mercy on me!

Othello: Amen, with all my heart!

Desdemona: If you say so, I hope you will not kill me.   35

Othello: Hum!

Desdemona: And yet I fear you, for you are fatal then
When your eyes roll so; why I should fear I know not,
Since guiltiness I know not; but yet I feel I fear.

Othello: Think on thy sins.

The fearful summons *Othello asks his wife if she has she prayed and warns her to repent of any sins she may have committed before he kills her, as he would not kill her soul by sending her unprepared to face judgement in the next world. Desdemona is terrified, saying that her only sin is loving Othello and remembering how she deceived her father to elope with Othello. The unhappy couple's fragmented dialogue reflects the disharmony between them.*

Desdemona: They are loves I bear to you.   40

Othello: Ay, and for that thou diest.

Desdemona: That death's unnatural that kills for loving.
Alas, why gnaw you so your nether lip?
Some bloody passion shakes your very frame:
These are portents; but yet I hope, I hope,   45
They do not point on me.

Othello: Peace, and be still!

Desdemona: I will so. What's the matter?

Othello: That handkerchief which I so loved and gave thee,
Thou gavest to Cassio.

Desdemona: No, by my life and soul!
Send for the man, and ask him.   50

Othello: Sweet soul, take heed,
Take heed of perjury; thou art on thy deathbed.

Desdemona: Ay, but not yet to die.

Othello: Yes, presently:
Therefore confess thee freely of thy sin;
For to deny each article with oath   55
Cannot remove nor choke the strong conception
That I do groan withal. Thou art to die.

Desdemona: Then Lord have mercy on me!

Othello: I say, Amen.

Desdemona: And have you mercy too! I never did
Offend you in my life; never loved Cassio   60
But with such general warranty of heaven
As I might love: I never gave him token.

Othello: By heaven, I saw my handkerchief in his hand.
O perjured woman! Thou dost stone my heart,
And makest me call what I intend to do   65

---

43 nether: lower

45 portents: bad signs for the future

52 perjury: untruthfulness

53 presently: at once

55 article: accusation (legal term)
56 conception: suspicion
57 do groan withal: am pained by

61 warranty: approval

Perjury *There is a great deal of legal language in this scene. Othello almost assumes the role of judge and executioner. He remains obsessed with the so-called evidence of the handkerchief, demanding an explanation from Desdemona. She tells him to send for Cassio, who can explain that she never gave it to him. Angrily, Othello refuses to accept her explanation and wants her to 'confess thee freely of thy sin' as she is on her deathbed and so should not commit perjury. Desdemona continues to protest her innocence, begging for mercy.*

	A murder, which I thought a sacrifice: I saw the handkerchief.	66 sacrifice: *an act of offering up something for a higher purpose*
Desdemona:	He found it then; I never gave it him: send for him hither; Let him confess a truth.	
Othello:	He hath confessed.	
Desdemona:	What, my lord? 70	
Othello:	That he hath used thee.	71 used: *i.e. sexually*
Desdemona:	How? Unlawfully?	
Othello:	Ay.	
Desdemona:	He will not say so.	
Othello:	No, his mouth is stopped; Honest Iago hath taken order for it.	
Desdemona:	O, my fear interprets: what, is he dead?	
Othello:	Had all his hairs been lives, my great revenge 75 Had stomach for them all.	76 stomach: *appetite*
Desdemona:	Alas! He is betrayed and I undone.	77 undone: *ruined*
Othello:	Out, strumpet! Weepest thou for him to my face?	78 strumpet: *whore*
Desdemona:	O, banish me, my lord, but kill me not!	
Othello:	Down, strumpet! 80	
Desdemona:	Kill me tomorrow: let me live tonight!	
Othello:	Nay, if you strive—	81 strive: *struggle*
Desdemona:	But half an hour!	
Othello:	Being done, there is no pause.	83 Being done, there is no pause: *now I've started, I can't stop*
Desdemona:	But while I say one prayer!	
Othello:	It is too late.	

He smothers her

Unfounded accusations *Othello continues to accuse the innocent Desdemona of giving the handkerchief to Cassio, even going so far as to say that Cassio has confessed. Desdemona replies that Cassio will not say so. Othello then informs her that he will say nothing since he is dead. Desdemona is appalled: 'Alas! He is betrayed and I undone.' Blinded by paranoia, Othello thinks she is crying for Cassio. His petrified wife pleads with him for time: 'Kill me tomorrow: let me live tonight!'.*

Emilia: [*Within*] My lord, my lord! What, ho! My lord, my lord! 85

Othello: What noise is this? Not dead? Not yet quite dead?
I that am cruel am yet merciful;
I would not have thee linger in thy pain.
So, so.

'I have no wife.'

Emilia: [*Within*] What, ho! My lord, my lord!

Othello: Who's there? 90

Emilia: [*Within*] O, good my lord, I would speak a word with you!

Othello: Yes: 'tis Emilia. By and by. She's dead.
'Tis like she comes to speak of Cassio's death.
The noise was high. Ha! No more moving?
Still as the grave. Shall she come in? Were it good? 95
I think she stirs again — no. What's best to do?
If she come in, she'll sure speak to my wife:
My wife! My wife! What wife? I have no wife.

94 high: *loud*

The murder *Despite Desdemona's heartbreaking pleas, Othello suffocates her. Emilia arrives, demanding to speak to him. He believes she has news of Cassio's death and fears she will want to speak to his wife.*

O insupportable! O heavy hour!
Methicks it should be now a huge eclipse   100
Of sun and moon, and that the affrighted globe
Should yawn at alteration.

Emilia: [*Within*] I do beseech you
That I may speak with you, O, good my lord!

Othello: I had forgot thee: O, come in, Emilia.   105
Soft, by and by. Let me the curtains draw.
Where art thou?

Unlocks the door
Enter Emilia

What's the matter with thee now?

Emilia: O, my good lord, yonder's foul murders done!

Othello: What, now?

Emilia: But now, my lord.

Othello: It is the very error of the moon,   110
She comes more nearer earth than she was wont,
And makes men mad.

Emilia: Cassio, my lord, hath killed a young Venetian
Called Roderigo.

Othello: Roderigo killed!
And Cassio killed!

Emilia: No, Cassio is not killed.   115

Othello: Not Cassio killed! Then murder's out of tune,
And sweet revenge grows harsh.

Desdemona: O, falsely falsely murdered!

Emilia: Alas, what cry is that?

101 affrighted globe/Should yawn at alteration: *the terrified world should erupt at what has occurred*

106 Let me the curtains draw: *on the Globe stage, the bed would have been in a recess*

110 error of the moon: *the moon alters its course and this was thought to make men mad*
111 was wont: *used to do*

116 tune: *place*

The new reality *Othello realises what he has done and is so horrified that he thinks the whole earth should reflect what has happened: 'Methinks it should be now a huge eclipse.'*

Out of tune *Nothing is as it ought to be. Othello draws the curtains around Desdemona to hide the body before he allows Emilia to enter. She tells the Moor that Roderigo has been killed, but shocks him with news that Cassio is still alive. Suddenly, Desdemona's voice is heard from behind the curtains: 'falsely, falsely murdered'. Emilia cries out for help. For a brief moment, there is a glimmer of hope that Iago's evil will not prevail.*

Othello: That! What?

Emilia: Out, and alas! That was my lady's voice.   120
Help! Help, ho! Help! O lady, speak again!
Sweet Desdemona! O sweet mistress, speak!

Desdemona: A guiltless death I die.

Emilia: O, who hath done this deed?

Desdemona: Nobody; I myself. Farewell:
Commend me to my kind lord: O, farewell!   125   125 Commend: *speak well of*

Dies

Othello: Why, how should she be murdered?

Emilia: Alas, who knows?

Othello: You heard her say herself, it was not I.

Emilia: She said so: I must needs report the truth.

Othello: She's like a liar gone to burning hell,   130
'Twas I that killed her.

Emilia: O, the more angel she,
And you the blacker devil!

Othello: She turned to folly, and she was a whore.

Emilia: Thou dost belie her, and thou art a devil.   133 belie: *falsely accuse*

Othello: She was false as water.

Emilia: Thou art rash as fire, to say   135
That she was false: O, she was heavenly true!

Othello: Cassio did top her; ask thy husband else.   137: top: *make love to*
O, I were damned beneath all depth in hell,   137 else: *if it was otherwise*
But that I did proceed upon just grounds
To this extremity. Thy husband knew it all.   140   140 extremity: *final punishment*

Emilia: My husband!

Innocence Desdemona proclaims her innocence and tries with her dying breath to exonerate Othello from implication in her murder. Some critics interpret her final act of forgiveness as reflecting her Christ-like character.

Denial For a brief moment, Othello sinks to a new low, denying that he is responsible for the murder. But his jealous rage and loss of honour quickly return. He tries to justify his actions to Emilia, who bravely challenges him: 'the more angel she,/And you the blacker devil'.

Othello: Thy husband.

Emilia: That she was false to wedlock?

Othello: Ay, with Cassio. Nay, had she been true,
If heaven would make me such another world   145
Of one entire and perfect chrysolite,
I would not have sold her for it.

145 chrysolite: *semi-precious stone*

Emilia: My husband!

Othello: Ay, 'twas he that told me first:
An honest man he is, and hates the slime
That sticks on filthy deeds.

Emilia: My husband!   150

Othello: What needs this iteration, woman? I say thy husband.

151 iteration: *say repeatedly*

Emilia: O mistress, villainy hath made mocks with love,
My husband say that she was false!

152 made mocks with: *mocked*

Othello: He, woman;
I say thy husband: dost understand the word?
My friend, thy husband, honest, honest Iago.   155

Emilia: If he say so, may his pernicious soul
Rot half a grain a day! He lies to the heart:
She was too fond of her most filthy bargain.

156 pernicious: *villainous*

Othello: Ha!

Emilia: Do thy worst.   160
This deed of thine is no more worthy heaven
Than thou wast worthy her.

Othello: Peace, you were best.

162 Peace, you were best: *you had better keep quiet*

Emilia: Thou hast not half that power to do me harm
As I have to be hurt. O gull! O dolt!
As ignorant as dirt! Thou hast done a deed –   165
I care not for thy sword; I'll make thee known,
Though I lost twenty lives. – Help! Help, ho! Help!
The Moor hath killed my mistress! Murder! Murder!

164: gull, dolt: *stupid person*

Enter Montano, Gratiano, Iago, and others

Disbelief *A shocked Emilia condemns the man she never really knew. Her repetition of 'My husband' suggests that she has been unaware of his true maliciousness all along. She immediately condemns him.*

Shakespeare Focus: Othello

Montano: What is the matter? How now, general!	
Emilia: O, are you come, Iago? You have done well,	170
That men must lay their murders on your neck.	
Gratiano: What is the matter?	
Emilia: Disprove this villain, if thou be'st a man:	
He says thou toldest him that his wife was false.	
I know thou didst not, thou art not such a villain.	175
Speak, for my heart is full.	176 full: *filled with passion*
Iago: I told him what I thought, and told no more	
Than what he found himself was apt and true.	
Emilia: But did you ever tell him she was false?	
Iago: I did.	180
Emilia: You told a lie, an odious, damned lie;	181 odious: *hateful*
Upon my soul, a lie, a wicked lie.	
She false with Cassio! Did you say with Cassio?	
Iago: With Cassio, mistress. Go to, charm your tongue.	184 charm: *hold still*
Emilia: I will not charm my tongue; I am bound to speak.	185
My mistress here lies murdered in her bed—	
All: O heavens forfend!	187 forfend: *forbid*
Emilia: And your reports have set the murder on.	188 set the murder on: *caused the murder*
Othello: Nay, stare not, masters: it is true, indeed.	
Gratiano: 'Tis a strange truth.	190
Montano: O monstrous act!	
Emilia: Villainy, villainy, villainy!	
I think upon it, I think: I smell it: O villainy!	
I thought so then – I'll kill myself for grief –	
O villainy, villainy!	
Iago: What, are you mad? I charge you, get you home.	195 195 charge: *order*
Emilia: Good gentlemen, let me have leave to speak:	
'Tis proper I obey him, but not now.	
Perchance, Iago, I will never go home.	197 Perchance: *perhaps*

The truth emerges *The other Venetians arrive with Iago. Emilia confronts her husband, demanding to know* 'did you ever tell him she was false?' *Iago admits it and Emilia refutes the charge as an* 'odious, damned lie'. *Iago tells her to be quiet, but Emilia is now incensed and says it was Iago's reports that caused the murder, and Othello agrees.*

Othello: O! O! O!

He falls on the bed

Emilia: Nay, lay thee down and roar;
For thou hast killed the sweetest innocent   200
That ever did lift up eye.

Othello: [*Rising*] O, she was foul!
I scarce did know you, uncle: there lies your niece,
Whose breath, indeed, these hands have newly stopped.
I know this act shows horrible and grim.

Gratiano: Poor Desdemona! I am glad thy father's dead.   205
Thy match was mortal to him, and pure grief
Shore his old thread in twain: did he live now,
This sight would make him do a desperate turn,
Yea, curse his better angel from his side,
And fall to reprobation.   210

Othello: 'Tis pitiful; but yet Iago knows
That she with Cassio hath the act of shame
A thousand times committed; Cassio confessed it:
And she did gratify his amorous works
With that recognizance and pledge of love   215
Which I first gave her I saw it in his hand:
It was a handkerchief, an antique token
My father gave my mother.

Emilia: O heaven! O heavenly powers.

Iago: Come, hold your peace.

Emilia: 'Twill out, 'twill out: I hold my peace, sir? No!   220
No, I will speak as liberal as the north:
Let heaven and men and devils, let them all,
All, all, cry shame against me, yet I'll speak.

Iago: Be wise, and get you home.

Emilia: I will not.

Iago threatens to stab Emilia

206 mortal: *fatal*

207 Shore: *cut*
207 thread: *hold on life*

210 reprobation: *state of damnation*

212 act of shame: *adultery*

214 amorous works: *seduction*

215 recognizance: *keepsake*

221 liberal: *freely*

Tragedy *Emilia now begins to realise the whole truth and asks that she be excused from obeying Iago, begging leave to speak. She describes Desdemona as the 'sweetest innocent'. Othello loses control and collapses. Gratiano says he is glad Desdemona's father is dead and not a witness to this terrible tragedy. Othello still clings to the flimsy evidence of the handkerchief: 'I saw it in his hand'.*

 Shakespeare Focus: Othello

Gratiano:	Fie!	
	Your sword upon a woman?	225
Emilia:	O thou dull Moor, that handkerchief thou speakest of	
	I found by fortune and did give my husband;	
	For often, with a solemn earnestness,	
	More than indeed belonged to such a trifle,	
	He begged of me to steal it.	
Iago:	Villainous whore!	230
Emilia:	She give it Cassio! No, alas! I found it,	
	And I did give it my husband.	
Iago:	Filth, thou liest!	
Emilia:	By heaven, I do not, I do not, gentlemen.	
	O murderous coxcomb! What should such a fool	
	Do with so good a woman?	
Othello:	Are there no stones in heaven	235
	But what serve for the thunder? Precious villain!	

228 belonged: was appropriate

234 coxcomb: fool

He runs at Iago. Iago, from behind, stabs Emilia, and exit

Gratiano:	The woman falls; sure he hath killed his wife.	
Emilia:	Ay, ay. O, lay me by my mistress' side.	
Gratiano:	He's gone, but his wife's killed.	
Montano:	'Tis a notorious villain. Take you this weapon,	240
	Which I have here recovered from the Moor:	
	Come, guard the door without. Let him not pass,	
	But kill him rather. I'll after that same villain,	
	For 'tis a damned slave.	

241 recovered: taken

Exeunt Montano and Gratiano

| Othello: | I am not valiant neither, | |
| | But ever puny whipster gets my sword: | 245 |

245 whipster: youngster

The truth *Emilia insists on speaking, even as Iago attempts to stab her. She tells the true story of the handkerchief: 'I found by fortune and did give my husband'. Iago had been begging her to steal it. Iago foully declares her a liar. Intent on ensuring that true justice is served, Emilia also exposes Othello as a 'murderous coxcomb'. Is her final act enough to redeem her?*

	But why should honour outlive honesty?	
	Let it go all.	
Emilia:	What did thy song bode, lady?	247 bode: *foretell*
	Hark, canst thou hear me? I will play the swan	248 play the swan: *sing before I die*
	And die in music.	

Singing

Willow, willow, willow –
Moor, she was chaste, she loved thee, cruel Moor.   250
So come my soul to bliss, as I speak true;
So speaking as I think, I die, I die.

Dies

Othello:	I have another weapon in this chamber;	
	It is a sword of Spain, the ice-brook's temper –	254 ice-brook's temper: *steel strengthened by being plunged into an icy stream*
	O, here it is. Uncle, I must come forth. 255	
Gratiano:	[*Within*] If thou attempt it, it will cost thee dear:	
	Thou hast no weapon, and perforce must suffer.	
Othello:	Look in upon me then and speak with me,	
	Or, naked as I am, I will assault thee.	259 naked: *unarmed*

Re-enter Gratiano

Gratiano:	What is the matter?	
Othello:	Behold, I have a weapon; 260	
	A better never did itself sustain	
	Upon a soldier's thigh: I have seen the day,	
	That, with this little arm and this good sword,	
	I have made my way through more impediments	
	Than twenty times your stop: but, O vain boast! 265	265 your stop: *your force as a guard*
	Who can control his fate? 'Tis not so now.	
	Be not afraid, though you do see me weaponed;	
	Here is my journey's end, here is my butt,	268 butt: *goal*
	And very sea-mark of my utmost sail.	269 sea-mark: *beacon*

Another victim *Emilia asks to be laid beside Desdemona's body. Her poignant song echoes her mistress, whom she defends to the very end: 'she loved thee, cruel Moor'. Emilia dies speaking of Desdemona's purity. Her death heightens the overwhelming sense of tragedy in this scene.*

Shakespeare Focus: Othello

Do you go back dismayed? 'Tis a lost fear; 270
Man but a rush against Othello's breast,
And he retires. Where should Othello go?
Now, how dost thou look now? O ill-starred wench!
Pale as thy smock! When we shall meet at compt,
This look of thine will hurl my soul from heaven, 275
And fiends will snatch at it. Cold, cold, my girl!
Even like thy chastity. O cursed slave!
Whip me, ye devils,
From the possession of this heavenly sight!
Blow me about in winds! Roast me in sulphur! 280
Wash me in steep-down gulfs of liquid fire!
O Desdemona! Desdemona! Dead!
Oh! Oh! Oh!

271 Man but a rush: *aim just a reed (of no use)*

273 ill-starred: *ill-fated*

274 compt: *Day of Judgement*

'Cold, cold, my girl!'

The end *Othello speaks of past military glories, but all is changed now. He fears Judgement Day and being condemned to Hell for killing an innocent woman.*

Othello's language *It has been argued that Othello's speech marks a return to his former nobility as a renowned military leader. His language, complete with poetic metaphors and exaggeration, has a formal grandeur that will remind audiences of his earlier greatness.*

Enter Lodovico, Montano, Cassio carried in a chair, and Officers with Iago, prisoner

Lodovico: Where is this rash and most unfortunate man?

Othello: That's he that was Othello: here I am. 285

Lodovico: Where is that viper? Bring the villain forth.

286 viper: *snake*

Othello: I look down towards his feet; but that's a fable.
If that thou be'st a devil, I cannot kill thee.

287 fable: *a reference to the story that the devil is supposed to have cloven feet*

Wounds Iago

Lodovico: Wrench his sword from him.

Iago: I bleed, sir; but not killed.

Othello: I am not sorry neither: I would have thee live; 290
For, in my sense, 'tis happiness to die.

Lodovico: O thou Othello, thou wert once so good,
Fallen in the practice of a damned slave,
What shall be said to thee?

293 practice: *schemes*

Othello: Why, any thing:
An honourable murderer, if you will; 295
For nought I did in hate, but all in honour.

Lodovico: This wretch hath part confessed his villainy:
Did you and he consent in Cassio's death?

Othello: Ay.

Cassio: Dear general, I never gave you cause. 300

Othello: I do believe it, and I ask your pardon.
Will you, I pray, demand that demi-devil
Why he hath thus ensnared my soul and body?

302 demi-devil: *half-man, half-devil*

Iago: Demand me nothing: what you know, you know:
From this time forth I never will speak word. 305

Why? *Othello looks at Iago's feet to check if they are the cloven feet of Satan. He continues to associate himself with Christianity, perhaps comparing himself to a vengeful God.*

The demi-devil *Iago fascinates Othello, who asks, 'If that thou be'st a devil, I cannot kill thee.' Iago is wounded but doesn't die, leaving audiences to draw their own conclusions. The villainous ensign plays his final trump card and refuses Othello the satisfaction of an explanation: 'From this time forth I never will speak word'.*

Lodovico: What, not to pray?

Gratiano: Torments will ope your lips.

306 Torments: *torture*
306 ope: *open*

Othello: Well, thou dost best.

Lodovico: Sir, you shall understand what hath befallen,
Which, as I think, you know not. Here is a letter
Found in the pocket of the slain Roderigo;   310
And here another: the one of them imports
The death of Cassio to be undertook
By Roderigo.

308 befallen: *occurred*

311 imports: *suggests*

Othello: O villain!

Cassio: Most heathenish and most gross!

314 heathenish: *savage*
314 gross: *terrible*

Lodovico: Now here's another discontented paper,   315
Found in his pocket too; and this, it seems,
Roderigo meant to have sent this damned villain;
But that, belike, Iago in the interim
Came in and satisfied him.

317 belike: *it is likely*

318 satisfied him: *stopped his complaints*

Othello: O the pernicious caitiff!
How came you, Cassio, by that handkerchief   320
That was my wife's?

319 pernicious caitiff: *villainous wretch*

Cassio: I found it in my chamber:
And he himself confessed but even now
That there he dropped it for a special purpose
Which wrought to his desire.

Othello: O fool! Fool! Fool!

Cassio: There is besides in Roderigo's letter,   325
How he upbraids Iago, that he made him
Brave me upon the watch; whereon it came
That I was cast: and even but now he spake,
After long seeming dead, Iago hurt him,
Iago set him on.   330

326 upbraids: *criticises*

327 Brave: *insult*

328 cast: *dismissed*

Lodovico: You must forsake this room, and go with us.
Your power and your command is taken off,
And Cassio rules in Cyprus. For this slave,

332 taken off: *removed*

Final details *Iago is told he will be tortured. Meanwhile, Lodovico takes control and investigates the case. Two letters have been found in Roderigo's pocket, one of which explains the part Roderigo played in Cassio's attempted murder. Cassio explains that he found the handkerchief in his lodging and that Iago had confessed he placed it there to incriminate him. Othello is horrified.*

If there be any cunning cruelty
That can torment him much and hold him long,   335
It shall be his. You shall close prisoner rest,   336 close: *closely guarded*
Till that the nature of your fault be known
To the Venetian state. Come, bring him away.

Othello: Soft you; a word or two before you go.   339 Soft you: *Just a moment*
I have done the state some service, and they know it.   340   340 service: *military service*
No more of that. I pray you, in your letters,
When you shall these unlucky deeds relate,
Speak of me as I am; nothing extenuate,   343 extenuate: *tone down*
Nor set down aught in malice: then must you speak
Of one that loved not wisely but too well;   345
Of one not easily jealous, but being wrought   346 wrought: *confused*
Perplexed in the extreme; of one whose hand,
Like the base Indian, threw a pearl away   348 base Indian: *American Indians were said to be ignorant about precious gems*
Richer than all his tribe; of one whose subdued eyes,
Albeit unused to the melting mood,   350
Drop tears as fast as the Arabian trees
Their medicinal gum. Set you down this.
And say besides, that in Aleppo once,   353 Aleppo: *Alexandria*
Where a malignant and a turbaned Turk
Beat a Venetian and traduced the state,   355   355 traduced: *insulted*
I took by the throat the circumcised dog,
And smote him, thus.

Stabs himself

Lodovico: O bloody period!   357 period: *conclusion*

Gratiano: All that's spoke is marred.   358 marred: *ruined*

Othello: I kissed thee ere I killed thee: no way but this;   359 ere: *before*
Killing myself, to die upon a kiss.   360

Falls on the bed, and dies

Punishments Othello is stripped of his command and is due to be imprisoned. Cassio will be promoted while Iago is to be treated severely.

The real Othello? Othello's final words could suggest that he has regained some nobility or that he remains arrogant and self-centred. Speaking about himself in the third person, he distances himself from the murder, seemingly unwilling to accept responsibility. Is the Moor still preoccupied with his reputation? To what extent is his suicide honourable? Is it a cowardly escape? Or a final act of redemption to atone for the killing of his young wife?

150   *Shakespeare Focus: Othello*

Cassio: This did I fear, but thought he had no weapon;
For he was great of heart.

Lodovico: [*To Iago*] O Spartan dog,
More fell than anguish, hunger, or the sea!
Look on the tragic loading of this bed.   365
This is thy work. The object poisons sight,
And seize upon the fortunes of the Moor,
For they succeed to you. To you, lord governor,
Remains the censure of this hellish villain;
The time, the place, the torture: O, enforce it!   370
Myself will straight aboard: and to the state
This heavy act with heavy heart relate.

Exeunt

363 Spartan dog: *savage hound*
364 fell: *cruel*

367 fortunes: *possessions*

369 censure: *sentence*

372 heavy: *sorrowful*

The new order is established *Lodovico awards Othello's possessions to Gratiano and orders Cassio, the new general, to decide on Iago's punishment. Cassio pays his own tribute to Othello as a man who was 'great of heart'. Lodovico will return to Venice 'with heavy heart'. For the time being, order has been restored and evil has been defeated, but at a terrible price.*

Key Points

- The setting in Othello and Desdemona's bedroom is significant. Although it is their personal space, the events are very public. Their entire relationship has always been under scrutiny.

- Emilia seems to redeem herself. Her loyalty to Desdemona is remarkable as she defiantly confronts both her husband and the Moor.

- Othello's realisation of what a fool he has been leads him to commit suicide. Although he tries to regain his nobility, his own death leaves many unanswered questions about his true character.

- Iago's final act of villainy is to deny Othello the satisfaction of an explanation.

- The scene is full of religious imagery as the fate of each character's soul becomes a focus.

- The new order is finally established, but at the cost of many lives.

Analysis of Key Scenes

Act 1, Scene 1

'Images of animals and images of Heaven and Hell predominate in Shakespeare's play, *Othello*.' Discuss the use of such images and the purpose they serve in the play. Support your answer with accurate quotation.

Sample Paragraph

Shakespeare's dramatic tale of Othello, the brave respected general in the employment of Venice, is compellingly opened with a dark Venetian street scene full of intrigue. Othello has just eloped with the beautiful aristocratic Venetian, Desdemona. The malevolent Iago bitterly resents the Moor, but has decided to stay in his service 'to serve [his] turn upon him'. Iago frequently uses crude animal imagery. He despises loyalty in a servant, likening him to a 'master's ass', merely working for food. He lewdly describes Othello as a 'black ram' and Desdemona as a 'white ewe'. Iago seems incapable of comprehending a refined notion of romantic love between a couple. Instead, he refers to Othello as a 'Barbary horse'. He remarks that the result of Desdemona's elopement with Othello will be to give Brabantio heirs like 'coursers' and 'gennets'. His grandsons will 'neigh' like horses. Here is a foul mind that destroys all that it comes into contact with. Most of the references to Hell are also uttered by Iago. He describes Cassio as a 'fellow almost damned in a fair wife'. Othello is a devil who will make a grandsire of Brabantio. Iago refers to 'hell-pains' and 'if the devil bid you'. This immediately associates Iago in the audience's mind with the dark forces of evil. The only mention of Heaven is by a weary Brabantio as he forlornly wonders, 'O heaven! How got she out?' This weak remark is no match for the malevolent Iago, whose language and imagery reveal a vulgar man with no moral scruples.

Examiner's Comment

- Impressive range of relevant images accurately quoted.
- Informative discussion on their effectiveness in the play.
- Clear expression, varied and controlled.
- Grade A standard.

Class Activities

1 **A different viewpoint** Imagine there are two servants from Brabantio's house who witness the commotion of Act 1, Scene 1. Improvise a 'below-stairs' scene where the two servants comment on what has just occurred. Write the drama script for their conversation.

2 **Opening scenes** Imagine you are a director making a new film version of *Othello*. Consider what mood or atmosphere you are trying to create – tragic, mysterious, intriguing, evil, etc. How will your film begin? Where will it be set? What music or sound effects will you use? What costumes will your characters wear? Write a proposal outlining your plans for filming Act 1, Scene 1.

Class / Homework Exercises

1 'Disappointment, jealousy and bitterness are powerfully conveyed in Act 1, Scene 1 of Shakespeare's play, *Othello*.' Based on your study of Act 1, Scene 1, write a developed paragraph in response to this statement. Support the points you make with close reference to the text.

Sample Paragraph

I thought Iago was a very jealous person. This is powerfully conveyed in the first scene. He was jealous of everyone, Cassio and Othello. Roderigo is very disappointed because Othello eloped with Desdemona. He was very disappointed that Iago didn't tell him because he was paying Iago money to help him attract Desdemona. He tells Iago 'You have had my purse'. Brabantio is very bitter when he discovers Desdemona has run off with Othello. He complains, 'Who would be a father!' He wishes Roderigo, whom he had already rejected as a suitor for Desdemona, had married her instead of Othello, saying 'would you had had her'. Iago really shows his resentment towards the Moor, calling him 'a thick-lips' and 'devil'. Basically, he is totally racist. He thought he had shown how good he was because he had fought on the battlefield. The whole scene is filled with jealousy and Iago makes it clear that he is out for revenge on Othello, 'I will follow him to serve my turn against him'.

Examiner's Comment

- Some good reference to jealousy.
- More emphasis could be placed on Iago.
- Expression could be improved and quotes checked.
- Average C grade standard.

2 Redraft this paragraph in light of the examiner's comments.

3 'Shakespeare's *Othello* is a dark play of innocence and intrigue.' Write one paragraph discussing this statement, using your study of Act 1, Scene 1 to support your views.

4 Copy the table below into your own notes and fill in critical comments about the last two quotations.

Key Quotes

A fellow ... That never set a squadron in the field (Iago: lines 21–2)	Iago's seething jealousy of Cassio, who has been promoted above him by Othello, is evident in this disparaging remark about Cassio's ability as a soldier. Iago ridicules the young lieutenant for only knowing the theory of warfare, not its practice.
I am not what I am. (Iago: line 65)	
Is there not charms *By which the property of youth and maidhood* *May be abused?* (Brabantio: lines 171–3)	

Act 1, Scene 3

'Irony is a powerful dramatic device used by Shakespeare to heighten the tragic dimension of his play, *Othello*.' Discuss this view, supporting your answer by reference to or quotation from the play.

Sample Paragraph

Dramatic irony is used by Shakespeare to great effect in his tragedy, *Othello*. We, the audience not only have the pleasure of the unfolding story, but also have the added enjoyment of knowing more than the characters on the stage. So our emotions are intensely engaged as we look back and project forward as well as looking at what is happening before our eyes. Having witnessed Iago plotting with Roderigo to bring about the downfall of Othello, we are then appalled as Othello entrusts the care of his young wife, Desdemona to his 'ancient' Iago. Ironically, he is a man whom Othello regards as of 'honest and trust'. But we know he is 'following' Othello 'to serve his turn upon him'. But it is Iago's soliloquy at the end of Act 1 Scene 3 which really heightens the audience's appreciation of this tragic story. We can see Iago hatching the evil plan to ensnare his so-called friend. His understanding of others is breath-taking as he dismisses Roderigo, the foolish Venetian 'snipe', while using him as a source of money. Coldly and astutely, he sums up Othello as 'a free and open nature'. We wonder can these characters ever escape his 'monstrous' plan or will he be able to lead them 'by the nose/As asses are'. Shakespeare has involved us as we see Iago's duplicity and we look forward with unease for the hapless victims. Shakespeare has greatly increased our sense of the fatal aspect of his play through irony.

Examiner's Comment

- Focused well on ironic elements.
- Suitable supportive quotes used effectively.
- Expression varies, but is awkward at times.
- Good grade B standard.

Class Activity

1   The soliloquy

A soliloquy is where a character speaks his or her thoughts aloud. The audience becomes aware of his or her motives and state of mind. The soliloquy at the conclusion of Act 1, Scene 3 is the audience's first opportunity to hear Iago's version of events. If you were a director, how would you get the actor playing Iago to present this speech?

- Directed towards the audience?
- As if Iago is talking to himself?
- As a voiceover while the actor looks thoughtful?

Choose one option and consider:

- How the actor would speak the lines.
- What movements would be required.
- Which aspects of Iago you wish to represent – his inherent evil, his cunning nature, his ability to manipulate, etc.
- What reactions you wish to elicit from the audience – horror, excitement, sympathy, collusion, etc.

Class/Homework Exercises

1   'We have reason to cool our raging emotions.' Based on your study of Act 1, Scene 3, write a developed paragraph in response to this statement. Support the points you make with close reference to the text.

Sample Paragraph

I thought Desdemona was madly in love with Othello, 'My downright violence and storm of fortunes'. But I don't really think she thought things through. I think she was just filled with Othello's stories of his adventures, 'with a greedy ear/Devour my discourse'. It seemed to me as if it was his adventures that she fell in love with, 'if I had a friend that loved her,/I should but teach him my story'. This is like the girl who thinks falling in love is like a gushy romantic novel with a big happy ending. She also insists on going to war with Othello, 'if I be left behind, As a moth of peace'. She is putting her personal feelings

before the safety of the state. Surely she knows as a soldier's wife she should wait at home for him? So I do think she has 'raging motions' which she needs to control with her reason. She needs to love more moderately, 'reason to cool'.

Examiner's Comment

- Suitable supportive quotes used effectively.
- Note-like and repetitive expression.
- Some inaccurate quotations.
- Basic grade C standard.

2   Redraft this paragraph in light of the examiner's comments.

3   'Othello is a character at once great and flawed.' Write one paragraph discussing this statement, using your study of Act 1, Scene 3 to support your views.

4   Copy the table below into your own notes and fill in critical comments about the last two quotations.

Key Quotes

Valiant Othello, we must straight employ you, *Against the general enemy Ottoman.* (Duke: lines 48–9)	The Duke greets Othello warmly, as he depends on him to lead the attack against the Turkish invasion in Cyprus. At this point in the play, Othello is highly regarded for his prowess on the battlefield.
Look to her Moor, if thou hast eyes to see *She has deceived her father, and may thee.* (Brabantio: lines 288–9)	
These Moors are changeable in *their wills ... fill thy purse with money.* (Iago: lines 336–7)	

Act 2, Scene 1

'Iago's schemes are largely successful because of his astute perception of other characters.' Discuss this statement, supporting your answer with accurate quotation.

Sample Paragraph

In Act 2, Scene 1, Iago's shrewd appraisal of other characters' weaknesses and virtues shows how his plan, although as yet unformed, will be successful. Desdemona, Cassio and Iago await the arrival of Othello, who has been delayed at sea by a ferocious storm. Cassio is a refined Venetian given to displays of courteous behaviour. Iago stands watching Desdemona and Cassio chatting. He is thinking, 'I will catch you in your own courtesies'. Observing Cassio's flamboyant actions, he remarks to himself, 'it had been better you had not kissed your three fingers so oft'. Iago intends to use Cassio's chivalrous manners against him. But he also intends to use his weakness, his tendency towards rash behaviour, to further his plan for revenge against Othello. He incites the foolish and besotted Roderigo to pick a quarrel with Cassio because he is 'very sudden in choler'. Iago has a keen insight into the proud character of Othello. He recounts how he won Desdemona as his wife by 'bragging and telling her fantastical lies'. He has a real awareness of the weakness in their relationship. He tells Roderigo how Othello lacks 'sympathy in years, manners and beauties'. Othello is older, an outsider to the ways of sophisticated Venetian society and uneducated except in warfare. Iago intends to play on Othello's superstition, as the Moor is only recently a convert to Christianity. He knows Othello's dislike of uncertainty. Although Iago acknowledges Othello's qualities of honour and nobility, he is determined to bring him low, 'Even to madness'. The audience's attention is held fast by the ingenuity of Iago's scheming, which is based on such insightful observation of character.

Examiner's Comment

- Addresses the question directly.
- Shows a close understanding of the scene.
- Uses suitable reference and quotations effectively.
- Impressive, well-controlled expression throughout.
- Very good A grade standard.

Class Activity

1 **'An excellent courtesy.'**

   Cassio has greeted Desdemona with a bold display of chivalry. He then proceeds to kiss Emilia. First he apologises to Iago, ''tis my breeding/That gives me this bold show of courtesy'.

As a director, how would you instruct the actor to interpret Cassio's behaviour not only towards Desdemona, but also towards Emilia?

- He's a naturally polite man.
- He's a womaniser.
- He's attempting to keep things normal as they anxiously await Othello's arrival from sea.
- He's trying to annoy Iago because he knows Iago is prone to jealousy.
- Some other approach.

Would you have the actors portray the kiss as a courteous peck on the cheek or as a more passionate act?

How would you suggest Emilia should react: flattered, embarrassed, annoyed, afraid, etc.?

How would you suggest Iago should react: ignore what is happening, be charmed at the attention his wife is receiving or would he move to reclaim Emilia?

Class/Homework Exercises

1 'You are pictures out of doors.' Iago believes that women are not to be trusted. Based on your study of Act 2, Scene 1, write a developed paragraph in response to Iago's views on women. Support the points you make with close reference to the text.

Sample Paragraph

I think Iago does not like women at all. Back in Shakespeare's time, the audience enjoyed clever wordplay and would have loved Iago's list of complaints about women. He calls them 'wild-cats' and 'bells'. He thinks they are fit 'only to chronicle small beer'. In other words, not to be taken seriously. He even has a very cynical view of the 'divine Desdemona'. He thinks her 'eye must be fed'. He thinks women flirt constantly. In short, I think he is a bit of the woman hater or misogynist. He has serious issues respecting Emilia and Desdemona and is so totally jealous of Cassio who is popular.

Examiner's Comment

- Some worthwhile points, but lacking development.
- Expression is casual and repetitive.
- Basic grade D.

2 Redraft this paragraph in light of the examiner's comments.

3 'Shakespeare uses the raging sea storm in *Othello* as a symbol of the destructive forces at work in human life and within man himself.' Write one paragraph discussing this statement, using your study of Act 2, Scene 1 to support your views.

4 Copy the table below into your own notes and fill in critical comments about the last two quotations.

Key Quotes

O, you are well tuned now! *But I'll set down the pegs that make this music* (Iago: lines 199-200)	Iago comments that Othello and Desdemona are in harmony now, but he will soon have them acting on his wishes. Iago's language develops the imagery of music, which Othello uses to greet Desdemona as he arrives safely at Cyprus after the terrible storm at sea.
Her eye must be fed; *and what delight shall she have to look on the devil?* (Iago: lines 224-6)	
yet that I put the Moor *At least into a jealousy so strong* *That judgement cannot cure.* (Iago: lines 294-6)	

Act 3, Scene 3

'Othello is a noble character, flawed by insecurity and a nature that is naive and unsophisticated.' Would you agree or disagree that Shakespeare presents the character of Othello in this way in his play, *Othello*? Support your answer with suitable reference to the text.

Sample Paragraph

For me, Shakespeare presents Othello as the man of the moment, the military hero with a proven track record. He possesses the soldierly qualities that Venice needs so desperately to safeguard their trade routes against the Turks. He is an ambitious outsider who desires to be accepted in Venice. So in Act 3, Scene 3, he is ripe for picking by the scheming Iago. The so-called casual remark of Iago, 'Ha! I like not that', begins the destruction of the noble Moor. Iago plays on Othello's lack of awareness as an outsider when he ridicules white women, 'In Venice they do let heaven see the pranks/They dare not show their husbands'. The apprehensive Othello responds, 'Haply, for I am black/And have not those soft parts of conversation/That chamberers have'. This is a general used to the battlefield. He is speedily led by Iago to agree that Desdemona has already been deceptive before when she eloped with him without her father's knowledge, 'And so she did'. Othello's self-image is based on his military skills and when he is set 'on the rack' of 'green-eyed' jealousy, he knows that 'Pride, pomp and circumstance of glorious war' is gone forever. The Moor is easy prey for Iago, who soon turns him against his innocent wife. As a soldier, Othello demands certainty, preferring suicide to dishonour, 'If there be cords, or knives … I'll not endure it'. The noble warrior accepts death as part of his job description without complaint, and so likewise he accepts his destiny, that of the cuckolded husband, ''tis the plague of great ones …'Tis destiny, unshunnable, like death'. I fully agree that Shakespeare has created a noble character who is deeply flawed by insecurity, naivety and a complete lack of sophistication.

Examiner's Comment

- Focuses clearly on addressing the question.
- Shows a very close understanding of the text.
- Uses appropriate quotes effectively.
- Assured and varied expression throughout.
- Grade A standard.

Class Activity

The story of the handkerchief

This group role play exercise explores the importance of Desdemona's 'napkin'.

(Emilia accidentally finds the decorated handkerchief, a gift from Othello to Desdemona, and gives it to her husband, Iago, in response to his insistent requests for it.)

Choose five students to represent Othello, Desdemona, Emilia, Bianca and Iago.

Pass a handkerchief from one character to another.

While holding the handkerchief, each character briefly explains:

- His/her name and background.
- How he/she came to be in possession of the handkerchief.
- What importance the handkerchief has for him/her.

Finally, another student is chosen to be a representative of the audience.

He/she states what the viewers' opinion is about the significance of the handkerchief.

Class/Homework Exercises

1   'This fellow's of exceeding honesty.' Based on your study of Act 3, Scene 3, write a developed paragraph in response to this statement made by Othello about Iago. Support the points you make with close reference to the text.

I think that Othello is very blind in judging characters as he keeps going on about how honest Iago is. I really don't understand if he is a general in an army with lots of soldiers under his command why he cannot see through Iago. After all he did not choose him for promotion. He chose Cassio. There must have been some reason he didn't choose him. He says in Act 3, Scene 3 'for I know thou art very full of love and honesty'. Well, if he thinks that, then why didn't he give him the job? He says he is 'of exceeding honesty'. Othello is very, very easily tricked. He believes everything Iago says. He also condemns Desdemona without giving her a fair chance to defend herself. He passes judgement very quickly on very flimsy evidence, e.g. the flimsy hanky. Iago knows he is smarter than Othello and lies about Venetian women two-timing their husbands. It doesn't say very much about Othello as a commander if he doesn't look a little closer. I wouldn't put him in charge of an army.

Examiner's Comment

- Slight attempt at addressing the question.
- General lack of development.
- Language could be much more controlled.
- Over-use of 'very'.
- Basic grade D.

2   Redraft this paragraph in light of the examiner's comments.

3   'Shakespeare's *Othello* is an intriguing display of manipulation and cunning schemes.' Write one paragraph discussing this statement, using your study of Act 3, Scene 3 to support your views.

4   Copy the table below into your own notes and fill in critical comments about the last two quotations.

Key Quotes

O, that's an honest fellow. (Desdemona: line 5)	Iago's ability to seem what he is not is very evident in this scene. None of the characters is aware of Iago's true nature. Emilia has just said that Iago is grieved because Cassio has been demoted. Ironically, Desdemona continues to think Iago is 'honest'.
Ha! I like not that. (Iago: line 35)	
O, now, for ever *Farewell the tranquil mind! Farewell content!* (Othello: lines 353–4)	

Act 5, Scene 2

'Iago is not only an unredeemed villain, but towers above all others in his evil genius.' Discuss this view of Iago's character. Support your answer with accurate quotation.

Sample Paragraph

As I finished reading Shakespeare's *Othello*, I was left wondering whether Iago, the 'Spartan dog', had really got away with it. This villain seems to have triumphed as witnessed by 'the tragic loading of this bed' with its poisonous sight of three dead bodies, the pure Desdemona, the noble Othello and the loyal Emilia. When asked to explain, Iago sneers insolently, 'Demand me nothing: what you know, you know'. He reminded me of a fundamentalist on trial for mass murder for his own twisted reasons. Neither shows the slightest regret for the carnage and suffering they have caused others. Both are unredeemed villains. Iago's final remark, 'From this time forth I never will speak word', hisses with absolute hatred and defiance. Here is a man glorying in his handiwork. This was something only he with his superior intelligence could have carried out. He rose to every challenge, used every opportunity given, recognised and exploited every weakness shown. Just as we sit in amazement at the lack of contrition by the fundamentalist mass murderer, so we sadly realise that Iago probably won't break even under torture. To the last he outwits all, he is still capable of maintaining control, now over his tongue. He denies the new order the satisfaction of a contrite villain. Lodovico will return to Venice to perform the only duty left to him, 'This heavy act with heavy heart relate'. Iago, the unredeemed villain, still towers above all others in his evil genius. Just like Othello, who looked 'down towards his feet', we wonder how anyone could be so diabolical.

Examiner's Comment

* Addresses the question directly.
* Focuses well on Iago's dominance throughout.
* Uses suitable supportive quotes effectively.
* Assured and varied expression.
* Solid grade A standard.

Class Activity

1   **Presenting a freeze-frame to a class** (group activity for five or six)

Imagine the action of the play stops at three key moments:

* Emilia (line 192): 'I think upon it, I think: I smell it: O villainy!'
* Othello (lines 274–6): 'when we shall meet at compt,/This look of thine will hurl my soul from heaven,/And fiends will snatch at it'
* Iago (line 305): 'From this time forth I never will speak word'

For each key moment, create a still picture.

- Each student chooses a character.
- Hold the frozen action for 10 seconds.
- One key character steps out of the freeze-frame and outlines his/her personal thoughts at this precise moment in Act 5, Scene 2.

Class/Homework Exercises

1 'Shakespeare spoils his tragic masterpiece with an anti-climax; all that happens at the end is predictable.' Based on your study of Act 5, Scene 2, write a developed paragraph in response to this statement. Support the points you make with close reference to the text.

Sample Paragraph

I did not think that the ending was totally expected and boring. I did feel Desdemona would die at Othello's hands, but I wasn't expecting Iago to stab Emilia who died as a swan singing 'Willow, willow'. I was a little surprised that Iago was caught. I thought he was so cunning he would have possibly escaped. I was very surprised that he was going to say nothing, 'Demand me say nothing'. I thought he would have wanted to boast about how clever he was with all his schemes and how he destroyed Othello with no real evidence. But it was Othello who boasted calling himself an 'honourable murderer'. The tragedy has really been happening ever since the Moor became jealous and his deep love turned to revenge. I thought the ending was actually very true to what had been happening all along. All the hatred was going to destroy the main characters. So I don't really think anyone would know exactly what was going to happen at the end. The play wasn't spoiled at all for me by the tragic ending.

Examiner's Comment

- Includes some personal interaction with the text.
- Note-like and repetitive expression.
- Some worthwhile points needed more development.
- Quotations not completely accurate.
- Basic grade C standard.

2 Redraft this paragraph in light of the examiner's comments.

3 'Despite the striking portrayals of goodness and nobility, the play *Othello* leaves the audience with a dismal sense of despair.' Discuss this view, supporting your answer by quotation from or reference to the play.

4 Copy the table below into your own notes and fill in critical comments about the last two quotations.

Key Quotes

Yet she must die, else she'll betray more men. (Othello: line 6)	Othello sees himself as the bloody avenger dispensing justice on a wicked woman. He has been totally corrupted by the poisonous suggestions of Iago. The noble Moor is no more.
My friend, thy husband, honest, honest Iago. (Othello: line 155)	
Of one that loved not wisely but too well; *Of one not easily jealous, but being wrought* *Perplexed in the extreme* (Othello: lines 345-7)	

Character Study

Othello

First Impressions

THE PLAY'S PROTAGONIST is an unusual tragic hero. Othello is a combination of contradictions. In the beginning, he is proud, patient and self-confident, but once he falls victim to his passions, he behaves in a most inhuman manner. From the outset, there are tensions underlying Othello's twin roles as dutiful soldier and loving husband.

Our initial impression of Othello's character comes from his enemies, Iago and Roderigo, who depict him in a completely hostile way. Throughout the opening scenes, their obvious hatred and prejudice suggest that because he is a North African, Othello is viewed as a black man in a white world, a cultural and racial outsider. Iago describes him as 'an old black ram' and the 'lascivious Moor', a boastful figure who has used witchcraft to seduce Desdemona, Brabantio's daughter.

When he first appears, however, this negative impression is immediately contradicted. Responding to his irate father-in-law, Othello is self-controlled and diplomatic: 'Good signor, you shall more command with years/Than with your weapons'. Audiences are already likely to feel a certain amount of sympathy for Othello because of the offensive way others treat him. We do not even hear his actual name until well into Act 1, Scene 3, when the Duke of Venice acknowledges his military abilities and leadership. 'Valiant Othello' is clearly a trusted servant of the Venetian state. In public, even his enemies pretend to respect him since he holds such an important position as general of Venice's armies.

Othello has other character traits. Iago's insightful comment that 'The Moor is of a free and open nature' is both a strength and a weakness. Othello is undoubtedly a fearless soldier and an able general. His knowledge comes from the battlefield, where he has spent most of his days. As a result, he is used to military life and the need to act quickly and decisively. As the leader of the Venetian troops, he is indispensable to the defence of territories controlled by Venice. For this reason, he is sent to fight the Turks and protect Cyprus. Othello himself is proud of his military reputation. But since he has spent so much of his life on the battlefield, he is unfamiliar with Venetian society and the wickedness that can sometimes exist in human nature.

Although Othello claims that he is 'rude' and inarticulate in his own use of language ('little blessed with the soft phrase of peace'), his seemingly rehearsed explanation about winning his 'fair lady's love' is polished and persuasive. Is this false modesty? Does it suggest that Othello is really tying to impress? We can only wonder about his egotism and whether it shows an underlying insecurity.

Audiences will also question Othello's understanding of romantic love. He says that Desdemona loved him 'for the dangers' he had experienced and that he in turn loved her because 'she did pity them'. Throughout the play's opening scenes, Shakespeare has intentionally created an aura of romance and mystery around the dark Moor, and Othello's poetic expression and thoughts strengthen this image.

But although Othello first inspires confidence in his character, the question of his elopement causes unease. The circumstances surrounding his secret marriage to Desdemona are never explained, but it is Othello who is initially blamed for the deception. Once again, the fact that the couple have flaunted civilised Venetian behaviour raises questions about both their characters.

Whether he is using Desdemona to flatter his own ego or is simply infatuated with her, Othello's intense feelings are undeniable. In response to Brabantio's ominous warning ('She has deceived her father, and may thee'), Othello confidently proclaims his trust in his wife – 'My life upon her faith!' – as he leaves the care of Desdemona to 'honest Iago'.

Othello's Development

At the start of Act 2, Othello has triumphed over tremendous obstacles: cultural prejudice, Brabantio's hostility and the threat of the Turkish fleet. When he and his wife are reunited in Cyprus, Othello can hardly express his happiness ('it is too much of joy'). But less than two days later, the marriage is utterly destroyed, and with it the lovers themselves. The fact that Othello is unable to control his powerful emotions is ominous. Critics have argued that the hero's tragic downfall results primarily from his failure as a husband.

From Act 3, Scene 3 onwards, Othello's suffering is intense. Over and over again, he struggles with raging anger, confusion and jealousy. He is acutely aware of the precarious nature of success and happiness. 'But I do love thee!/And when I love thee not,/Chaos is come again.' These are the words of someone who fears uncertainty and believes himself to have been rescued from it by true love. Increasingly tortured by doubts about Desdemona, he is easily manipulated by his 'demi-devil' ensign. It is important to remember that Iago is so exceptionally plausible and cunning that he is able to deceive many others as well as Othello. Iago's chilling influence is evident in Othello's language, which echoes the imagery of his ensign as the play progresses.

Throughout the second half of the drama, Othello's noble character is transformed for the worse as he becomes ever more 'ensnared' by Iago. Why Othello should trust his ensign more than his own wife has always intrigued audiences. That his enormous pride has been hurt is certain – 'Othello's occupation's gone'. The Moor's cruel behaviour is crude and irrational. Yet his obsession with honour and Desdemona's apparent unfaithfulness might suggest that he is an idealistic character. Central to Othello's demise is an overwhelming desire for revenge that brings together his crucial roles as soldier and husband. Tragically, his misplaced insistence on honour can be seen as both his redemption and downfall.

Final View

Othello remains a complex and enigmatic figure who continues to divide opinion. We are left considering the extent to which he is a vulnerable victim or a pompous villain. He describes himself as an 'honourable murderer'. His numerous dying claims infuriate and fascinate: 'one that loved not wisely but too well'. Othello's assertion that he was 'not easily jealous' must leave many people asking if he ever really knew himself.

However, it is possible to feel some sympathy for the Moor although we can never condone his actions. In his final moments, he appears to be almost entirely self-centred and concerned with his reputation. Is he essentially narcissistic and self-dramatising? It is characteristic that Othello judges himself before carrying out his own execution and dying alongside his love.

The Moor's killing could be seen as an attempt to regain his honourable military identity. Whether his suicide is an act of redemption or an effort to restore his reputation is open to debate. Some critics view Othello's violent death as a cowardly escape from taking responsibility for his actions. For others, his decision to die 'no way but this' is an acceptance of his inevitable fate as a wretched hero.

On the surface, of course, Iago is the undeniable architect of Othello's downfall. Yet it could be argued that it is the tension between Othello's experience as an outsider adapting to a foreign culture and his own personal trauma that makes him a truly tragic figure. At any rate, the protagonist's story forces audiences to consider the nature of his character flaws as well as his difficulty in acknowledging his own destructiveness.

In the end, fate is cruel to Othello. But in his final speeches, there are some glimpses of the protagonist's former greatness: his military achievements, loyalty to Venice, the intensity of his love and his terrible realisation that, by killing Desdemona, he has destroyed the best in himself.

Key Characteristics of Othello	
• Othello: 'one not easily jealous'	• Accomplished, heroic, idealistic
• Honourable, dignified, calm	• Insecure, naive, foolish, tragic
• Jealous, paranoid, violent, uncontrolled	• Arrogant, self-obsessed, egotistical

Iago

First Impressions

IAGO IS ONE OF THE MOST NOTORIOUS and compelling villains in all of literature. His capacity for cruelty seems limitless, and no motivation he gives for his actions is enough to explain the incredible destruction he wreaks on the lives of those around him. At first, Iago is portrayed in stark contrast to Othello. The audience is presented with a false and manipulative character who promises the gullible Roderigo that he will help him win Desdemona's affections and even brings him into his confidence by admitting, 'I am not what I am'.

Although Iago says 'I will wear my heart upon my sleeve', he is really deceitful, plotting against Othello, Cassio and Roderigo. We also get the clear impression that he is extremely spiteful and racist, almost unable to contain the ingrained resentment and jealousy he feels towards Othello: 'I hate the Moor'.

Iago's manipulation of others leads to the play's tragic climax: Desdemona's death and the downfall of many characters, including Iago himself. However, critics disagree over why he acts as he does. Some argue that Iago doesn't have a motivation and doesn't need one. Because he presents several different fronts to the other characters, audiences are also left wondering which is the real Iago.

As Othello's 'ancient' or 'ensign', Iago has worked his way through the ranks to become a junior army officer who was overlooked for promotion. His anger at Othello, who chose Michael Cassio as his lieutenant, provides an obvious motive to explain his revenge. The deep-rooted hostility is evident in his egotistical comment, 'I know my price'. Another possible reason for Iago's hatred is his suspicion that his wife, Emilia, has committed adultery with both Othello and Cassio. It seems that Iago's unhappy life is filled with envy and jealousy, feelings that he will soon use to ruin others.

Iago dominates the opening scenes. The language he uses immediately demonstrates his vulgar, sinister nature. He is frequently racist and misogynistic. Iago delights in telling Desdemona's father, Brabantio, 'An old black ram is tupping your white ewe', reducing the love between two human beings to the level of animals. However, Iago's language – which is mainly in prose as opposed to verse – is in keeping with his role as a rough-talking soldier. His speech is full of crude imagery straight from the barrack-room.

Consumed by a warped sense of sexual jealousy, bitterness and self-interest, the embittered ensign devises a plan to destroy Othello by making him believe that his wife is having an affair with his lieutenant. For Iago, the destruction of his enemy soon turns into an obsessive game in which the Machiavellian schemer displays his skills at deception. 'Let us be conjunctive in our revenge against him,' he tells Roderigo. 'If thou canst cuckold him, thou dost thyself a pleasure, me a sport.'

While it might well appear that Iago is entirely evil, Shakespeare adds depth to his character, at times making him amoral (beyond right and wrong), as opposed to the typical immoral villain. Yet the obsessive ensign always believes that his actions against the Moor are justified: 'nothing can or shall content my soul/Till I am evened with him'. In his insatiable scheming, he manages to fool everyone, especially Othello, who constantly refers to him as 'honest Iago'. He is also trusted by Desdemona and soon takes advantage of her basic good nature to 'enmesh them all' in his paranoid revenge.

Iago's Development

As the story develops, Iago gains the confidence of all the main characters and is able to control them by taking advantage of their failings. He delights in manipulating his enemies, in being the one who is truly in command. Iago is highly intelligent and clearly enjoys ruining people's lives. Always pragmatic and plausible, he does it with a sense of craftsmanship, appreciating his own clever ingenuity and the thrill of the risks he takes.

Ruthless versatility is another of Iago's most notable characteristics. He turns every occasion to his advantage, constantly improvising in unexpected situations and adapting his language to suit whoever he is speaking to. He flatters Roderigo ('Why, now I see there's mettle in thee') simply to gain his trust. When Iago is with Desdemona, his words are tenderly supportive: 'Do not weep, do not weep. Alas the day'. With Othello, he resorts to giving graphic details about Desdemona's infidelity that reflect the jealous Moor's worst fears. Iago understands that Othello is compassionate and naive, 'of a free and open nature', and he takes full advantage of this at every opportunity.

Cassio's weakness for drink makes him an easy target. While appearing to offer seemingly practical advice, Iago exploits this character flaw to have the lieutenant demoted. Throughout the play, he displays contempt for women, suggesting that they are all promiscuous. His attitude to Emilia typifies his innate disrespect for people in general. Knowing that she is desperate to please him, he uses her to steal Desdemona's handkerchief and then dismisses her as 'a foolish wife'.

However, it is in Act 3, Scene 3 (often referred to as the jealousy or temptation scene) that we see the ensign in his true element. His relationship with Othello is complex, veering at times between hatred and love. Iago pretends to be an honest, but reluctant, witness. His 'Ha! I like not that' is a subtle indication that he is genuinely concerned about Othello's marriage. Iago is also lucky in that Desdemona dooms herself by repeatedly pleading on Cassio's behalf.

Having planted general doubts in Othello's mind, the ensign becomes more confident, specifically reminding the Moor of how Desdemona has already deceived

her father. As Othello increasingly falls under his control, Iago presents him with further 'evidence' of Cassio's dream and introduces the sensitive matter of the handkerchief. In convincing the Moor that he has made a dreadful mistake in trusting Desdemona, Iago has his greatest triumph. His pride is satisfied when he is appointed lieutenant, but his treachery still knows no bounds.

Despite – or perhaps because of – his obvious villainy, Iago fascinates audiences, who are always aware of the irony surrounding him. He also appeals (both to the audience and other characters) because of his sense of humour, entertaining others with his crude stories, often joking about his own 'honesty' and denying brazenly that he is playing the villain.

Final View

Iago cares for nobody, yet he devotes his whole life to revenge rather than walking away in disdain. Towards the end of the play, he takes greater chances as his scheming grows more and more convoluted. Fearing that Roderigo is becoming unreliable, he plots to have him kill Cassio. Both men are equally expendable. So too is Emilia, who exposes the startling truth about her husband's crucial role in Desdemona's death.

It would be out of character for Iago to show any remorse and he remains unrepentant to the end. As a result, his true nature and motives continue to intrigue. It has often been suggested that he is simply the embodiment of evil ('motiveless malignity', as Coleridge claimed). Even his asides and soliloquies are never quite enough to fully reveal his personality. Iago's refusal to explain himself to Othello illustrates his ultimate victory and highlights Othello's tragic failure.

Perhaps the merciless ensign has no explanation for what happened. Is Iago an evil genius? A self-absorbed psychotic? His final statement, 'what you know, you know:/From this time forth I never will speak word', presents audiences with a powerful mystery. As always, Shakespeare leaves us with more questions than answers about human behaviour.

Key Characteristics of Iago	
• Iago: 'I know my price'	• Intelligent, resourceful, shrewd, superior
• Bitter, dishonourable, warped, malevolent	• Sadistic, violent, heartless
• Vulgar, racist, obsessive, misogynistic	• Vicious, self-obsessed, defiant
• Insecure, paranoid, amoral, cynical	

Desdemona

First Impressions

DESDEMONA IS BRABANTIO's beautiful young daughter. Like so many others in the play, she is a contradictory character. Initially she appears strong-willed and independent, but becomes increasingly submissive as the story develops. Desdemona refuses to choose any of the rich, handsome Venetian men everyone expects her to marry. Instead, she elopes with Othello, an older black man and an outsider to Venetian society.

When we fist hear of Desdemona, she is at the centre of a major scandal. Iago takes great delight in spreading sensational gossip about this wealthy upper-class socialite marrying outside her race. He suggests that she is a victim of Othello's lust. But while Desdemona's act of rebellion seems to reflect her unconditional love for Othello (something which is never in any doubt), it raises questions about her attitude to all those she deceives. However, she herself is fully aware that because of her marriage, she now has a 'divided duty' to her father and husband.

For his part, Brabantio thinks of his only daughter as a 'jewel'. She is his pride and joy, 'a maiden never bold;/Of spirit'. This description of an innocent young girl is in sharp contrast to the confident Desdemona we meet in the senate scene. With dignity and quiet intelligence, she asserts her independence as a newly married woman. At no point does she explain her elopement, but focuses primarily on her romantic feelings and loyalty towards Othello.

However, the exact nature of Desdemona's relationship with Othello is of crucial interest. For her, he is the hero of exciting and dangerous adventures. In addition, Othello is an important figure in Venice, and his heroic past would presumably make him attractive to many young noblewomen. As the Duke says, 'I think this tale would win my daughter too.' In light of the tragedy ahead, audiences will wonder about Desdemona's impetuous judgement in marrying the Moor. Is she blinded by infatuation? Does she really know her husband? Has she fallen in love with an idealised image of Othello? Or perhaps because he was different to all the other men she knew?

Yet although Desdemona was 'half the wooer', she fully accepts her husband's authority: 'my heart's subdued/Even to the very quality of my lord'. She is keen to support Othello by leaving the familiar comforts of Venice to travel with him to Cyprus, happy to play the role of his 'fair warrior'. Unfortunately for her, all her good qualities will soon work against her as she becomes central to Iago's devious plans to destroy his enemies. It does not take long for him to exploit her natural decency and 'out of her own goodness make the net/That shall enmesh them all'.

Character Development

Like Othello, Desdemona undergoes a dramatic transformation over the course of the play. For the most part, she is portrayed as a chaste and virtuous young woman – although she seems happy enough to join in with Iago's crude conversation at the beginning of Act 2. As the story develops, however, Desdemona begins to display just how naive she is about human behaviour. Trusting everyone around her, she takes up Cassio's cause and does all she can to persuade her husband of his lieutenant's qualities: 'I'll intermingle every thing he does/With Cassio's suit'. She genuinely believes that a reconciliation will benefit both men.

However, Desdemona soon becomes vulnerable to Othello's increasingly uncontrollable jealousy. She is understandably shocked when he insults her in public, striking her and calling her a 'strumpet' and a 'whore'. Despite such abuse, Desdemona remains as dignified as she can ('I have not deserved this') before defending her husband's behaviour: 'we must think men are not gods'. She blames herself for Othello's anger, promising to be even more dutiful as a true and loyal wife who 'must not now displease him'. Ironically, Iago persuades Othello of his wife's apparent infidelity partly because she betrayed her father by marrying in secret.

Confused and demeaned by her husband's relentless accusations, Desdemona is reduced to a state of innocent helplessness: 'I am a child to chiding.' Her unworldly nature seems strangely out of touch with reality, particularly when she discusses the subject of unfaithful wives with Emilia: 'I do not think there is any such woman.' Once again, audiences will wonder about the extent to which Desdemona is a victim of her own gullible nature.

Final View

By the end of Act 4, Desdemona seems resigned to her 'wretched fortune' and is prepared for the worst. The haunting song she sings reflects her own tragic life and foreshadows her eventual fate. Not once does she blame Othello for her unhappiness; indeed, she forgives all his failings: 'even his stubbornness, his checks, his frowns ... have grace and favour in them'. Throughout the play, Shakespeare has emphasised her essential Christian virtues by associating 'the divine Desdemona' with heaven and light.

Her death—smothered by her husband on her marriage bed—could hardly be more ironic. She proclaims her innocence to the end, insisting that the only sins she has committed are 'loves I bear'. She dies bravely, asserting the right to defend her honour: 'I never did/Offend you in my life'.

As she dies 'a guiltless death', Desdemona's final words are ambiguous and intriguing. Responding to Emilia's desperate question about 'who hath done this deed', she replies: 'Nobody; I myself.' Is she protecting the man she loves once again? Does her passivity reflect her innate naivety and powerlessness? Or is she taking responsibility at last for her own part in her own tragic downfall?

It is obvious that Desdemona is the victim of a patriarchal society. In one way or another, she is abused by the men in her life. She is insulted and rejected by Brabantio, cruelly used by Iago and finally misjudged and murdered by Othello. As one of Shakespeare's best-known heroines, Desdemona has been the subject of much critical attention. For some, she is a saintly goddess, often described as goodness personified. Other critics argue that she is too good to be true and too guileless to be convincing. Yet the playwright has presented her devotion to her husband in a sympathetic way. In contrast to Othello, who alternately idolised and then demonised Desdemona, she herself remains submissively loyal and forgiving to the end. Does this make her a stereotype of female passivity?

At any rate, few would deny the enduring sense of pathos associated with Desdemona's sad demise. She remains a highly compelling figure, whether we regard her well-meaning intentions as admirable or foolish. It is not surprising, therefore, that audiences continue to see Desdemona as the sacrificial victim of this tragic play.

Key Characteristics of Desdemona	
• Desdemona: 'your true and loyal wife'	• Naive, insecure, obedient, submissive
• Sophisticated, beautiful, virtuous	• Dignified, loyal, pathetic, tragic
• Strong-willed, romantic, innocent	• Unfortunate, forgiving

Cassio

First Impressions

LIKE MANY OF THE OTHER central characters in the play, Michael Cassio is introduced to us by Iago. It is a typically unflattering portrayal based on envy and prejudice. From the embittered ensign's viewpoint, Cassio is a shallow character, a lady's man and a native of Florence. Iago resents this fussy outsider, an 'arithmetician' and mere scholar who has been promoted to the rank of lieutenant despite not having any real experience in warfare.

Iago presents Cassio as a somewhat effeminate intellectual, comparing him to a 'spinster' and mocking his military record as 'mere prattle, without practice'. How such a man has become the general's second in command is beyond his understanding. However, when we first meet the lieutenant, he seems chivalrous and sincere. Othello considers him a friend who was aware of his courtship of Desdemona. Cassio's loyalty towards the general is never in doubt and he expresses his concern for his safety as he awaits Othello's arrival in Cyprus: 'O, let the heavens/Give him defence against the elements'.

From the outset, it is clear that Cassio's easy charm and good looks make him attractive to women: 'A fellow almost damned in a fair wife'. His polished language and mannerly behaviour are certainly in keeping with Iago's description: 'a proper man'. He is obviously proud of his breeding and shows every courtesy to Desdemona as well as greeting Emilia with a kiss. Keen to promote this refined, cultured image to the world, Cassio frequently uses exaggerated language to flatter women, comparing the 'divine' Desdemona to a chaste goddess. Unfortunately, this flirtatious charisma will soon be used by Iago to convince Othello that Cassio is having a secret affair with his wife.

Character Development

Cassio's high regard for Desdemona is sincere and he is always extremely respectful of her. He resists all Iago's efforts to discuss her relationship with Othello in crude terms. Naturally gallant and polite, he describes her as 'a most exquisite lady'. But although he is somewhat aware of his personal failings, the lieutenant lacks the strength of character to change his behaviour, particularly his weakness for drink: 'I have very poor and unhappy brains for drinking'. His response to getting drunk with Iago is decidedly half-hearted: 'I'll do it; but it dislikes me.' This is a failing that the devious ensign fully exploits.

As a direct result, Cassio loses his important position as lieutenant after a drunken brawl with Roderigo and Montano. The embarrassing public row occurs when questions are raised about Cassio's public image and reputation – something that means a great deal to him. Indeed, his repeated use of the word 'reputation' highlights how significant it is to him. Cassio is greatly concerned about how others see him. He is thoroughly ashamed of his reckless behaviour, telling Othello, 'I pray you, pardon me; I cannot speak.' It is not altogether surprising that he accepts Iago's support in solving his immediate problems.

Reduced to self-pity about his loss of military honour, Cassio resorts to relying on Desdemona to take up his cause for reinstatement. His obvious pride – a trait he shares with most of the play's male characters – exposes other character flaws. Desperate to regain Othello's confidence, he admits that he is too self-conscious to confront the general directly: 'I am very ill at ease,/Unfit for mine own purposes'. It could, of course, be argued that Cassio's use of women is somewhat cowardly, revealing a petulant self-interest that is far from admirable. Rather than face the truth about his obvious indiscipline, he feels sorry for himself, maintaining that he is 'past all surgery'. Characteristically, he exaggerates his feelings over his demotion: 'I have lost the immortal part of myself, and what remains is bestial.'

However, it is his relationship with his lover, Bianca, that is most unsettling. When they are together in private, Cassio is his usual charming self. He calls her his 'most fair Bianca' and 'sweet love'. At other times, Cassio treats her with contempt, dismissing her cruelly because he does not want to be found 'womaned'. Ironically, she is much more honest than he is. Cassio is quite happy to use the relatively lower-class Bianca when it suits him, but he will also mock his courtesan mistress behind her back when he 'cannot refrain/From the excess of laughter'. Whether this makes Cassio a plausible hypocrite or just another selfish 'customer' is debatable, but it certainly suggests that he is much more concerned with keeping up appearances than treating people with genuine regard.

Nearly all of Shakespeare's characters mirror one another in certain ways. Just as Othello categorises his own wife at different times, Cassio also tends to see women either as virgins or whores. When he talks about Desdemona, we can tell that he sees her as a kind of goddess. On the day she arrives in Cyprus, he uses reverential imagery to elevate her to a seemingly divine level: 'Ye men of Cyprus, let her have your knees.' By contrast, he demeans the vulnerable Bianca and doesn't want to be seen in public with her.

Final View

Notwithstanding his various faults, it is important to remember that Cassio is yet another unwitting victim of Iago's villainy. Like everyone else, he is unable to resist the ensign's persuasive scheming. As the object of Iago's jealousy, Cassio is soon caught up in this tragic revenge story. Overall, he is an innocent bystander. Indeed, Iago simply despises the 'daily beauty' of Cassio's life and punishes him severely for his youthful charm and flirtatious behaviour.

Shakespeare Focus: Othello

In the play's final scene, Cassio is wounded. He reveals important evidence against the 'heathenish' Iago, renews his friendship with Othello and pays generous tribute to the Moor: 'For he was great of heart'. The senate appoints Cassio as the new governor of Cyprus to replace Othello, a final indication, perhaps, that his many qualities outweigh his occasional failings. It is ironic that Iago's plans to destroy Cassio eventually lead to even greater promotion and status. In the end, audiences are left with a relatively lightweight figure who is primarily concerned with his own popularity and the idea of himself as a gentleman. However, in a tragedy where more complex characters, such as Othello and Iago, acted extremely and irrationality, it seems appropriate that Cassio is given final responsibility for 'the censure of this hellish villain'.

Key Characteristics of Cassio	
• Cassio: 'O, I have lost my reputation'	• Easily led, false, popular
• Cultured, sophisticated, intellectual	• Selfish, vain, thoughtless
• Romantic, loyal, well-intentioned	• Honest, sincere, honourable

Roderigo

THROUGHOUT MOST OF THE STORY, Shakespeare presents Roderigo as a foolish character with no saving graces. To a great extent, this rich Venetian nobleman is a figure of ridicule, an easy target for Iago's exploitation. From the outset, the ensign's merciless control of the 'poor trash of Venice' reveals much about both their characters. Roderigo is infatuated with Desdemona – and Iago exploits such unrealistic feelings to the utmost.

Even though he is sometimes aware that the quick-witted ensign is manipulating him, Roderigo continues to look up to Iago and is seemingly incapable of thinking for himself. At the start of the play, his racist comments about Othello echo Iago's vulgar abuse. He has no hesitation in provoking Brabantio's anger, telling him that his daughter has been reduced to 'the gross clasps of a lascivious Moor'. At other times, Roderigo displays more gentlemanly qualities and is simply overcome by Desdemona's 'most blessed condition'.

But he is essentially gullible and prone to self-delusion. Roderigo may have no moral sense, but he does have money – something that makes him particularly appealing to Iago, who boasts, 'Thus do I ever make my fool my purse'. Roderigo is also convinced that he can buy Desdemona's love, even after her marriage to Othello. The fact that there is not the slightest indication that she has any feelings whatsoever for him further emphasises his image as an impulsive fantasist. Indeed, if Roderigo is typical of the 'curled darlings' who wish to marry Desdemona, it is understandable why she decided to elope with Othello.

Iago takes full of advantage of his young friend's stupidity and uses him to destroy Michael Cassio. But while Roderigo is a very willing accomplice, he is not a particularly competent one. Although he admits to having 'no great devotion to the deed', he agrees to kill Cassio. The murder attempt is a complete fiasco, with Roderigo himself ending up wounded.

It could be argued that such typically ludicrous antics make Roderigo more of a comic caricature than a fully rounded character. He is so weak and inept that Iago sees him as a somewhat pathetic figure of fun, a mere 'fool'. Occasionally, he is even aware of his own overwhelming hopelessness, complaining at one point about being 'exceedingly well cudgelled'. Predictably, as soon as he has outlived his usefulness, Iago literally stabs him in the back and tries to blame everything on the hapless young nobleman.

Some critics maintain that Roderigo does not deserve such a violent fate. Unable to control his feelings and lacking any real strength of character, he stands no chance against the opportunistic ensign. Shortly before he is fatally stabbed in public, Roderigo eventually acknowledges his own wrongdoing ('O, villain that I am!') and tries to expose Iago's true evil ('O inhuman dog!') with his dying breath.

As much a villain as a victim, Roderigo's major dramatic function is to highlight the true character of his devious mentor, Iago. He also provides an interesting foil to Othello. Both men are subject to irrational jealousy while being completely unaware of Iago's deception. Despite his miserable life and unfortunate death, however, it is hardly surprising that audiences tend to have little or no sympathy for Roderigo.

Emilia

OLDER AND MORE WORLDLY than Desdemona, Emilia develops a close relationship with the young married woman during the course of the story. Despite their different social backgrounds, Emilia and Desdemona have much in common, particularly their troubled marriages. While both women are eager to please their military husbands, Emilia is much more spirited, responding to Iago's vulgar criticisms of Venetian women with, 'You shall not write my praise.'

Shakespeare's characterisation of Emilia creates an interesting foil to Desdemona. Her cynical views on married life contrast with Desdemona's more romantic idealism. Discussing the subject of husbands, Emilia says they 'eat us hungerly, and when they are full,/They belch us'. It is obvious that she has an unhappy relationship with Iago, who rarely, if ever, shows her any affection. Yet she remains loyal to him until she discovers the true extent of his treachery.

For the most part, Emilia is desperately seeking some appreciation from her husband, openly admitting, 'I nothing but to please his fantasy.' But she remains disappointed, even when she presents Iago with Desdemona's special handkerchief. He snatches it from her, saying 'leave me'. Later on, it seems as if Emilia has been thinking about Iago's hunger for power and wishes she could gratify it. At one stage, she asks her mistress, 'who would not make her husband a cuckold to make him a monarch? I should venture purgatory for it'.

As Desdemona's lady-in-waiting, her one dishonest act of stealing the handkerchief turns out to have devastating consequences. This is what convinces Othello that Desdemona is guilty of infidelity, so Emilia's seemingly harmless theft contributes greatly to the final tragedy.

Throughout the second half of the drama, Emilia plays a more significant role by supporting the increasingly submissive Desdemona. She repeatedly defends her mistress's honour, vowing to lay down her own soul 'to wager she is honest'. Although she is deceived by Iago, Emilia comes close to understanding Othello's obsessive jealousy and realises that 'The Moor's abused by some most villainous knave'.

In the play's final scene, she courageously exposes her husband's evil deception and confirms Desdemona's innocence: 'she was chaste, she loved thee, cruel Moor'. Emilia's angry condemnation of Othello ('such a fool') is likely to reflect the feelings of most audiences. However, although her dying words seem to reflect her basic honesty – 'So come my soul to bliss, as I speak true' – it has been suggested that Emilia might have acted earlier to save Desdemona. She herself hints at this when she comments on Iago's evil behaviour: 'I think I smell it; O villainy!/I thought so then – I'll kill myself for grief'.

Nevertheless, there is no denying Emilia's sense of outrage when she finally confronts Othello and defies Iago. Whether or not she can be taken altogether seriously as a reliable judge of character is less certain. Yet she is essentially loyal to her mistress and eventually sacrifices her own life to clear Desdemona's good name. To a large extent, Emilia is a woman of her time who tries hard to make the most of life in a man's world. She is a genuinely engaging character whose good-humoured nature adds vitality to the play. It is also an interesting irony that Iago, who is so good at controlling most people's behaviour, underestimates the one person he should have known best.

Brabantio

Brabantio is defined by the twin roles of respectable Venetian senator and dutiful father to Desdemona. He is highly regarded by his fellow senators – and also by himself. The Duke admits to relying on his 'counsel' in moments of political crisis. His relationship with Desdemona is not as clear-cut, however, and the elopement with Othello raises interesting questions about how well Brabantio knows her.

During Elizabethan times, fathers often arranged marriages for their daughters. Brabantio seems to have been more liberal, however, allowing Desdemona to reject various suitors from 'The wealthy curled darlings of our nation'. Having always considered his only daughter as a shy, nervous person, 'A maiden never bold', Brabantio is embarrassed and outraged to learn that she has deceived him by secretly marrying outside of her race. Her shameful behaviour is simply unacceptable to him and he describes it as a 'gross revolt'.

He reacts emotionally to the scandal, immediately blaming the 'foul thief' Othello for stealing his 'jewel' and quickly lapsing into self-pity ('Who would be a father?') and selfish anger ('I had rather to adopt a child than get it'). While it is possible to have some sympathy for the deceived father, Brabantio's racist insults about Othello ('such a thing') only highlight his hypocrisy. According to Othello, Brabantio had been quite welcoming and friendly towards him before the elopement occurred.

Brabantio's prejudiced views lead to accusations of witchcraft ('foul charms') against the Moor. For the proud senator, interracial marriage is 'Against all rules of nature'. His hysterical outburst is in sharp contrast to Othello's controlled explanation of falling in love with Desdemona. Yet although he misjudges his daughter and treats her unkindly, Brabantio is the first person to foreshadow the awful tragedy which awaits the newlyweds: 'She has deceived her father, and may thee'.

Brabantio is an ambiguous character whose fatherly feelings are thrown into turmoil by Desdemona's unacceptable marriage. He is both a victim of unfortunate circumstances and the product of a patriarchal era. Like others in the play, he is blinded by appearances, failing to recognise his daughter's true nature and unable to accept Othello as an equal.

Bianca

Like Desdemona and Emilia, Bianca is abused by the male characters in the play. She is largely defined by her profession as a courtesan, although this is never explicitly stated. Critics disagree on whether or not she is a prostitute, although Cassio describes himself as her 'customer'. Bianca's love for Cassio is not in doubt, however, and she always behaves affectionately towards him. Unfortunately, he does not take her very seriously and she fares badly as his mistress.

As a courtesan in Cyprus, Bianca is seen as a promiscuous and dishonest woman. However, she challenges such expectations, particularly in the final scene, where she is treated viciously by Iago to divert attention from himself. But she shows true spirit, defending herself against his accusations of treachery: 'I am no strumpet; but of life as honest/As you that thus abuse me.' All through the play, Shakespeare uses Bianca as a foil to the chaste Desdemona. However, in his vengeful jealousy, Othello mirrors Iago's misogyny, eventually seeing no difference between the two women.

Bianca also shares many similarities with Othello. They are both outsiders who are paid for their services. The two of them become extremely jealous about their respective lovers, mainly because of Desdemona's special handkerchief. But Bianca reacts much more generously and invites Cassio to explain himself: 'you'll come to supper to-night'.

Somewhat ironically, despite her low status and vulnerability, Bianca is the only female character to survive. She is primarily defined by her relationships with men and must work hard to maintain whatever rights she can establish as Cassio's mistress. However, her sincere feelings for her lover and her efforts to survive in a predominately patriarchal society usually make her a sympathetic figure for modern audiences.

Shakespeare's Themes

Themes are the basic ideas or issues that are central to the story. Shakespeare explores many fascinating subjects in *Othello*. Perhaps the most obvious themes are revenge and jealousy. There are many others, including race, gender, deception, love, identity, conflict, judgement, tragedy, and appearance and reality. All of these major themes overlap and cannot be dealt with in isolation.

Jealousy

Many characters in *Othello* experience jealousy, although none of them has any real cause. Nonetheless, jealousy is a powerfully destructive force that is central to much of the play's action. Shakespeare presents jealousy as an overwhelmingly negative and all-consuming compulsion. Both Iago and Othello are eaten up with jealous feelings that they cannot control. Even minor characters, such as Roderigo and Bianca, are also affected adversely by envy. However, audiences are most likely to remember this great tragedy for the protagonist's own rapid descent into an obsessive jealousy that all too quickly overpowers his potential for greatness.

Iago's jealous feelings towards Cassio (who has been promoted to Othello's lieutenant) clearly undermines his ego and encourages him to take revenge. Iago reveals this deep sense of envious resentment from the start: 'I know my price, I am worth no worse a place'. He is furious that career success appears to be based on favouritism and complains that 'Preferment goes by letter and affection'. As Othello's 'ancient', the relatively low-ranking ensign is determined to regain what he believes to be his rightful status by plotting against the 'great arithmetician', Cassio.

However, his jealous hatred is not only professional; he despises the young lieutenant's 'daily beauty' and boyish charm. The embittered ensign is also suspicious that his wife, Emilia, and Cassio might be lovers. Such sexual jealousy – which is directly related to feelings of masculine insecurity – provides the idea for Iago's eventual plan to destroy Othello.

Ironically, the Moor's compulsive jealousy is as extreme as his initial devotion to Desdemona. In Act 3, Scene 3 (the play's crucial turning point), Othello admits his deep-rooted insecurities about age and racial background. He quickly loses his capacity for rational behaviour and is prepared to accept the handkerchief as proof of his wife's infidelity. Caught between frustrated anger and self-pitying shame, the military side to his personality takes over and he sees Desdemona as the enemy he must destroy. Like Iago, he has lost something that is important to him. The resulting resentment transforms both men into vengeful killers.

Othello's increasingly vulgar language reflects his loss of judgement. Abrupt outbursts – 'I'll tear her all to pieces' – illustrate his anger and desperation. Iago has always associated jealousy with poison ('pestilence') and observes that the Moor is 'eaten up with passion'. It is the ensign who pretends to warn Othello of 'the green-eyed monster which doth mock/The meat it feeds on'. Shakespeare uses disturbing, hellish imagery to suggest the natural effects of jealousy. In his half-deranged state, Othello becomes obsessed with blood revenge: 'Arise, black vengeance, from the hollow cell'. The playwright develops the metaphor of jealousy as a monster that feeds on itself. In a sense, Iago personifies this consuming force, delighting in mocking his unfortunate victims. Emilia also describes jealousy as a devouring 'monster/Begot upon itself'.

Critics continue to disagree about the protagonist's final assessment of himself as 'one not easily jealous'. It can be argued that the Moor's sexual jealousy emerges from excessive affection and that he was a man who 'loved not wisely but too well'. At the end of the play, Othello himself claims that Iago created such extraordinary circumstances that it was impossible to avoid becoming jealous. This view is supported by the fact that Othello defended his wife's honour for some time, trusting Desdemona, who 'had eyes, and chose me'. He also demanded 'ocular proof' of her guilt.

However, the Moor's defence that he was 'Perplexed in the extreme' can also be challenged. Iago's apparent evidence, particularly the report about Cassio's alleged dream, is not exactly credible. That such insubstantial evidence could convince a loving husband of his wife's betrayal highlights just how powerful and irrational jealousy can be.

Unlike Bianca, who allowed her lover to explain how he found Desdemona's handkerchief, Othello chose a very different response and presumed that his wife was unfaithful without giving her a chance to redeem herself.

Shakespeare's themes are all closely interlinked and cannot be studied effectively in isolation. The play's complex characters and the prevailing culture of Elizabethan times must always be considered. In *Othello*, the playwright has presented us with a terrifyingly evil force that is at the heart of this unhappy story. Jealousy corrupts love and honour, transforming the tragic hero into a self-centred murderer. Along the way, many others are victims of this wildly destructive force, which is repeatedly and aptly described as a 'monster'.

Race

Since the earliest productions of *Othello*, critics have differed over Shakespeare's presentation of the protagonist. Although Othello's actual race and colour are never precisely defined, there is broad consensus that the playwright introduced a black hero to address the idea of difference and explore the experience of the outsider in a white patriarchal society. In Elizabethan drama, black characters were usually typecast as villainous, reflecting the racial prejudice that was prevalent in European society at the time.

This negative view of black people is particularly evident at the beginning of the play, when Iago fuels Brabantio's overtly racist opposition to Desdemona's elopement with Othello. Interracial marriage is said to be 'Against all rules of nature'. Bestial images of the 'lascivious' Moor as 'a Barbary horse' and 'an old black ram' depict Othello as a savage creature. Brabantio refers to his son-in-law as a 'thing', and there are recurring references to evil and witchcraft. To Iago, Roderigo and Brabantio, of course, the Moor's colour offers a basis for expressing their personal hatred of Othello. Ironically, such prejudice is likely to make audiences feel sympathy for the hero.

For the most part, Othello himself uses his race positively. In his earliest comments, he seems proud, almost boastful at times, about his exotic origins: 'I fetch my life and being/From men of royal siege'. His eloquent speech to the senators stresses the fact that his unique Moorish history attracted Desdemona, who acted freely in selecting a husband for herself: 'she had eyes, and chose me'. Nevertheless, by commenting on the 'Cannibals that each other eat', Othello appears to distance himself from the uncivilised realities of his past.

At any rate, Desdemona has no reservations about race or colour. She defends her husband at every opportunity, saying, 'I saw Othello's visage in his mind'. Her attitude is exceptional, of course, and some would say it typifies her blind – and possibly naive – love. Almost every other character in the play sees Othello's race as problematic. On some occasions, of course, the hero's colour is less important, especially when Venice itself is under threat. The Moor seems be held in high esteem as a 'valiant' military leader, recognised by the Duke as 'more fair than black'. Whether this is a genuine compliment or an expedient attempt to encourage the general to concentrate on his military responsibilities is uncertain. However, the comment is yet another reminder that in Shakespeare's time, fairness and whiteness equate with goodness.

It could be argued that under Iago's increasing influence, Othello eventually displays some of the negative racial characteristics he was first accused of, such as his superstitions about Desdemona's handkerchief and his uncontrollable violence. Othello clearly turns to 'savage madness', such as when he strikes his terrified wife in public. Of course, the extent to which the white devil Iago brings out the black devil in the Moor is highly debatable. Iago's persuasive expertise infects Othello's view of himself, and towards the end of Act 3, Scene 3, he is horrified to think of Desdemona's name as 'begrimed and black/As mine own face'.

Negative references to the protagonist's race are present throughout the story. It is interesting that in the moments leading up to the murder, Othello focuses on his sleeping wife's colour, seemingly obsessed with the 'monumental alabaster' of her skin, once again challenging his own preconception of whiteness representing goodness. It is not surprising that some critics define the hero's tragic character in terms of his essentially untenable position as a black mercenary who is hopelessly unsuited to a hostile culture. Furthermore, in challenging the established social conventions of Venice, the Moor's controversial marriage to an upper-class white woman is guaranteed to end in disaster.

When she confronts Othello after the murder, Emilia compares him to his wife, emphasising the moral divide between the couple: 'the more angel she,/And you the blacker devil'. Whether or not the tragic hero ever reaches an understanding of the part played by race in his downfall is never altogether clear. Ultimately, audiences will probably see Othello's colour in relation to his exclusion from white Venice. As a victim of racism, he highlights the culture of Elizabethan times.

Male–Female Relationships

Shakespeare's audience would have sympathised with Brabantio's outraged reaction to Desdemona's elopement. Elizabethan society was largely patriarchal. Men were generally considered to be physically, intellectually and socially superior to women. Daughters depended on their fathers, who had responsibility for finding them appropriate husbands. Brabantio expects complete 'obedience' and Desdemona recognises that she has a 'divided duty' to both her father and Othello. Such tensions resulting from gender, sexuality and male–female relationships are central to much of the conflict in the play.

The 'masculine world' of *Othello* is dominated by men of action who put great emphasis on military honour. It is Othello's daring heroism that first attracts Desdemona. The 'warlike Moor' defines himself by his

'dearest action' and views his wife's infidelity as a failure of his masculinity. Iago boasts of being a seasoned soldier, unlike the inexperienced Cassio, whom he describes as a 'spinster'. But the young lieutenant is also obsessed with his professional reputation and is devastated at losing his position as Othello's second in command. When the male characters find that their honour and ego are being challenged, their usual reaction is to revert to violence.

Initially, Desdemona challenges patriarchal values by asserting her independence in choosing her own husband and defying her father by secretly marrying someone from outside her own race. She is also rebellious in her desire to accompany her husband to Cyprus. Her unconventional behaviour clearly highlights how men try to control women throughout the play. Brabantio loses his 'jewel'. Iago refers to Desdemona as if she were part of her father's possessions, similar to his 'house' and 'bags'. In his jealous rages, Othello constantly reasserts his control over her, both physically and verbally: 'we can call these delicate creatures ours,/And not their appetites'.

During the 16th century, Venice was known not only for its wealth and sophistication, but also for its loose morals. There were many courtesans in the city and Venetian women were often seen as promiscuous, something that Iago uses effectively to suggest that Desdemona is unfaithful. Only half-jokingly does he accuse all women of being prostitutes who 'go to bed to work'. As a courtesan, Bianca is presumed to be untrustworthy, but she challenges these assumptions by being much more honest than her lover Cassio, who treats her with little respect, seeing her as a mere 'bauble'. Emilia also struggles to gain any happiness in her loveless marriage. In questioning the double standards about infidelity for men and women, she blames husbands who 'change us for others' while criticising wives who might be adulterous.

Emilia's pragmatic attitude to men is understandable, considering the years she has spent being controlled by Iago. Her calamitous decision to steal Desdemona's handkerchief results from fear of displeasing him, even though this conflicts with her loyalty to her mistress. Like the other female characters who try to assert themselves, Emilia is viewed as a threat simply because she dares to challenge the balance of power in a predominantly masculine hierarchy. To some extent, Iago is also threatened by Desdemona (the general's 'general'), who now has more power over Othello than he can bear.

Nevertheless, despite Iago's misogyny, Shakespeare does not present all female sexuality in a negative light. Bianca expresses genuine feelings for Cassio and is determined to defy their divisive social backgrounds. Initially, Othello also loves Desdemona very dearly. However, his apparent devotion to his 'soul's joy' is a reminder that women were regarded as either chaste or promiscuous.

For the most part, however, Shakespeare supports the traditional Elizabethan stereotypes about gender throughout the play. Among the many ironies is the fact that while Othello and Iago see themselves as powerful men, both are subject to personal insecurities and petty jealousies that define their severely dysfunctional marriages. Overall, there are no happy relationships between men and women in this tragic story, which must always be seen within its destructive patriarchal context.

However, modern audiences are still left with much to consider about gender and sexuality in *Othello*. Some critics view Desdemona as passive and unconvincing, while others admire her independent spirit. In the end, we are left to consider a fascinating world where public honour is very highly rated and to make up our own minds about the many issues explored through same-sex and male–female relationships.

Style

Irony

- Irony is the use of words to convey a meaning that is the opposite of its literal meaning.

- Irony usually signals a difference between appearances and reality.

- Irony involves collusion between the playwright and the audience. We know something that the characters on stage don't.

The purpose of irony is to create suspense. Audiences imagine what will happen next. Irony also adds interest as we begin to consider, 'I wonder if...?' Shakespeare uses three types of irony in *Othello*: situational irony, verbal irony and dramatic irony.

Situational irony is when the result of an action is different from what was expected or considered appropriate. In the play, a clear case of situational irony occurs when Cassio not only survives the best efforts of his rival Iago to have him murdered, but he is also reinstated as lieutenant. Ironically, it is Iago's reputation that is destroyed. Equally ironic is the scene when Desdemona kneels before a secretly delighted Iago and pitifully begs for help from the man who is poisoning her husband's mind against her, asking, 'What shall I do to win my lord again?'

Another case of situational irony is that both wives, Desdemona and Emilia, are murdered even though they are innocent. Iago has used his wife as an instrument against Desdemona. He took the 'lost' handkerchief from Emilia, who does not know that he intends to use it to destroy the reputation of the 'chaste' Desdemona. Later on, Emilia is so shocked when she is informed of this by Othello that she keeps repeating 'My husband' in utter disbelief. The purpose of situational irony is to make the storyline more fascinating and absorbing.

In tragedy, events often turn out to have the opposite result of what was originally intended. Desdemona is murdered by her husband on their marital bed. For the audience, this heightens the sense of misfortune, as reality seems to conspire against the characters.

Verbal irony is when the opposite of what is spoken turns out to be true. Othello has absolute trust in Iago. He refers many times to 'honest Iago'. He calls him 'brave Iago, honest and just' and he even considers him 'wise'. The Moor asks for advice about his doubts in his changing relationship with Desdemona, fearing that Iago is so good that he won't want to tell him the horrible truth, that his 'honesty and love doth mince this matter'.

Yet the audience is aware that Iago is inflaming Othello's suspicions and systematically dismantling his relationship with Desdemona for his own diabolical ends. Iago's duplicity creates verbal irony. He lies

brazenly. He even tells Othello, 'My lord, you know I love you', while the audience has already been informed that 'I hate the Moor'. He issues a bogus warning to Othello, which turns out to be tragically true: 'O, beware, my lord, of jealousy'. One purpose of verbal irony can be to add humour, often black humour, to appal and to terrify, as a character believes what is not true and doubts what is while the audience sits in the privileged position of being fully aware of the truth.

Dramatic irony captivates the audience by creating feelings of sympathy, anger, awe and disbelief. The audience experiences the story through the emotions stirred in them by the skill of the playwright. These aroused feelings are not accidental, but created on purpose by Shakespeare when he places certain events together or when he explains a character's thoughts and emotions.

Iago continually communicates with the audience through his soliloquies: 'This is the night/That either makes me or fordoes me quite'. This is how the audience knows more than the characters on stage. Therefore, their reaction to a character has been shaped into viewing them with sympathy or disgust. They certainly agree with Emilia when she calls Othello a 'dull Moor'. The audience is always aware that Desdemona is innocent, Iago is crooked and that Othello knows neither of these facts. Indeed, he believes Iago to be 'honest' and Desdemona to be a 'strumpet'. This is a powerful irony.

The audience is in a superior position during the highly-charged scene where Othello is tricked into watching Iago and Cassio talking about Bianca. Iago has already signalled what will happen when the suspicious Moor observes Cassio boasting about his success with women: 'As he shall smile, Othello shall go mad'. Inevitably, when the lieutenant speaks disparagingly about his mistress, the audience immediately knows that Othello thinks Desdemona is being discussed. Iago's secret delight is also evident. By presenting a multifaceted view of the event, Shakespeare enhances the experience of the story for the audience.

All of the characters who are betrayed and destroyed by Iago – Othello, Desdemona, Emilia, Roderigo – trust him implicitly. Roderigo believes Iago is his friend – 'I am for you' – when he hands over a fortune in jewels for him to pass on to Desdemona in his desperate quest to woo her. Yet Iago contemptuously regards Roderigo as a 'fool' whom he has made his 'purse'. Iago is the consummate actor. He is only true with the audience; all the rest of the time he is 'seeming so'.

The bitter ensign masterminds situations ingeniously, such as when he instructs Roderigo, 'Here, stand behind this bulk; straight will he come'. Then when the scuffle breaks out between Roderigo and Cassio, he emerges as if only discovering the fracas, asking, 'Whose noise is this that cries on murder?' He doesn't care about who is killed – both would suit, as then he would not be discovered. Iago has many selves, acting as friend and adviser to Roderigo, but also as his betrayer and murderer.

However, the greatest irony of the play is that Othello eventually learns the truth that Desdemona is blameless – 'Cold, cold, my girl!/Ever like thy chastity' – but only after murdering her. He cannot comprehend why Iago has manipulated him into believing otherwise: 'Why he hath thus ensnared my soul and body?' But the audience has been aware all along of Iago's seething resentment at being passed over for promotion and because he believes Othello has been Emilia's lover. We know the true Iago – 'I am not what I am' – who chillingly declares to Roderigo, 'In following him, I follow but myself ... for my peculiar end'. Thus, the audience is forced into a position of feeling intimately connected with Iago's villainy.

Irony plays an important role in *Othello*. For example, the Moor is a good man who commits a heinous crime. Meanwhile, the evil Iago masquerades as an honourable man throughout. Irony is a powerful technique that takes advantage of the difference between what is said and what is meant, or what is supposed to happen and what actually happens. It increases the audience's involvement in the play and heightens the sense of tragedy.

Imagery

The main function of imagery in *Othello* is to aid our understanding of characters and events as well as establishing the dramatic atmosphere in the play. The antagonist, Iago, is defined through many different images, such as the use of poison, to show his true sadistic nature.

Othello's character is also shaped by imagery, such as the animalistic, water, light and darkness, war and recurring references to black and white. The characterisation of women is heavily influenced by images that emphasise the patriarchal attitudes of Shakespeare's time.

The playwright defines the power of jealousy by memorable images, including Desdemona's handkerchief, the green-eyed monster and cuckolding images that are prominent throughout the story.

Patterns of imagery are closely interwoven and enhance our awareness of major themes in the play. Some of the key images are discussed below.

Poison

The satanic character of Iago is depicted through his sadistic plans to 'poison [Brabantio's] delight' with coarse gossip about Desdemona's sexuality. Later on, outlining his malicious intent to make the Moor jealous, he vows to 'pour this pestilence into [Othello's] ear'. Figurative language like this continues throughout the play with lines such as 'The Moor already changes with my poison' and 'Not poppy, nor mandragora,/Nor all the drowsy syrups of the world,/Shall ever medicine thee to that sweet sleep/Which thou owedst yesterday'.

References to poison are appropriate to Iago's venomous character, whose natural behaviour is lethal. In Act 3, Scene 3, he informs us that 'Dangerous conceits are, in their natures, poisons'. When Othello is considering how he will kill his young wife, Iago advises him, 'Do it not with poison, strangle her in her bed'. The audience will, of course, be only too aware of the irony that the real poisoner has already contaminated the Moor's mind.

Hell

Iago is invariably identified with diabolical imagery. Lodovico calls him a 'viper', comparing the ensign's malicious nature to a dangerous snake. The Machiavellian persona of Iago is also suggested through his own numerous references to the Devil. He ends his Act 1, Scene 3 soliloquy planning Othello's downfall with the chilling promise, 'Hell and night/Must bring this monstrous birth to the world's light.' There is never any doubt that Iago delights in the 'Divinity of hell'.

Othello's language becomes equally preoccupied with Hell and damnation. In his jealous rage, he shouts 'Fire and brimstone!' and calls Desdemona 'Devil' when he strikes her in public. Frustrated beyond reason, he turns on Emilia, saying that she 'keeps the gate of hell' for his cheating wife. Ironically, when the truth eventually emerges, it is Emilia who echoes these words, describing the Moor as 'the blacker devil' who has killed his 'angel' wife.

Shakespeare makes effective use of contrasting heavenly imagery to highlight Desdemona's innocence. Her essential goodness is reflected in Cassio's description of her as 'the divine Desdemona' and Roderigo also idolises her 'most blessed/condition'.

In his final moments of despair, a shocked Othello tries to make sense of Iago's evil and concludes, 'If that thou be'st a devil, I cannot kill thee'. The Moor's overwhelming sense of defeat is clearly evident at the end of this tragic story when he can only regret his tragic association with the 'demi-devil' and 'hellish villain' who still refuses to explain his motives.

Animals

Othello is strongly characterised by references to animals. Iago routinely expresses his loathing of the Moor in racist language, calling him a 'Barbary horse' and 'an old black ram'. Such references reflect the prejudice both of characters in the play and of Shakespeare's contemporary audience. Iago also debases human relationships to their lowest physical level, depicting Desdemona and Cassio's friendship in animalistic terms, 'as hot as monkeys'.

In Act 1, Scene 3, the cynical ensign tells Roderigo, 'Ere I would say, I/would drown myself for the love of a guinea-hen, I/would change my humanity with a baboon'. His language frequently suggests his warped hatred for all his victims. Iago is convinced that Othello will be 'led by the nose/As asses are' and predicts that 'With as little a web as this I will ensnare as great a fly as Cassio'.

As Othello becomes more and more influenced by his ensign, his own language deteriorates, revealing his deep personal misery: 'I had rather be a toad', he cries, 'Than keep a corner in the thing I love/For others' uses'. After publicly humiliating Desdemona, he retreats in rage, shouting, 'Goats and monkey!' By the start of Act 4, the once noble general has been reduced to a 'horned' 'beast'.

Other references to animals convey a sense that the laws of nature, rather than those of society, are the primary forces governing the lives of characters. In the final scene, for example, Emilia says that she will 'play the swan./And die in music'. Once again, the playwright is imaginatively using evocative poetic language to create a poignant atmosphere and heighten the tragic nature of Emilia's death.

Sea and Storms

Not all of the play's imagery is associated with tragedy. The initial love between Othello and Desdemona reflects the calm before the storm. The Moor pledges his love for 'the gentle Desdemona' and swears that he 'would not my unhoused free condition/Put into circumscription and confine/For the sea's worth'.

As the story unfolds, however, the sea motif is increasingly used to signify danger and to foreshadow disaster. In Act 2, storm and flood imagery represents Iago's deceitful plans and Othello's impending demise. The main characters arrive in Cyprus during a great storm, clearly symbolising the disorder that is about to engulf Othello's mind.

The disharmony that affects the Moor's marriage soon leads Othello to take his revenge: 'Like to the Pontic sea,/Whose icy current and compulsive course/Never feels retiring ebb'. Again, the imagery suggests a loveless relationship that is already doomed. Just before he kills himself, Othello reflects on his 'journey's end' and recognises the agonising moment as the 'very sea-mark of my utmost sail'. This final glimpse of his former heroism is all the more tragic as we witness the extent of his downfall and the unbearable loss of his devoted wife.

Sample Essays

Sample Essay 1

'Shakespeare's play *Othello* presents audiences with an intriguing world of prejudice and jealousy.' Discuss this statement, supporting your answer with suitable reference to the text.

1   Although several themes drive the action of *Othello*, I believe that audiences are primarily fascinated by the widespread effects of prejudice in this absorbing drama. Central to Shakespeare's tragic story is the envious Iago whose intense hatred of Othello transforms this once loving husband and turns him against his devoted Desdemona.

2   As the play opens, we are drawn into the city of Venice. A predominantly white society which the audience would expect to be sophisticated. However, almost immediately, we are faced with unpleasant characters who are filled with bitter resentments. Roderigo has failed to attract Desdemona and is clearly jealous of her marriage to Othello. Iago despises Othello and cannot hide his staunch hostility towards the army general who has promoted the inexperienced Cassio – 'a great arithmetician' – over Iago himself to the more prestigious position of lieutenant. Because of this, he plans to use Othello's insecurities to make him believe that his wife Desdemona is unfaithful. For the audience, the scene is ready for inevitable tragedy.

3   In his anger, Iago makes no secret of his prejudice, referring to Othello as 'the thick-lips' and 'an old black ram'. In most cases, the abuse depicts Othello in animal terms. More interestingly, as the story develops, Othello himself seems to hold this same prejudiced view. On a number of occasions he

describes himself in similarly unflattering racial terms. Ironically, his inhuman treatment of Desdemona will eventually symbolise this irrational image.

4   Although Iago's anger may have started on a professional level, his contempt quickly deteriorates to obvious racism. This causes a recurring paradox in the play. While Othello is an extremely powerful man in a political and military context, his race makes him inferior. Especially in white Venetian society. As Othello becomes obsessed with Cassio, the inventive Iago can confidently trick his master and manipulate him on a consistent basis. When I watched a performance of the play earlier this year, I was very impressed by Act 3, Scene 3, the so-called 'jealousy scene' where Iago and Othello play an explosive cat-and-mouse game.

5   What was most evident was the tense balance between truth and lies. One wrong move from Iago and Othello might easily have murdered him. Iago poisons the already suspicious Othello by seeming to defend Cassio with vague comments until Othello loses patience: 'thou echo'st me,/As if there was some monster in thy thought'. Slowly but surely, Iago begins to control the distraught Othello, until he judges that it is safe to advise him against losing his 'good name' and warn him to beware of jealousy, 'the green-eyed monster'. What I think the audience found interesting was the changing body language between the two characters. As Iago began to control Othello, he circled him on stage. It seemed as though the hypocritical Iago was actually growing in height as he increasingly towered over his pitiful enemy. Iago took more chances then, knowing that Othello would believe almost anything about his wife. This compelling exchange was typical of many scenes where the audience is involved in the central conflict.

6   Another interesting aspect of the play is the prejudice against women. Iago's misogyny is fairly typical of the way women characters are seen only in sexual terms, and often as dishonest. Cassio never takes Bianca seriously while Iago constantly insults women – 'In Venice they do let heaven see the pranks/ They dare not show their husbands'. His description of Desdemona's elopement is cleverly used to highlight her treachery: 'She has deceived her father and may thee'. Later on, Othello's arrogant killing is conveniently justified to suit his ego: 'Yet she must die, else she'll betray more men'. Ironically, he first idealised his wife. But has quickly become just as convinced that she is no better than Bianca. Behind all this resentment and racism is male insecurity. Roderigo is a pathetic figure. Cassio is decent but weak. Iago's pride ('I know my price') has been wounded. He shows signs of inferiority, unable to accept that he is past his prime and even suspicious of Emilia's faithfulness to him. Othello is also extremely insecure, relying on his past glories and overwhelmed by the thought of being ridiculed in public.

7   I think most audiences will have some sympathy for Emilia who is less naive than Desdemona throughout. Her experience of life with Iago has made her hate all men: 'They are all but stomachs, and we all but food'. Emilia defends Desdemona in life and death: 'she loved thee, cruel Moor'. As the tragedy unfolds, she courageously confronts her husband and condemns Othello's jealous actions. It is in keeping with her character that she resorts to racial stereotyping when she discovers Othello's role in the murder: 'O, the more angel she, and you the blacker devil!'

8   As the play ends, Othello's love is restored, although it is much too late, and some of his nobility returns as well. Audiences must wonder then why Othello takes his own life. Does he delude himself as one 'not easily jealous'? For me, he is a flawed hero, a man who mirrored Iago in many ways. Both of them were more self-interested than honourable. Shakespeare leaves the audience to consider important universal

themes, still relevant to today's society. Did evil jealousy destroy a great tragic hero? Or did Othello eventually adopt the same prejudiced behaviour of which he himself was a victim? Questions about the complexity of human experience are at the heart of this unhappy story, which ultimately comes down to the age-old conflict between good and evil.

(approx. 920 words)

GRADE: A1

P   = 18/18
C   = 16/18
L   = 14/18
M   = 6/6
Total = 54/60

Examiner's Comment

- Well-sustained and focused personal response.
- Very good overall knowledge of the play.
- Interesting points supported with apt reference.
- Impressive exploration of misogyny.
- Some very well-controlled and lively discussion.
- Expression flawed in places.

Sample Essay 2

'The villain Iago fascinates and repels us in the play *Othello* as he contrives clever, complex stratagems.' Discuss this view, supporting your answer with suitable reference to the text.

Marking Scheme Guidelines

Candidates are free to agree and/or disagree with the statement, but they should engage with the terms 'fascinates and repels' and 'clever, complex stratagems', though not necessarily with equal emphasis.

Possible areas of discussion:

- 'Honest Iago' – an intriguing mix of bitterness and revenge.
- His cynical charm fools everyone.
- An inventively treacherous sociopath.
- Skilled manipulator who delights in evil.
- Iago's action and language dominate the play.
- Remains enigmatic to the end.

1   A man who declares unashamedly, 'I am not what I am', cannot fail to captivate not only his poor trusting victims, but also his audience. Iago alienates, disgusts and offends us as he devises plans with skill and subtlety that will wreak havoc on all around him. Yet this example of glittering evil compels rapt attention not only by the audacity of his tricks, but also by the playwright's skilful use of dramatic irony. We know what Iago is up to, we watch as if a slow-motion car crash is taking place in front of us, repelled, yet unable to tear ourselves away.

2   Shakespeare interests his audience in this character by carefully setting up Iago's motivation. He reveals that he hates 'the Moor' because Othello has passed him over for promotion in preference to Michael Cassio. Iago despises him as a theoretician, 'Mere prattle, without practice/Is all his soldiership'. He bitterly comments that 'Preferment goes by letter and affection/And not by the old gradation'. Later he discloses another motive for following Othello to 'serve my turn upon him'. Iago also suspects Othello of being his wife's lover, 'And it is thought abroad that 'twixt my sheets/He's done my office'. He also says he suspects Cassio of doing the same, 'For I fear Cassio with my night-cap too'. Although there is no evidence for these last two suspicions, Iago has set out plausible reasons for complaint, and the scene is set for black revenge.

3   Iago displays a breathtaking cynical and very realistic knowledge of his victims' characters. He accurately sums up Othello as 'loving his own pride and purposes/Horribly stuff'd with epithets of war'. He acknowledges that Desdemona possesses a nature 'so free, so kind, so apt, so blessed' that Othello's 'constant noble loving nature' would make him a 'most dear husband' to her, yet he is prepared to prey on all of them and devise a plan from 'her own goodness' he will 'make the net/That shall enmesh them all'. We watch spellbound and horrified.

4   Carefully feeling his way, deftly adapting to changing circumstances, Iago hatches his devious plans, quickly deciding that he will 'abuse Othello's ear' with the insinuation that Cassio 'is too familiar with his wife'. He gleefully notes that with 'as little a web as this' he 'will ensnare as great a fly as Cassio', because he will use Cassio's trademark gallantry against him, 'I will catch you on your courtesies'. He will use Cassio's weaknesses also, particularly his 'poor and unhappy brains for drinking'. Indeed, he plays Cassio so well that Cassio ends up saying to him, 'You advise me well'.

5   Iago also completely fools Othello, who repeatedly speaks of his honesty, 'A man he is of honesty and trust'. He regards him as of 'exceeding honesty'. Yet all the time we are so aware that this is most decidedly what Iago is not. Shakespeare is using dramatic irony to great effect. We are seeing Iago plot to 'put the Moor/At least into a jealousy so strong/That judgement cannot cure'. He plots to make the Moor, like Cassio, 'thank me, love me and reward me/For making him egregiously an ass'. We are appalled. Persuasive insinuation is used to smear Cassio when Othello and he come across Desdemona and Cassio chatting, 'Ha I like not that'. He ratchets up the 'guilt' by the comment that Cassio has sneaked 'away so guilty-like'. Othello's peace of mind is shot, 'Chaos is come again'. The Moor stumbles into the carefully constructed web asking, 'what didst not like?' Deliciously ironical as always, Iago replies, 'Men should be that they seem'. Shakespeare now has Iago speak the truth to Othello, as he advises him to 'beware, my lord, of jealousy'. We are astounded, because at the same time he is playing on the fact that Othello is an outsider to Venetian society and does not really know Venetian women, 'In Venice they do let heaven see the pranks/They dare not show their husbands'. He cleverly reminds Othello that Desdemona 'did deceive her father' and refused Venetian suitors with 'a will most rank'.

6   Audiences will feel that Iago is a man who is not afraid to act and act swiftly, 'Dull not device by coldness and delay'. He now decides to involve his own wife Emilia as a pawn in his deadly game, 'My wife must move for Cassio to her mistress, I'll set her on'. He decides to produce the 'ocular proof' Othello demands by getting a handkerchief, a gift from Othello to Desdemona during their courtship, stolen and placed in Cassio's lodgings knowing that 'Trifles light as air/Are to the jealous, confirmation strong'. At last, he has Othello 'on the rack'. Triumphantly Iago watches, 'Work on/My medicine work: thus credulous fools are caught'. Even when he has finally been found out by his own wife, he will not give Othello any relief from his pain, 'why he hath thus ensnared my soul and body'. Iago is malicious to the last, 'what you know you know/From this time forth I will never speak word'. Even though Lodovico swears to 'torment him much', we sense that Iago will have this final victory over his enemies.

7   So this 'demi-devil' uncaring at the 'tragic loading of this bed' remains a repulsively fascinating epitome of evil. We, like Othello, 'look down at his feet; but that's a fable'. He has sworn by the two-faced Roman god, Janus, and he has 'set down the pegs that make this music'. Iago has skilfully hypnotised his victims and us with 'his work'.

(approx. 930 words)

GRADE: A1

P   = 18/18
C   = 16/18
L   = 15/18
M   = 6/6
Total = 55/60

Examiner's Comment

- Shows a very good knowledge of the play.
- Clear points supported with detailed reference.
- Wide-ranging and generally controlled discussion.
- Well-sustained and focused response.
- Somewhat over-reliant on quotations.

Sample Essay 3

'Despite the experience of individual suffering in Shakespeare's *Othello*, the essential tragic vision is uplifting.' Discuss this statement, supporting your answer with suitable reference to the text.

1   The classical form of tragedy concerned a great man brought low by a fault in his character, and who after much suffering grows in self-knowledge. The old corrupt order is swept away and a new order is established, so the essential tragic vision is uplifting. However, the women in the story are victims of male ego and cruelty. Suffering dominates the play. Othello, Desdemona, Emilia, Roderigo, Brabantio and Cassio all endure torment. Yet it is not completely clear to me that the concluding tragic vision is entirely uplifting. While Othello eventually realises the truth about Desdemona, his focus is on his own reputation. He states, 'I have done the state some service and they know it'. The new order does not seem secure. Iago, the embodiment of evil, survives. Has evil been truly eradicated? Is Cassio really a strong leader for the future good of Cyprus?

2   Othello is first presented as dignified and noble, he is of 'royal siege'. He handles the bigoted Brabantio well, refusing to be drawn into a public brawl. A brave, intelligent army commander, he knows his worth to the Senate: 'My services which I have done the signiory/Shall out tongue his complaints'. His flaw, insecurity, is exploited with devastating consequences by the cunning Iago, who is furious at being passed over for promotion. Othello knows he is different from the sophisticated Venetians. His skin colour elicits racist comments, 'sooty bosom'. He is seen as a sexual predator by some and one who even engages in witchcraft, 'thou hast enchanted her'. He is deeply worried and desperately desires to be accepted.

3   The Moor suffers dreadfully at the hands of Iago. He admits 'thou hast set me on the rack'. But he must accept some of the blame for his tragic downfall. He rushes to judge. He accepts Iago's insinuations, 'Ha! I like not that'. Perhaps it is his inferiority complex, his insecurity as an outsider that leaves him

vulnerable to being deceived into believing his wife is unfaithful. Within a short space he is calling her a 'lewd minx'. He realises he has squandered his beloved 'occupation' of military life. He is in such anguish that he wants to commit suicide: 'If there be cords, or knives ... I'll not endure it'. Othello demands 'ocular proof' while remaining blind to reality. He has sunk so low that he readily submits to being placed as an eavesdropper by Iago. He is then tormented to the delight of Iago by 'the jeers, the jibes and notable scorns' of Cassio, who gossips about Bianca, while the 'dolt' Othello believes that he is speaking about Desdemona.

4   Yet at the play's conclusion, I do not believe Othello really knows himself. He is a 'fool' who really sank low when he shabbily denied murdering Desdemona to Emilia: 'You heard her say herself, it was not I'. He still insists Desdemona is 'foul' and he clings desperately to the so-called evidence of the handkerchief. 'How came you, Cassio by that handkerchief/That was my wife's?' Rather than being fully focused on his unjust murder of an innocent woman, he is very concerned with how he will be regarded in Venice. He asks, 'Speak of me as I am'. Then he proceeds to outline how he wishes to be reported on, excusing himself as one who 'loved not wisely but too well'. So, in my opinion, he only partially gains self-knowledge. He does not act in a convincingly noble way. This is why I do not find the ending of the play fully inspiring.

5   Neither is Iago fully defeated. He frustrates both audience and the remaining characters by refusing to explain his actions. Instead, he sneers, 'what you know, you know'. So evil is left like a malingering dark presence over the new rule that has just been established in Cyprus. To me, there is a sense of weariness rather than hope in the last lines of the play as Lodovico states, 'and to the state/This heavy act with heavy heart relate'. A terrible price has been paid for the restoration of order, 'the tragic loading of the bed' heaped with three dead bodies, which 'poisons sight'. Yet evil has not been fully eradicated.

6   I am not convinced that Cassio has the strength of character to be an effective leader in Cyprus. He has been criticised by Iago, who is a very shrewd judge. Cassio has been described as 'a theoretician'. He is a 'bookish theoric'. Although he has refined Venetian manners, 'light behaviour', he was unreliable when given charge of the watch. He is very easily led and has a weakness for being unreliable: 'I have very poor and unhappy brains for drink'.

7   When Cassio has been dismissed by Othello, his first concern is his lost reputation, 'the immortal part of myself', rather than the crime he committed. He also is very impatient, wanting to be reinstated immediately, unwilling to wait for time to pass. He puts incredible pressure on Desdemona to plead his case with Othello. Cassio does not confront Othello himself. Instead he chooses to run away when he sees Othello approach. He gives Iago the perfect opportunity to remark that he has gone 'away so guilty-like'. I do not feel the new order is assured, that evil has been successfully squashed nor that the central character, Othello, has grown sufficiently in self-knowledge.

8   There is much heartbreaking individual suffering in *Othello*, but I cannot agree that the tragic vision is ennobling and empowering. I certainly did not feel uplifted.

(approx. 925 words)

GRADE: A2

P = 16/18
C = 15/18
L = 16/18
M = 6/6
Total = 53/60

Examiner's Comment

- Some clearly focused discussion points.
- Effective use of apt supportive reference.
- Shows a close understanding of the play.
- Good personal engagement.
- Impressive expression overall.

Sample Essay 4

'Shakespeare's play *Othello* is primarily concerned with examining the weakness of human love.' Discuss this statement, supporting your answer with suitable reference to the text.

Marking Scheme Guidelines

Candidates are free to agree and/or disagree with the statement, but they should engage with the term 'weakness of human love'.

Possible areas of discussion:

- Fragility/strength of family love.
- Joys/dangers of romance and passion.
- Triumph/failure of idealistic love.
- Platonic/unrequited love.
- Contrasting male–female friendships.
- Love as a powerful force for good/evil.

1   In *Othello*, Shakespeare dares to show audiences that human love is imperfect, flimsy and vulnerable to attack. He first presents familial love, which evaporates through deceit and bigotry. Passionate love is shown bursting into jealousy and hate. Pure, ideal love disintegrates under the force of evil of this world. Friendship does not hold because of duplicity and self-interest. Love is a survival instinct, a function to

keep human beings together against menaces. Iago, the evil but great source of truth remarks, 'We have reason to cool our raging motions'.

2   At the start of the play, familial love is portrayed in the story involving Brabantio, a Venetian senator, who is awoken to the vulgar comments of 'an old black ram/Is tupping your white ewe'. This refers to the secret elopement of Desdemona, Brabantio's daughter, with Othello, a Moor. The duped father is heartbroken, 'Who would be a father!' It seems so unnatural to him. He thinks she has to have been 'abused, stolen from me and corrupted/By spells and medicines bought of mountebanks'. He cannot understand how she could 'fall in love with what she feared to look on', feeling it is 'Against all the rules of nature'. He thinks she will be dishonoured, 'to incur the general mock'. I think Shakespeare has touched on an issue which resonates today for those who have moved to new countries, yet do not wish their daughters to marry outside their culture and race.

3   Desdemona answers these charges in front of the Senate. She says she has a duty to more than one man, 'My noble father/I do perceive a divided duty'. She acknowledges her debt to him, 'you are the lord of duty' but she has another commitment, But here's my husband'. Brabantio cuts the ties of familial affection forcefully, 'I have done'. He would 'rather adopt a child than get it'. To later chilling effect in the story, he warns Othello, 'She has deceived her father and may thee'. There is no further communication between father and daughter, only a sad epilogue when it is revealed to Othello that Brabantio had died, 'Thy match was mortal to him'. Desdemona's deception of her father had catastrophic consequences.

4   Sexual love is explored both in the Othello and Desdemona storyline. As well as that of Cassio and Bianca. In a blaze of passion, the two lovers elope. How did their love begin? Brabantio had invited Othello to their home and as the Moor told his strange stories of his military exploits, 'She wished she had not heard it, yet she wished/That heaven had made her such a man'. Desdemona also speaks of her strong feelings, 'That I did love the Moor to live with him'. Her passion for Othello is such that she refuses to be left behind. Yet, these two people have known each other a short time, they do not share a common background. Or culture. Nor are they the same age. Is Shakespeare suggesting that their careless desire is a terrible mistake?

5   Yet the audience still hopes that love will triumph. Othello lovingly calls Desdemona 'gentle love', 'sweeting'. But they are pulled apart not only by the cunning schemes of Iago, but also because Othello cannot really believe that Desdemona has accepted him even though he declares that 'she had eyes and chose me'. He is riddled with insecurity, 'Haply for I am black and have not those soft parts of conversation that chamberers have, or for I am declined into the vale of years'. So Iago works his evil magic reminding Othello that white Venetian women 'let heaven see the pranks/They dare not show their husbands'. From the start, the playwright is challenging the view that love is a positive force.

6   In Cyprus, love soon turns to hate and jealousy. Othello declares 'She's gone, I am abused'. Now she is called a 'fair devil'. Chaos indeed has come as Othello plots the death of Desdemona, 'let her rot ... my heart is turned to stone'. He becomes concerned with justice, agreeing with Iago to strangle her 'even in the bed she hath contaminated'. He sees himself as a minister of justice, although he has judged and condemned his wife without allowing her any right of reply, basing his case on gossip. Also on the flimsy evidence of a handkerchief. 'Yet she must die, else she'll betray more men'. Shakespeare's tragedy centres on the idea that passionate love consumes itself.

7 Throughout the play, married love is seen almost as a war between the sexes, as Emilia and Iago battle it out, 'Then let them use us well; else let them know,/The ills we do, their ills instruct us so'. But Emilia proves the only true friend loyally defending Desdemona, 'O thou dull Moor! that handkerchief/I found by fortune and did give my husband'. She will not be silenced, defying all the men around her, '"Twill out, 'twill out: I hold my peace, sir? No!' But she is killed for her loyalty, proving that genuine friendship and human love cannot survive this imperfect world.

8 As the play concludes, we come to the same conclusion as Othello – 'the pity of it' – that love which should conquer all is tripped up by small-minded human imperfections of deceit, self-interest, jealousy and hate. Love is eternal. But it can be tragic whether it is familial affection, passionate love or a platonic relationship. Shakespeare's tragedy makes it clear that being 'great of heart' does not protect a person against the weakness of human love.

(approx. 930 words)

GRADE: A2

P   = 16/18
C   = 16/18
L   = 15/18
M   = 6/6
Total = 53/60

Examiner's Comment

- Good introductory overview.
- Well focused on the question overall.
- Range of interesting discussion points.
- References and quotes used effectively.
- Some note-like expression and general commentary.

End Notes

The Critics

Almost all the criticism of *Othello* has been concerned with the relationship between the two male protagonists. It is only in more recent times that Desdemona's role has been closely examined. Over the years, leading critics have taken very different – indeed, contradictory – views of the play. Some of the earliest reviewers thought that *Othello* was unrealistic and could not be seen as classic tragedy. Others have concentrated on major themes in the story, such as love, race, religion and patriarchy.

Unsurprisingly, critics have disagreed about their attitudes to the central character. Some paint Othello in a positive light as a noble character, while others depict the Moor as a highly unsympathetic figure. As always, Shakespeare's great tragedy is open to many different readings. In the end, individuals are free to consider the views of others, but should interpret the play for themselves.

'... *the most lamentable play that ever appeared on any stage. A noble Venetian lady is to be murdered by our poet, in sober sadness, purely for being a fool.*'

Thomas Rymer (1693)

'[*Othello*] *does not belong in our world, and he seems to enter it we know not whence – almost as if from wonderland. There is something mysterious in his descent from men of royal siege; in his wanderings in vast deserts and among marvellous peoples; in his tales of magic handkerchiefs and prophetic Sibyls; in the sudden vague glimpses we get of numberless battles and sieges in which he has played the hero and has borne a charmed life.*'

A.C. Bradley (1904)

'*Othello, in his magnanimous way, is egotistic ... This self-centredness doesn't mean self-knowledge: that is a virtue which Othello, a soldier of fortune, hasn't had much need of.*'

F.R. Leavis (1952)

'*Othello is supreme in one quality: beauty. Much of its poetry, in imagery, perfection of phrase, and steadfastness of rhythm, soaring yet firm, enchants the sensuous imagination.*'

Helen Gardner (1955)

'Iago is still serviceable to us, as an objective correlative of the mindless inventiveness of racist aggression.'

Germaine Greer (1986)

'In loving and marrying each other, Othello and Desdemona instinctively act according to principles of racial equality and sexual freedom which are still not normative, still far from generally accepted and practised even in our own day, let alone in Shakespeare's.'

Kiernan Ryan (1989)

Othello on Screen

Othello has been adapted for the sceen many times, including four silent movies between 1907 and 1922.

Films

* 1952 *Othello* directed by, and starring, Orson Welles as Othello.
* 1965 *Othello* with Laurence Olivier, Maggie Smith, Frank Finlay and Joyce Redman.
* 1995 *Othello* with Kenneth Branagh, Laurence Fishburne and Irene Jacob. Directed by Oliver Parker.

Television

* 1981 *Othello* part of the BBC's Complete Works of Shakespeare. Starring Anthony Hopkins and Bob Hoskins.
* 1990 *Othello* a film version of the Royal Shakespeare Company production starring Michael Grandage, Ian McKellen, Clive Swift, Willard White, Sean Baker and Imogen Stubbs. Directed by Trevor Nunn.

Leaving Certificate Questions

The Single Text English Higher Level question is allocated 60 minutes in the exam and is worth 60 marks in total.

1 'Despite his deep sense of honour, what ultimately causes Othello's downfall is his own impulse towards self-destruction.'
  Write your response to this statement, supporting your views with reference to the play *Othello*.

2 'The tension between Othello's twin roles as soldier and husband is central to the tragedy that unfolds during the course of the play.'
  Discuss this statement, supporting the points you make by suitable reference to the text.

3 'Honesty and love triumph over hatred and jealousy in *Othello*.'
  Write your response to this statement, supporting your views with suitable reference to the play.

4 'In Shakespeare's play *Othello*, the stories of Othello and Iago mirror each other closely in interesting ways.' Discuss this view of the play, supporting your answer by suitable reference to the text.

5 'The play *Othello* portrays a disturbing society of prejudice and patriarchy.' Write your response to this statement, supporting your views with appropriate reference to the text.

6 'Shakespeare's effective use of language and imagery heighten the dramatic impact of *Othello*.' Discuss this view of the play, supporting your response with close reference to the text.

7 'In *Othello*, Shakespeare presents a morally chaotic world where hatred and love can be equally destructive forces.' Discuss this view, supporting your response by reference to the play.

8 'Shakespeare's play *Othello* has all the main elements of compelling drama.' Discuss this statement, supporting your answer by suitable reference to the text.

Literary Terms

antagonist: an important character, such as Iago, who provides the main opposition to the protagonist.

aside: when a character says something that is only heard by the audience.

blank verse: unrhymed verse in iambic pentameter, relatively close to spoken English.

catharsis: the purging of emotion (usually pity and fear) that the audience experiences.

characterisation: how a playwright creates characters so as to attract or repel audience sympathy.

courtesan: a prostitute who usually had upper-class or wealthy customers.

cuckold: a male character who is unaware that his wife is unfaithful.

dramatic irony: when the audience knows something that some of the characters don't. On certain occasions, characters may speak in a dramatically ironic way when they are not fully aware of the significance of their words.

feminism: in literature, a movement concerned with how women are presented by writers.

foil: a contrasting character, such as Emilia, whose realistic attitudes highlight Desdemona's naivety.

genre: type or classification of literature, e.g. drama, tragedy.

hyperbole: exaggeration deliberately used for dramatic effect.

iambic pentameter: 10-syllable lines in which each unstressed syllable alternates with a stressed syllable.

imagery: figurative or literary language (including symbols, metaphors and similes) that creates pictures in the mind.

irony: in speech, saying one thing and meaning another. Some of Iago's sarcastic comments imply the opposite to what he actually says.

Machiavellian: a villainous character, such as Iago, may get involved in immoral behaviour out of self-interest and then delights in his own manipulative evil. Based on the reputation of the Italian writer Niccolo Machiavelli (1469–1527).

mercenary: someone who is paid to provide a service; usually a soldier in a foreign army.

metaphor: a direct comparison, e.g. 'the green-eyed monster'.

metre: the arrangement of stressed and unstressed syllables to create rhythm in poetry.

misogyny: hatred of women.

Moor: term used to describe natives of the Barbary coast in North Africa. During Elizabethan times, it usually referred to people with a darker skin tone than white Europeans.

oxymoron: a figure of speech linking two contradictory ideas, e.g. 'honest knaves' or 'fair devil'.

pathos: a quality in a text that arouses feelings of pity or deep sorrow.

patriarchy: a society where men hold most of the power and where women are dominated.

personification: type of metaphor in which an object is described as if it were alive.

poetic justice: the idea that characters should get what they deserve, based on their behaviour.

protagonist: the central or main character in a story.

pun: word-play using ambiguity between words to create humour.

rhetoric: the use of language techniques to make speech or writing more powerful and persuasive.

rhythm: the pace or movement of language.

sibilance: the repetition of musical or hissing *s* sounds.

simile: a comparison describing something (or someone) by saying it is like something else using the words 'like' or 'as'.

soliloquy: a speech during which a character reveals his or her thoughts and feelings exclusively to the audience.

symbol: an object that represents something else, e.g. Desdemona's handkerchief becomes a symbol of infidelity.

tone: dominant mood or feeling suggested by the writer. A tone can be joyful, bitter, angry, etc.

tragic flaw: the main fault or character weakness that leads to the tragic hero's downfall, e.g. Othello's jealousy.

villain: anti hero, vice character who personifies evil. Iago is often said to be based on this stereotypical figure from 16th-century morality drama.